6/95

CROSS-CULTURAL LITERACY

Global Perspectives on Reading and Writing

FRAIDA DUBIN
NATALIE A. KUHLMAN

EDITORS

D0219584

REGENTS/PRENTICE HALL
Englewood Cliffs, New Jersey 07632

Library of Congress Cataloging-in-Publication Data

Cross-cultural literacy / Fraida Dubin and Natalie A. Kuhlman.
  editors.
    p.   cm.
  Many of the chapters in this book have grown out of the authors'
  participation in cross-cultural literacy colloquia at TESOL
  conventions.
  Includes bibliographical references and index.
  ISBN 0-13-194408-8
    1. Literacy.   2. Intercultural education.   I. Dubin, Fraida.
  II. Kuhlman, Natalie A.
  LC149.C75   1992   91-32115
  302.2'244—dc20   CIP

Acquisitions Editor: Anne Riddick
Editorial/Production Supervision and
  Interior Design: Kala Dwarakanath and
  Noël Vreeland Carter
Copy Editor: Sandy Di Somma
Cover Design: Ray Lundgren Graphics, LTD.
Prepress Buyer: Ray Keating
Manufacturing Buyer: Lori Bulwin
Scheduler: Leslie Coward

Permissions:

The editors gratefully thank the following publishers and individuals for permission
to quote from their materials:

Article by W. Smalley in *Southeast Asian Refugee Studies Newsletter.* (Chapter 3)

Paper presented by Lynn Huenemann at TESOL Summer Meeting at Flagstaff,
Arizona, July, 1988. (Chapter 11)

Printed in the United States of America
10 9 8 7 6 5 4 3 2 1

0-13-194408-8

Prentice-Hall International (UK) Limited, *London*
Prentice-Hall of Australia Pty. Limited, *Sydney*
Prentice-Hall Canada Inc., *Toronto*
Prentice-Hall Hispanoamericana, S.A., *Mexico*
Prentice-Hall of India Private Limited, *New Delhi*
Prentice-Hall of Japan, Inc., *Tokyo*
Simon & Schuster Asia Pte. Ltd., *Singapore*
Editora Prentice-Hall do Brasil, Ltda., *Rio de Janeiro*

Contents

PART FOUR: ACADEMIC SETTINGS IN THE UNITED STATES

*Innovative modes of instruction; recognition of cultural and
individual diversity; culturally derived attitudes*

The Dimensions of Cross-Cultural Literacy

WHAT IS CROSS-CULTURAL LITERACY?

Background

Our use of the term "Cross-Cultural Literacy" began in 1984 as the title for a Colloquium which Natalie Kuhlman and I organized at the annual TESOL Convention. At that time, we defined "literacy" simply as reading and writing. The more complex part of the title was "cross-cultural." By using it, we wanted to call attention to the existence of co-occurring cultures in many of the settings in which literacy skills in English are taught. We selected "cross-cultural," too, because unlike "inter-cultural" it is neutral in regard to fostering mutualism or adaptation; and, unlike "multicultural," it emphasizes the contrastive elements between two cultures, rather than the co-existence of many. Most important, it underscores the signifigance of two literacy systems, the student's and the target, or English language system. Moreover, the term cross-cultural acknowledges all individuals' rights to their native language and culture.

Many of the chapters in this book have grown out of the authors' participation in the Colloquia at TESOL Conventions over the years. Some were presentations at TESOL Conventions and other conferences which the editors felt would add significantly to the collection. In all cases, the papers included in *Cross-Cultural Literacy* have not appeared in other sources.

In defining the parameters for the first Cross-Cultural Literacy Colloquium in 1984, we recognized that our focus was separate from the area which has come to be known as "contrastive rhetoric." For while the later is concerned with analyzing written texts in other-than-English languages, Cross-Cultural Literacy has emphasized the nature of the users and producers of literacy. It has been inevitable, therefore, that papers presented at Cross-Cultural Literacy Colloquia over the years have dealt with questions of societal, cultural, and political issues concerning literacy. The stated purpose of the colloquia has been to foster research on topics that deal with the beliefs and attitudes about reading and writing that people bring to the task of learning a new literacy, or values reflecting another cultural background.

Reading and writing are often considered topics that involve young students—children. Yet post-secondary schools in North America have had a burgeoning expansion of skill-building, learning skills, and language development programs which offer instruction in various aspects of reading and writing—for an adult population. With this student audience in mind, the focus in the Cross-Cultural Literacy Colloquia, as it is in this collection, has been on post-secondary learners in settings within and outside of classrooms, ranging from basic literacy to academic reading and writing.

v

An Educational Imperative

The motivation to produce this book began with an educational imperative: we realized the importance of bringing information and awareness about literacy in other countries to the attention of a broad audience in North American education. All teachers of content area courses face the challenge today of dealing with large numbers of students whose cultural patterns for reading and writing were developed in other parts of the world. At the same time, ESL teachers encounter those students whose English language skills are not yet sufficiently developed for them to do regular classroom work. In North America, in secondary schools, community colleges, four-year colleges, and adult schools, educators recognize that their classes are filled with students who may have received their early exposure to reading and writing in an other-than-English mother tongue. They also encounter students who are learning through the medium of English, yet their background in the reading/writing of their native language may have been scant or interrupted. With such dramatic changes in student populations today, traditional approaches for presenting content material must be re-examined in light of the multiethnic mix of students who pursue various educational goals.

The Metaphoric Meaning of Literacy

On the way to becoming a book, the "literacy" part of our title has taken on meanings that go beyond the simple definition of "reading and writing" as we had conceived of it in 1984. In many ways, literacy has become both a cause and a "national scandal," (Kozol). While eschewing discussions that profess simple cause and effect relationships between literacy and societal elements—for example "literacy and crime," "literacy and drop-out rates," or even the term "illiteracy"—we acknowledge that the word literacy itself has come to mean competence, knowledge and skills (Dubin). Take, for example, common expressions such as "computer literacy," "civic literacy," "health literacy," and a score of other usages in which literacy stands for know-how and awareness of the first word in the expression. In fact, metaphorically speaking, cross-cultural literacy implies the knowledge and sensitivity which educators require in order to work in most North American classrooms today given the multilingual, multicultural backgrounds of large numbers of students.

Another example of the metaphoric use of literacy occurs in the widely discussed work by Hirsch (1987) which presents the case that so-called educated people in any particular society possess a shared body of knowledge; to be culturally literate in the United States today, according to Hirsch, demands taht one has knowledge of facts, names, events, dates, and concepts largely related to the sweep of western civilization. One of the contributors to this volume, Field, takes on Hirsch's argument but advances it by relating it to the needs of people whose origins are non-western or whose languages are non-European, in other words, the population in our schools, colleges, and universities today.

Contemporary Scholarship in Literacy

Literacy is not a unified field by any means. Many academic disciplines lay a claim to at least some part of its territory, including history, economics, linguistics, anthropology, and English. A few scholars have seen the need to try to make sense out of defintions, assumptions and points-of-view (Langer, Scribner, Street). Contributing to the current interest in the need for a theory-base for literacy, the authors in this collection present a cohesive perspective by emphasizing social, cultural, and political dimensions, or literacy situated in a social context.

A prevailing and familiar paradigm in literacy studies has been called the high-culture, or "literacy-as-a-state-of-grace" (Scribner) view. In this frame of reference, literacy is a primary requisite for achieving entry to status and achievement. Another term that captures this idea is to speak of literacy as representing "authority." This view holds that the success of western civilization in the history of our species has been strongly influenced by its well-developed literacy traditions, made possible by its system of alphabetic literacy. Within this scholarly view, claims are made for the causal link between literacy and patterns of thinking, modes of expression, orientations towards cognitive processes, and even creativity (Ong, Havelock).

A corollary to literacy as authority places emphasis on literacy as a profound technological development in the history of man. The alphabet, according to this view, influenced the development of scientific thought in western civilization, a way of looking at the world through elements which can be dissected and analyzed. The influence was profound, bringing about new understanding of the physical world through biology, physics, physiology, astronomy and all other sciences. In this collection, Topping draws on this viewpoint in presenting a historical perspective on the impact of western literacy on South Pacific island cultures.

While the view of literacy which is most familiar to educators emphasizes literacy as an individual achievement, it is not the one which underlies the work of many of the authors in this collection. Instead, we have concentrated on a more recently developed perspective, that literacy reflects social-cultural norms of behavior. However, the individual view underlies the whole technology of quantification through testing, scoring, calculating grade level equivalences, etc. The traditions of scholarly research about the processes of both reading and writing have been strongly influenced by the view of literacy as an individual achievement.

The past decade has been marked by significant new directions in literacy research brought about by questions which seek to discover how literacy functions in families (see Henze's chapter), in communities (see Long's chapter) and in workplaces (see Summer & Plaister's chapter). What does it mean to be "literate" as a member of a particular culture? What are the patterns of literacy use within fields of work, within professions, within age-groups?

Street's work (1984) contributed to theoretical perspectives by establishing a dichotomy between opposing ways of viewing literacy, or in his terms, the "ideological" view vs. the "autonomous." Literacy as an individual accomplishment lies in the latter sphere, while the emphasis on literacy generally presented in the chapters in this book is that of the former, "ideological," though we prefer to capture the idea of social and cultural views of literacy by calling them "pragmatically" oriented, a term less likely to create misunderstandings of our intent.

A groundbreaking study about the literacy patterns in two communities in southeastern United States by Shirley Brice Heath (1983) has become a beacon for inspiring researchers to look at literacy through pragmatic lenses. Indeed, some of the chapters in this collection, particularly those by Henze and Long, directly grow out of the kinds of questions regarding literacy that Heath's work has raised. Such issues reflect a pragmatic orientation towards literacy which, in fact, underlies the collection as a whole.

ORGANIZATION OF THE BOOK

The Four Parts

The thirteen chapters are arranged in four Parts, *Macroliteracy, Family, Community and Workplace Settings, Academic Settings in Asia and Eastern Europe,* and *Academic Settings in the United States.* This organization, in terms of settings, emphasizes the multifaceted characteristics of multiple literacies, instead of it being a single term, single concept construct. The term "Macroliteracy" creates a parallellism with "macrosociolinguistics," a field which encompasses language planning and policy studies. Dealing as she does with issues of language policy, Meisenhelder in Chapter One treats literacy as tied to national development. In Chapter Two, Topping deals with the consequences which result from a neglect of policy regarding local language maintenance in a large cultural area while in Chapter Three, Long discusses the choices which confront refugees as they move from one literacy sphere into another.

Part Two, "Family, Community and Workplace Settings," focuses on literacy as social practice among participants in locations as varied as within families in rural Greece as reported on by Henze, at a police station in Hawaii as studied by Summers and Plaister, and in an aboriginal community in Northern Australia, Eggington's territory. Parts Three and Four highlight globally dispersed academic settings including locations in Japan (Hino), China (Kohn), Korea (Scarcella and Lee), Eastern Europe (Kuhlman), as well as North America (Field, Murray and Nichols, Lewis).

Re-occurring Themes

A number of themes cut across this four-part organizational plan:

Literate/Oral Cultures Dichotomy. Many scholars have pointed out the fundamental gulf separating cultures which depend upon oral recitation of their histories, lore, beliefs, myths, etc. and those that employ written literacy, (Ong, Havelock). This body of work on literacy has dealt with questions such as the relationship of literacy and cognition. For example, does the use of literacy affect the ways in which people think about the world they live in? and the consequences of the use of literacy in western civilization. While contemporary research has criticized the division of literate/oral as being too simplistic, specifically regarding the complexities of oral communication in the modern world (Tannen), the theme remains prominent in studies of literacy on a societal basis as illustrated by the references which authors in this book make to it, for example: Meisenhelder in regard to Botswana, Topping in the South Pacific area, Eggington in Australia, Long among the Hmong the people, Henze in rural Greece, and Summers and Plaister in reference to Hawaiian vernacular.

Literacy as Techonology. A prevailing view emphasizes that since literacy is an invention of man, it is primarily a tool in the anthropological sense of the term. It is an easy next step to view the invention of the alphabet as one of man's most significant technological developments because writing is an abstract representation of the stream of language. In fact, our concept of words as separate entities is a consequence of our alphabetic writing system (Havelock). A number of the authors in this book emphasize that literacy is a manifestation of this kind of technology, among them including Henze, Topping, Eggington and Long.

Literacy as a Social Change Agent. This theme can be viewed in various ways: in one sense people are affected by a force outside of themselves, something over which they have no control. The cultures of the South Pacific are viewed in this way by Topping. In another sense, the possibility for change which lies within literacy can be viewed as *empowerment* when it is used to bring about social change which improves the lives of people without power, a concept embodied in the educational philosophy of Paulo Freire (1985). The theme of literacy as an empowering force is discussed by Eggington, along with important references to it made by Meisenhelder, Long, and Henze. In many respects, it is implicit in the chapters by Summers and Plaister as well as in Field's.

Literacy Grounded in Specific Cultural Values. This is an important theme that has been made prominent in contemporary research, notably through Heath and Street's work. The latter deals with traditional or Koranic-based and modern or marketplace patterns of literacy use in Iran (1984). Henze's chapter on literacy in rural Greek families grows out of this research tradition. Others among our authors have been strongly influenced by it either directly or indirectly, notably as shown in Long's account of Hmong refugees. It is also evident in Scarcella and Lee's chapter on literacy in Korea, as well as in Kohn's report when he realized that his own American academic values had to bend to those of his Chinese university students', and in Lewis' study among Spanish-speaking basic literacy students.

Literacy in Multilingual Setting. This brings up questions about choices in regard to competing literacies since a great deal of literacy acquisition occurs in places where more than one language is used and where there is more than one system of writing, as in the case discussed by Long regarding the Hmong people in refugee camps and Meisenhelder in regard to national development policy in Botswana. That literacy in a specific language carries with it a whole complex set of values necessitating shifts in these beliefs when entering a new literacy tradition is illustrated by the findings of Scarcella and Lee as well as in the case studies of Murray and Nichols.

Literacy and Second/Foreign Language Learning. As a direct consequence of the Collections's focus on cross-cultural aspects, all of the contributors to it who deal with academic settings exemplify the difficulty in separating out issues of language learning and literacy learning. In fact, Hino shows how foreign language learning in Japan has been codified into a system of foreign literacy learning via word-by-word translation. Even the police, in Summers and Plaister's study of Hawaii, who received their education through the medium of the English language, are faced with problems in communication between "standard Mainland English" or standard English and HCE (Hawaiian Creole English), a spoken vernacular. At the same time, a consequence of dealing with literacy in a foreign language setting necessitates developing a *metalanguage* for referring to it as Kuhlman's students discovered when they attempted to trace their constrastive experiences in learning to write in their native Polish language and in English.

Qualitative Research

All of the chapters draw on the broad approach of qualitative, as opposed to quantitative, research methodology. While some of the authors are influenced by ethnographic techniques, for example Henze in studying a Greek rural family and Long in reporting on a refugee camp in Thailand, others utilize archival and historical records as the basis for data analysis and interpretation, as is the case with Meisenhelder's study of Botswana, Topping's of the South Pacific, Hino's of literacy traditions in Japan, and Kohn's of China.

The role of the researcher as a participant observer plays a significant part in the chapters by Summers and Plaister (Hawaii), Lewis (the U.S.), Kuhlman (Poland), Kohn (China), as well as in Long's and Henze's, while Eggington (Northern Australia), relies heavily on data from a key informant. The classroom as the locus for intensive study is paramount in the chapters by Kuhlman, Kohn, and Lewis, while Scarcella and Lee's chapters together with Field's make concrete suggestions to teachers who work in North American classrooms. Finally, our authors have also drawn on case study and life history research techniques, as in the case of Murray and Nichol's study of Vietnamese students, and questionnaires, as in Lewis' work.

References

Each of the authors' references in *Cross-Cultural Literacy* appear at the end of the chapter, rather than being compiled into a general reference section at the end of the book. The Editors purposely decided to keep the references with each author's work, even though there are inevitable duplicate entries, because we feel that the reference section reveals a great deal about the scholarly outlook of the writer and thus is an important guide to intelligent reading.

Discussion Questions

Following each of the chapters there is a set of Discussion Questions for use in teacher training courses. Both students and instructors are urged to pick, add, delete, and supplement these questions to suit their particular needs and concerns.

Fraida Dubin

REFERENCES

DUBIN, FRAIDA. 1989. "Situating literacy within traditions of communicative competence." Applied Linguistics 10:2; 171–181.

FREIRE, PAULO. 1985. *The politics of education.* So. Hadley, MA: Bergin and Garvey Publishers, Inc.

HAVELOCK, ERIC A. 1976. "Origins of western literacy." Monograph Series/14. Toronto: The Ontario Institute for Studies in Education.

HEATH, S.B. 1982. *Ways with Words.* Cambridge: Cambridge University Press.

HIRSCH, E.D. 1986. *Cultural Literacy: What Every American Needs to Know.* Boston: Houghton Mifflin.

KOZOL, JONATHAN. 1985. *Illiterate America.* Garden City, NY: Anchor Press/Doubleday.

LANGER, J.A. 1988. *"The state of research on literacy."* Educational Researcher. (April); 42-6.

ONG, WALTER. 1982. *Orality and Literacy: The Technologizing of the Word.* London: Methuen & Co.

SCRIBNER, S. 1986. "Literacy in three metaphors." In N. Stein (ed.): *Literacy and Schooling.* Chicago: Chicago University Press.

STREET, B.V. 1984. *Literacy in Theory and Practice.* Cambridge: Cambridge University Press.

TANNEN, DEBORAH. 1985. "Relative focus on involvement in oral and written discourse." In Olson, D.R., Torrance, N. Hildyard, A. (eds.) *Literacy, Language and Learning.* Cambridge: Cambridge University Press.

1

Literacy and National Development: The Case of Botswana

SUSAN MEISENHELDER

Introduction

From a global perspective, interest in basic literacy during the past four decades has been closely linked with national development. The history of many developing nations during this period often began by recognizing the fact that for the new nation to become economically viable, an educated work force is a prime requirement. Literacy is basic to education. This chapter outlines some of the most prominent issues that have emerged from basic literacy education in developing nations. In the first section, I sketch the broad perspective by discussing literacy and national development in general: where it has taken place, what success has been achieved, and what the key issues are. Then, in the second section, I describe the case of the national literacy program in Botswana, a developing country in southern Africa which borders on South Africa, Zimbabwe, Zambia, and Namibia.

LITERACY PROGRAMS IN DEVELOPING COUNTRIES

Numerous literacy programs have been launched in developing countries in the last thirty years. Major campaigns have taken place, for instance, in the People's Republic of China (1950s–1980s), Burma (1960s–1980s), Cuba (1961), Brazil (1967–1980), Tanzania (1971–1981), Somalia (1973–1975), and Nicaragua (1980). Under the auspices of the United Nations Educational, Scientific, and Cultural Organization (UNESCO), a major international effort was made to battle illiteracy from 1967 to 1974 through the Experimental World Literacy Program (EWLP). Although many nations participated in some form, the program focused on literacy programs in eleven countries: Algeria, Equador, Ethiopia, Guinea, India, Iran, Madagascar, Mali, Sudan, Syria, and Tanzania.

Features of Successful and Unsuccessful Programs

The accumulated history of these campaigns, assessed by Bhola (1984), Hamadache and Martin (1986), and UNESCO (1976) reveals some recurring features of successful literacy programs. Experience has shown, for instance, the importance of postliteracy activities and bridges to formal education systems. While it may seem obvious that learning to read and write is a meaningless or limited exercise unless new literates have ways to use their skills and further their education, the history of more than one country demonstrates the importance of planning these avenues in the early stages of the literacy program itself (UNESCO 1976, 140).

For Westerners, accustomed to equating educational success with the amount of money spent, the experience of literacy programs over the last thirty years points to the surprising conclusion that success has not depended on the wealth of the countries launching the programs. In fact, some of the most successful have been conducted in very poor countries with limited resources to devote to literacy work. Much more crucial is a social and political climate that makes it possible to muster the national will and to mobilize energies behind literacy efforts. The importance of this factor helps explain why some of the most successful campaigns have been launched in countries following revolutions for national independence or in countries moving toward greater social justice. (Hamadache and Martin 1986, 16)

Literacy campaigns in India and Nicaragua.

The history of recent literacy campaigns suggests that the success of literacy programs is intimately connected to larger social and political issues. How such factors can affect the outcome of literacy efforts is evident in a comparison of the campaigns conducted in India and Nicaragua.

In explaining unsuccessful results of the Indian campaign, despite its technical and pedagogical innovation, Bhola pinpoints the lack of sustained political commitment to the project as its most fundamental problem. This lack of commitment can best be understood, not as a personal failing of individual leaders, but as a reflection of the political situation in that country. Since independence, adult education and adult literacy have been low priorities, he argues, because of the upper-class composition and interests of the ruling elite. The failure of the adult literacy program undertaken reflects "th[is] political situation in the country and . . . the structures of privilege and poverty on which the Indian polity rests" (Bhola 1987, 267). India represents just one case, he concludes, demonstrating "a congruence between the political culture of a society and its adult literacy policy and performance" (Bhola 1987, 248).

In very different ways, the milieu in which the Nicaraguan literacy campaign was launched made it an extremely difficult endeavor. It was undertaken immediately after the revolution in 1979 in a war-torn country suffering extreme economic adversity. Arnove (1987) suggests, however, that one important factor in the country made possible the impressive success of Nicaragua's campaign. Because mass literacy was a crucial part of the political agenda after the revolution and a major symbol of the democratic restructuring envisaged, the new Government of National Reconstruction was able to achieve the mass mobilization and enthusiasm necessary to carry out the program (Arnove 1987, 269–71). While the success of the campaign also involved broader social and political effects, the sheer numbers tell an important story about the role of "political commitment" in literacy work: external sources have estimated that Nicaragua reduced its illiteracy rate from roughly 50 percent to 23 percent in only five months (Arnove 1987, 281).

Curriculum and Language Issues

A review of modern literacy campaigns also shows that political factors influence the specific characteristics of literacy campaigns. In developing countries, issues around curriculum and language especialy demonstrate that literacy campaigns are never conducted in a vacuum. As Arnove and Graff (1987) have pointed out, questions concerning what literacy learners should learn and in what language are always complicated questions with major political implications: "The language of insturction leads to the question of whose language and values form the medium and content of a literacy campaign. The power of dominant groups to shape the language policy and educational content is similarly reflected in what skills are developed in what populations as part of the literacy process" (Arnove and Graff 1987, 19).

The history of changes in the broad notion of curriculum—what people should learn—shows that this issue has been closely tied to political ideas about the nature of development. In answering questions such as "What kind of literacy?" and "Literacy for what?" literacy workers have generally agreed that traditional literacy—literacy for its own sake—is inappropriate in the social and political context of developing nations. Literacy, it has been assumed since at least the 1960s, has an important social and economic role to play in the overall development of a country. What has led to changes in the answer to "What kind of literacy?" have been changes in the answer to "What kind of development?"

4 Macroliteracy

The Concept of Functional Literacy.

A number of literacy campaigns, most notable perhaps the Experimental World Literacy Program (EWLP), have been based on the concept of functional literacy. This type of curriculum assumes that literacy should not be an end in itself but a contributor to community and national development. The predominant theory of development on which functionality was built involved the ideas that development meant economic expansion and that the key to economic expansion for developing countries was technical expertise.[1] In practice, this concept of functionality led to literacy projects of the EWLP that were work-oriented and tied to vocational training.

While functionality—the idea that literacy should not be an end in itself—is still at the core of literacy theorizing and practice today, the concept has undergone transformation in part as the result of changing notions about what constitutes development. During the 1970s, the argument was frequently advanced that development meant much more than mere economic expansion. National economic expansion, people began to realize, does not necessarily mean that the poorest people in a country will benefit from an overall increase in wealth unless political and social change makes it possible.

Acknowledging a change in the idea of development, the assessment study of EWLP explicity points to a shortcoming in the notion of functionality embodied in EWLP by stating that:

> A crucial lesson of EWLP seems . . . to be the need to avoid viewing or designing literacy as an over-whelming technical solution to problems that are only partly technical. A broad, multidimensional approach to both development and literacy is required. Indeed, it would seem that literacy programmes can only be fully functional—and development contexts can only be fully conducive to literacy—if they accord importance to social, cultural and political change as well as economic growth. (UNESCO 1976, 122)

From a somewhat different angle, social critics such as Paolo Freire have rejected a narrowly economic conception of functionality because it fails to foster political awareness in the process of learning to read and write. In *Pedagogy of the Oppressed* and other of his works, Freire stresses the importance of developing critical consciousness ("conscientization" in Freire's terms); new literates should learn not only to read the word but also to read the world if they are to take an active role in political and social life. Freire's ideas have formed the basis of several literacy campaigns (including the one in Nicaragua) and have played a major role in transforming the concept of literacy.

Many theorists now recognize two kinds of functionality when talking about literacy: economic and political. This distinction and the move away from

---

[1]For a full discussion of the background for and failings of the concept of functional literacy see Levine (1982).

narrowly economic ideas of functionality are recognized in a number of important documents concerning literacy. For instance, the assessment document of the EWLP, itself a massive exercise in economic functionality, raises specific questions about the problems of defining "mastery of the environment" in narrowly technical and economic terms:

> In acquiring this [technical and economic] kind of mastery of the milieu, to what extent has the new literate become dependent on . . . external socio-economic processes and forces? Has literacy enabled the new literate to know and understand these processes and forces? To come to grips with them? To have a voice in controlling them? What implications has the new literate's accession to mastery of the milieu for the fate of his or her less favoured neighbours and compatriots? (UNESCO 1976, 181)

The Declaration of the 1975 International Symposium for Literacy in Persepolis (UNESCO 1975) similarly stressed the importance of linking literacy to "meeting man's fundamental requirements, ranging from his immediate vital needs to effective participation in social change." Successes have been seen "when literacy programmes were not restricted to learning the skills of reading, writing and arithmetic, and when they did not subordinate literacy to the short-term needs of growth unconcerned with man" (Reprinted in Hamadache and Martin 1986, 128). The ideas of Freire are echoed in this document's broadened definition of literacy as

> . . . not just the process of learning the skills of reading, writing and arithmetic, but a contribution to the liberation of man and to his full development. Thus conceived, literacy creates the conditions for the acquisition of a critical consciousness of the contradictions of society in which man lives and of its aims; it also stimulates initiative and his participation in the creation of projects capable of acting upon the world, of transforming it, and of defining the aims of an authentic human development. It should open the way to a mastery of techniques and human relations. (Hamadache and Martin 1986, 128–29)

Indigenous Languages.

In addition to showing the political nature and ramifications of curricular decisions in literacy work, the history of literacy campaigns over the last thirty years shows that questions of language choice are crucial and often are also politically motivated. One general trend, fostered by the EWLP, has involved moving away from European languages and toward indigenous ones as the medium of instruction in developing countries. This change, in countries that have traditionally used colonial languages in education, has played an important political role in developing national unity in the postindependence period.

The general agreement to use indigenous languages rather than colonial ones certainly has not solved all the problems involved in deciding which language or languages to use. While it has become an accepted principle that acquiring literacy is most successful when it is carried out in the learner's mother tongue (UNESCO 1976, 170), the implementation of this principle in countries with large numbers of indigenous languages often becomes economically unfeasible. When planners have had to decide which of a number of languages to use in literacy training, they have had to consider not only practical issues but political and social ones as well. Needless to say, the problems have varied from country to country where they have been tackled, with varying degrees of success, in a variety of ways.

Language Choice in Tanzania and Ethiopia.

A comparison of the paths taken in the literacy programs of Tanzania and Ethiopia gives one a sense of the complex problems surrounding the language issue in literacy work. While Tanzania has speakers of many different languages, its literacy planners made the decision to teach literacy in a single language, Swahili, as one way to develop national unity. Generally, the decision has been seen as a wise one. Ryan has suggested that this language policy worked in Tanzania largely because many peope already understood Swahili even though it was not their first language (Ryan 1985, 162–65).

The situation and outcome was very different, he argues, in Ethiopia, where a single-language policy was also initially adopted in literacy work (Ryan 1985, 165–67). There, the language chosen, Amharic, was not widely known and was, in fact, the language of the dominant ethnic elite. A later change to fifteen indigenous languages in adult literacy not only allowed more people to learn in their mother tongues but also helped solve the political and social problems engendered in the single-language policy. The case of Ethiopia demonstrates strongly how closely tied are social and hence political issues in language policy.

Against this overview of some issues involved in literacy campaigns with a stress on the political nature of literacy work, I now turn to an account of one literacy campaign. As has been the case in other countries, the development of the literacy program in Botswana has been closely connected to larger social and political issues.

THE BOTSWANA LITERACY PROGRAM

The Botswana Literacy Program, begun in 1980 and continuing up to the present, has not been the success story seen in some other developing nations. The internal documents of the program point to numerous difficulties stemming from the lack of funds, infrastructure, and cooperation between government agencies. The purpose of this chapter is not to argue that these problems are not real, but rather to suggest that the specific issues are related to each other when the literacy program is examined in the broader context of the country's development goals and strategies.

Development Strategy

To see the relationship between the Literacy Program and larger social and economic issues in Botswana requires understanding the country's overriding development strategy. Botswana (formerly Bechuanaland) achieved its independence from Great Britain in 1966 without the kind of revolutionary activity evident in some other African states. Styling its government after Western democracies, with an elected President and legislative body, and its economy on a capitalist model, the new government immediately embarked on a development plan emphasizing the growth of diamond mining as a major source of government income. This strategy was seen as crucial for develoment, and income redistribution necessarily a "long range objective" (Colclough and McCarthy 1980, 76).

The overall results of this move were quite impressive. In 1966, Botswana was among the twenty poorest countries in the world; by 1976, its per capita product was higher than the average for Africa and Asia, excluding Japan (Colclough and McCarthy 1980, 74). As Colclough and McCarthy (echoing contemporary theories of development) argue, however, an increase in aggregate income does not necessarily mean that the rural population will be better off unless government expenditures focus on services for the masses. Despite the government's claim that mining resources would be used to improve the lives of Botswana's largely rural and poorly educated population, they argue that government expenditures have favored urban areas and infrastructure rather than areas that would benefit the masses.

As a result of these and other economic policies, distribution of wealth became more unequal in Botswana during the 1960s and 1970s (Colclough and McCarthy 1980, 202). While the focus on investment in mining (a capital-intensive, low-employment sector) has actually created a government revenue surplus, the rewards have been enjoyed by only a small part of the population. Colclough and McCarthy conclude that these development policies have "increased the power of [the elite] minority and its aspirations, changed its perceptions and brought its own interests into conflict with those of the majority of the people" (Colclough and McCarthy 1980, 243). Leepile (1986) and Cliffe (1984) argue that this trend continued in the 1980s.

This "trickle-down" approach to development has also influenced the country's educational planning. The first development plan emphasized "manpower training" and higher levels of education (Colclough and McCarthy 1980, 213) to enable locals to run the bureaucracy. Higher education, the first National Development Plan argued, was a necessary prerequisite for the betterment of the masses: "While there is a shortage of work for unskilled Botswana, there is a dearth of trained and skilled people without whom new jobs for the unskilled cannot be created" (quoted in Roth and Etherington 1981, 21). Even in the second National Development Plan (1970–1975) no mention was made of nonformal education to serve the needs of uneducated adults (Bhola

1985, 5) or of a literacy program for the largely illiterate population, estimated at 65 percent to 80 percent of the adult population in 1979 (Townsend-Coles 1979, 1). This general approach, Colclough and McCarthy argue, despite a general expansion of the educational system, has "done little to break down existing patterns of inequality within the communities" (Colclough and McCarthy 1980, 215).

Given this particular development strategy, it is not surprising that Botswana, unlike some other newly independent countries, did not immediately embark on a mass literacy campaign. Mass literacy would have provided little increase in aggregate income (compared to an investment in mining) regardless of its potential role in redistributing wealth. In fact, the government rejected a suggestion for a literacy campaign made by a UNESCO consultant in 1972 as "too ambitious and too demanding of existing extension services, which had other priorities" (Gaborone, Mutanyatta, and Youngman 1987, 1).

The National Literacy Program

A national literacy program was not launched until 1980, fourteen years after independence. After the program was started, it was consistently lauded by the government as an important part of the nation's development plans. The Minister of Education, for instance, speaking at the opening of the Meeting on the Eradication of Illiteracy stressed that "for the great majority of people, if life in modern society is to be lived to the full, they must be released from the bondage of illiteracy if they are to make their best contribution to their families, their communities, and their nation." (Morake 1979, 1).

The enthusiasm here for the value of literacy overshadows a nagging vagueness about how literacy and development will be related in Botswana, one that becomes explicit in the minutes of that meeting: "It was generally agreed that literacy should be linked to development but the extent to which this should be the case was not determined" (Department of Non-Formal Education 1979, 4). Even as late as 1987, the *Annual Report on the National Literacy Program: 1986* refers ambiguously (and tellingly in the role of literacy in development it bespeaks) to a "spillover benefit of literacy" (Ministry of Education 1987, 6).

External evaluators of the program have suggested, in fact, that the literacy program was never an integral part of Botswana's economic development plan. A study by consultants for one of the donor agencies commented that "as implied in the program's title (Go bala je tswetelopele—to read is to develop) literacy is often seen as a precondition for development. Its relationship to economic development was not emphasized in Botswana, though it was acknowledged that literacy could contribute in minor ways to increased productivity through for example, helping farmers read information about fertilizer seeds or the repair of equipment" (Roth and Etherington 1981, 57).

H.S. Bhola goes even further in concluding that

. . . the "Literacy for Development" plans of Botswana are an excellent example of technical rationality, duly codified in planning documents. But technical rationality is not the same thing as political reality; and codification in planning documents is not the same thing as implementation of planning actions. Political commitment to literacy may be less than total. The *belief* in the role of literacy in development is not permeated within the whole system of planning and actions at its various levels. (Bhola 1985, 8)

Related Problems.

Given the fact that the Literacy Program never played a central role in the kind of national development envisaged, several frequently noticed problems become intelligibly related. The lack of "top level commitment" by leaders (no official higher than Minister of Education is recorded in the archives as speaking out publicly in favor of the program) and the lack of coordination among ministries are not surprising difficulties besetting a program tangential to a government's focus. Neither is the low level of financial commitment on the part of the government for the program. Despite a government surplus as early as 19971-1972 (Colclough and McCarthy 1980, 106), the Literacy Program has been funded primarily by external donors (including Swedish and West German agencies).[2]

The Curriculum.

The fact that the Literacy Program was not envisaged as a means to redistribute wealth in Botswana also affects its curriculum. The general approach chosen was one of functional literacy, using key concepts drawn from developmental issues. Nowhere in the public archives of the program is there discussion of a Freirean model with an emphasis on critical consciousness or radical transformation of social reality. Theoretically, economic functionality was the goal, not political functionality as in Cuba or Nicaragua.[3] Through discussion of key

---

[2]The 1987 study of the Literacy Program estimates that donor agencies have provided 91 percent of the development expenditures and 72 percent of the total costs of the National Literacy Program. According to Hamadache and Martin, the extent of political, human, and material resources given to literacy is the most reliable indicator of a nation's commitment because of the frequent "chasm between words and acts" (Hamadache and Martin 1986, 22).

[3]Giroux has stressed the relationship between functional literacy and capitalism. In his view, the functional approach to literacy is

. . . geared to make adults more productive workers and citizens within a given society. In spite of its appeal to economic mobility, functional literacy reduces the concept of literacy and the pedagogy in which it is suited to the pragmatic requirements of capital; consequently, the notion of critical thinking, culture, and power disappear under the imperatives of the labor process and the need for capital accumulation. (Giroux 1983, 215-16)

concepts (for instance, to read, to plough, medicine, money, woman, porridge, vegetables, and rain) and from follow-up community action projects, individuals would, planners argued, be able to improve their personal economic situation.

Early on, it was clear that even this more conservative economic change was not the real focus of the program despite repeated official denigration of "literacy for its own sake." In the original *Working Paper on a National Approach to the Eradication of Illiteracy in Botswana* (Townsend-Coles 1979), the move was already toward literacy *per se:* "The keywords in the text will have significance to the participants and there will be some time for discussion of the themes, though the emphasis will be on learning to read and write" (Townsend-Cole 1979, 4). In the original planning meeting in March 1979, a discussion of the earlier pilot projects led to the view that "action topics were not very popular and at times counter-productive" (Ministry of Education, Department of Non-Formal Education 1979, 4) and to questions about the general concept of functional literacy. An official document reports that

> . . . following the report of UNESCO projects in various countries it was suggested that the term "relevant" literacy replace "functional" literacy. It was argued that literacy had to be functional in terms of including action because literacy for the sake of literacy was lifeless. After much discussion the issue of terminology was left unresolved but it was generally agreed that the sense of what was wanted in terms of literacy training was agreed upon. (Department of Non-Formal Education 1979, 5)

A study in 1981 by consultants for the West German donor agency, as part of their aid for the program, noted that discussion as a way for groups to discuss problems was "downplayed" and "not working satisfactorily" (Roth and Etherington 1981, 60). In the consultants' view, the problems with the functional component were severe enough to make them conclude: "it is doubtful whether a nation-wide functional literacy program could be carried out in Botswana at present" (Roth and Etherington 1981, 60). Their description of literacy classes observed suggests that the curriculum—and even the classroom atmosphere—early became one of traditional school literacy learning. They reported that

> . . . some groups have changed the nature of their sessions to more closely replicate a school. Thus the leaders are called "teacher," the learners become "pupils" and sit in rows not circles. Discussion of the keyword involves the learners asking the teacher for her opinion. Primers are marked with ticks and crosses, results are given as a score and the leader writes in comments in English such as "good." There are even reports of demands for uniforms. (Roth and Etherington 1981, 51)

Evidence in the government reports on the program suggest, however, that literacy learners were not satisfied with "literacy for its own sake." The Evaluation Report of 1984, based on the responses of literacy learners, found that "the learners themselves advocate a very functional practical approach, where they can help improve their own immediate life, but also for some thing that can help them earn a cash income" (Ministry of Education 1984, 20). The study, therefore, recommends a stronger functional component in the curriculum and in follow-up activities because the "learners' learning needs were found to demand such measures" (Ministry of Education 1984, 45). Nevertheless, an extensive study of the program in 1987 suggests that this element had not been incorporated successfully into the program. Noting that "the teaching of the primers remains theoretical rather than at a practical level" and that "there is too little student involvement and a tendency to stress memorisation," the study concludes, "The extent to which general education on a variety of development and social issues actually takes place is open to question" (Gaborone, Mutanyatta, and Youngman 1987, 65–66).

Language Policy

Evidence that the Literacy Program is not working to bring marginalized people into the political and economic life of the nation can also be seen in the language policy adopted. With English the official language of the country and Setswana the national language, the choice was made to teach literacy in Setswana. While this seems a reasonable decision, the language situation in Botswana makes the choice of language a more complicated issue. Although the majority of people do speak Setswana, there is a sizable minority (about 20 percent) with another first language. Predictable difficulties for these speakers in the literacy program arose since the same materials were used for all learners. Until 1987, however, the only study of the literacy experiences of these learners was a paper written by a university diploma student. Nganunu (1982) argues strongly that non-Setswana speakers have serious problems participating in the political life of Botswana and in the literacy program, explaining that

> . . . language policy in Botswana stresses that the official languages (Setswana and English) must be used in everything that concerns the government. This makes it difficult for Non-Setswana speakers to cope with developments and changes which occur in everyday life in this country. After the establishment of the Department of Non-Formal Education, literacy programs were started and carried out in various parts of the country, some parts of which do not understand the two languages. Despite this complication, the policy of this country's literacy program has continued to be the use of the National language regardless of the above mentioned problem. (Nganunu 1982, 4)

Discovering that 25 percent of the literacy learners in a community with another first language could not explain what was being taught because they did not speak Setswana, Nganunu concludes, "I have no hesitation in stating that the literacy program of the Department of Non-Formal Education is failing. I say this because, the program is about a year old in the village and there is no progress seen whatever" (Nganunu 1982, 4).

Even in the study of 1987, the problems of these individuals is not a primary concern. While the study tentatively concludes that results of a literacy test "suggested that mother-tongue is not a significant variable" in performance (Gaborone, Mutnyatta, and Youngman 1987, 50), several methodological features of the study make this a very tentative conclusion. Test respondents did not include dropouts and the questionnaire did not ask learners to specify their language identification (the results were based on inferences derived from the learner's geographical residence) (Gaborone, Mutanyatta, and Youngman 1987, 52, 64).

Despite early signals that non-Setswana speakers experienced special difficulties in literacy classes, teaching literacy in indigenous languages other than Setswana was never seriously considered. The political nature—and official avoidance—of this issue is suggested in the proceedings of the Botswana Library Association, (1985) which stated that

> . . . it was accepted that this [teaching literacy only in Setswana] is an important and difficult issue, with political implications. It was noted that the issue goes beyond literacy and even education, so that it is a national issue. It was suggested that educationally, mother-tongue initial education is always desirable but that economic constraints often made it difficult to provide. It was proposed that minority language groups might take the initiative in developing their own materials and put pressure on the government for an evolution in policy away from the current insistence on Setswana. (Botswana Library Association 1985, 33)

Even in 1986 the government response to this problem was a rather tentative consideration of special materials for these learners: "the long-term solution may lie in the development of special sets of instructional media through the assistance of bilingual design specialists" (Ministry of Education 1986, 4).

English as a Second Language.

Government action on teaching English as a second language follows a similar pattern. From the early days of the program, documents point to the inevitable demand for literacy in English. An extensive study in 1982 summarizes the learners' feelings: "They took it for granted that English would follow Setswana, as night follows day" (Alley 1982, 2). The study also points to an economic motive for this demand: in response to the question posed to literacy group leaders, "Would English help your learners to get work in their town or village?" every leader responded "yes" (Alley 1982, 5). The study's findings suggest the accuracy of this view. A month-long survey of newspapers conducted by these researchers revealed, for instance, that every job advertisement was published in English. Even a catalogue of government forms written in English at the time revealed much about the necessity of English to move beyond rural subsistence life. These English-only forms included, for instance, passport applications, departure from and arrival to Botswana forms, Self-Help Housing forms, and driver's license applications.

The government was slow to act on information such as this, moving only in response to strong demand by learners and then rather unenthusiastically. For example, a government publication stated that

> . . . a majority of neo-literates perceive and express a need to learn practical English and they continue to exert pressure on the Department to consider it as one of the components of the post-literacy package. As a central facet of the philosophy of non-formal education DNFE [Department of Non-Formal Education] feels committed to help participants satisfy this felt need. However, caution will be exercised to ensure that literacy in Setswana remains the basic tenet in programming. (Ministry of Education 1986, 6)

The evaluation of the program in 1987 explicitly questions an economic reason for inaction, pointing out that an external donor had been willing to pay schoolteachers to teach English (Gaborone, Mutanyatta, and Youngman 1987, 80). That study concluded that "DNFE has as yet done little to respond to the demand [for English] although a draft English primer was produced at the end of 1985. The Primer has not been used officially because a Leader's Guide has not yet been prepared" (Gaborone, Mutanyatta, and Youngman 1987, 81).

Postliteracy Planning

The government's failure to implement the demands of learners (and even its own policy statements) is also evident in the program's postliteracy planning. Throughout the program's history, action groups and income-generating activities had been deemed crucial. Characteristic of the rationale for these groups is a document stating that

> . . . it was agreed that this [postliteracy activities] was an important question which faces literacy workers and which raises the issue of the purpose of the literacy programme. It was pointed out that the concept of "Literacy for its own sake" had a limited appeal as people wished to see tangible benefits. The general aim of the programme is to improve the standard of living of the majority in the rural areas, especially by helping adults to engage in more productive activities. To this end, literacy groups were being encouraged to form production groups. (Botswana Library Association 1985, 34)

In a similar vein, the Ministry of Education's Report on the program in 1985 noted that the Department of Non-Formal Education continued "to mobilize groups to undertake income-generating activities" (Ministry of Education 1986, 6). This idea was also incorporated into the Policy Paper of the National Literacy Program which stated that

> . . . the intention is to make literacy functional rather than being an isolated experience and unrelated to life. It is envisaged that in the follow-up phase, accent would be put on the formation of project groups by advanced literacy groups or individual members so that they acquire functional skills and in order that they could embark on production and income-generating activities. (Ministry of Education 1986, 7)

The difference between technical rationality and implementation, however, is clear in the 1986 report. Despite promises to "encourage," "mobilize," and "accent[uate]" income-generating groups, only seven projects were actually in operation at that time, all but one funded by an individual or the group (Ministry of Education 1986, 8). The failure of this part of the literacy program is also evident in the 1987 study: "It is apparent that there are no clear policy guidelines regarding the setting up of income-generating activities for literacy graduates. The idea seems to have been 'sold' to the NLP participants as a way of sustaining their interest in the literacy programme without considering the wider implications of its implementation" (Gaborone, Mutanyatta, and Youngman 1987, 77).[4]

The learners' disappointment in this aspect of the program is evident in their interview responses in this study. One learner noted, "We can read and write now, but we don't use newly-acquired skills to earn a living like you" (Gaborone, Mutanyatta, and Youngman 1987, 73). A member of one defunct activity group comments bitterly, "We couldn't wait forever for assistance which was not forthcoming. You see, the people who tell us about these bright ideas are assured of a monthly income whether the projects succeed or not. We don't have a monthly income—this is the difference" (Gaborone, Mutanyatta, and Youngman 1987, 78).

Literacy Links to Formal Education

A literacy program aiming to improve people's economic situation also needs a link to the formal education system to allow people to progress beyond basic literacy. Again, a wide gap separates policy statements from implementation. In 1983, the Ministry of Education's own reports note the failure of this part of the program and establish it as a future priority: "The link to formal education was supposed to have been established already [a] long time ago. But somehow, all the parties involved seemed to be reluctant to work on it since the tasks involved are very huge, demanding, and not very promising at the same time. But now there is the demand of the learners that urge for actions to be taken" (Ministry of Education 1984, 74).

---

[4]One conclusion Hamadache and Martin draw from their survey of literacy campaigns applies to this aspect of Botswana's literacy program: "It is undoubtedly preferable to justify the campaign by means of political and social rather than economic arguments. It is always hazardous to dangle before future literacy learners the lure of a job or increased wages" (Hamadache and Martin 1986, 25).

Political Will

The history of the Botswana Literacy Program suggests the importance of political will for a successful campaign. As H. S. Bhola has argued, political will and the specific characteristics of a literacy campaign do not develop in a vacuum but ultimately grow out of a country's political ideology. He points out that

> . . . the prevailing ideology of a society will, first of all, determine whether universal adult literacy is indeed central to the achievement of overall national development goals. Ideology will also determine the articulation and maintenance of the "politicall will" to achieve universal literacy in a society—a necessary condition for a successful mass literacy campaign. At another level, the prevailing ideology . . . will determine the organization, mobilization, and implementation of a mass literacy campaign within a particular society. (Bhola 1984,177)

In the case of Botswana, the political will (at least that of government leaders) has been directed toward an area where mass literacy has not been crucial. As comments by literacy learners suggest, however, the popular will is another matter. In their demands for a literacy responsive to their needs lies a hopeful future for mass literacy in Botswana. The lesson Parsons (1984) draws from his historical study of education in Botswana echoes clearly in the history of its National Literacy Program: "Education is not just a 'social service' to be dispensed by central government to local communities like a tonic medicine. People can educate the government as much as, if not more than, the government can educate the people" (Parsons 1984, 43).

References

ALLEY, E. 1982. *English as a second language—An investigation into the feasibility of a course suitable for people who have just learned to read and write Setswana.* Gaborone: Department of Non-Formal Education.

ARNOVE, R. F. 1987. The 1980 Nicaraguan national literacy crusade. R. F. Arnove and H. J. Graff, eds. In *National literacy campaigns: Historical and comparative perspectives,* 269–92. New York and London: Plenum Press.

_____ and H. J. GRAFF, eds., (1987). *National literacy campaigns: Historical and comparative perspectives* New York and London: Plenum Press.

BHOLA, H. S. 1984. *Campaigning for literacy: Eight national experiences of the twentieth century, with a memorandum to decision-makers.* Paris: UNESCO.

_____ 1985. *Report card on a national literacy programme: The case of Botswana.* Paper presented at the Joint SIDEC/CIES Conference on Comparative Education and International Development, Stanford University, Stanford, CA.

_____ 1987. Adult literacy for development in India: An analysis of policy and performance. R. F. Arnove and H. J. Graff, eds., In *National literacy campaigns: Historical and comparative perspectives,* 245–67. New York and London: Plenum Press.

BOTWSANA LIBRARY ASSOCIATION. 1985. *Report of the conference on libraries and literacy.* Kanye, April 1985.

CLIFFE, L. 1984. A critique of Botswana's development path.In *Education for development: Proceedings of a symposium held by the Botswana society at the national museum and Art Gallery,* ed. M. Crowder, 59–77. Gaborone, 15–19 August, 1983. Gaborone: Macmillian Botswana Publishing.

COLCLOUGH, C., and S. MCCARTHY. 1980. *The political economy of Botswana: A study of growth and distribution.* Oxford: Oxford University Press.

CURRY, R. L. 1987. Poverty and mass unemployment in mineral-rich Botswana. *American Journal of Economics and Sociology* 46, no. 1 (January): 71–86.

DEPARTMENT OF NON-FORMAL EDUCATION. 1979. *Minutes of the meeting considering a national approach to the eradication of literacy in Botswana.* Gaborone: Department of Non-Formal Education.

FREIRE, P. 1970. *Pedagogy of the oppressed.* Trans. Myra B. Ramos. New York: Continuum.

GABORONE, S., J. MUTANYATTA, and F. YOUNGMAN. 1987. *An evaluation of the national literacy programme.* Gaborone: Institute of Adult Education, University of Botswana.

GIROUX, HENRY. 1983. *Theory and resistance in education: A Pedagogy for the opposition.* South Hadley, MA: Bergin and Garvey.

HAMADACHE, A. and D. MARTIN. 1986. *Theory and practice of literacy work: Policies, strategies and examples.* Paris: UNESCO.

LEEPILE, M. 1986. Twenty years of economic planning: A critique. *Mmegi wa Dikgang,* 3, no. 36 (27 September 1986): 6–7.

LEVINE, K. 1982. Functional literacy: Fond illusions and false economies. *Harvard Educational Review* 52 (3): 249–66.

MINISTRY OF EDUCATION, Department of Non-Formal Education. 1984. *National literacy programme: national evaluation exercise 1983. Recommendations.* Gaborone.

_____ 1986. *Annual report of programme: 1985.* Gaborone.

_____ 1986. *Policy paper on the national literacy programme.* Gaborone.

_____ 1987. *Annual report of programme: 1986.* Gaborone.

MORAKE, K. P. 1979. *Speech delivered at the opening of the meeting on the eradication of illiteracy in Botswana.* Gaborone.

NGANUNU, T. E. 1982. *The evaluation of the non-formal education literacy programme in Mapoka.* Institute of Adult Education. Gaborone.

PARSONS, Q. N. 1984. Education and development in pre-colonial and colonial Botswana to 1965. In *Education for development: Proceedings of a symposium held by the Botswana society at the national museum and art gallery, Gaborone. 15–19 August, 1983,* M. Crowder, ed. 21–45. Gaborone: Macmillan Botswana Publishing.

ROTH, K., and A. ETHERINGTON. 1981. *GTZ assistance to the national literacy programme of Botswana.* Bonn and Toronto: Hepworth.

RYAN, J. W. 1985. Language and literacy: The planning of literacy activities in multilingual states. In *Issues in planning and implementing national literacy programmes,* G. Carron and A. Bordia eds., 159–75. Paris: UNESCO.

TOWNSEND-COLES, E. K. 1979. *Working paper on a national approach to the eradication of illiteracy in Botswana* (n.p. Department of Non-Formal Education).

Udaipur declaration on international strategy for literacy promotion. 1982. Reprinted in H. S. Bhola, *Campaigning for literacy: Eight national experiences of the twentieth century, with a memorandum to decision-makers, 201–3.* Paris: UNESCO.

UNESCO. 1975. Declaration of Persepolis International Symposium for Literacy. Reprinted in A. Hamadache and D. Martin, *Theory and practice of literacy work: Policies, strategies and examples,* 128–31. Paris: UNESCO.

UNESCO. 1976. *The experimental world literacy program: A critical assessment* Paris: UNESCO.

Discussion Questions

1. Why does the author make a distinction between economic and political functionality?

2. How have Paulo Freire's ideas of education been linked with literacy education in developing countries?

3. For a developing country, what are the benefits and drawbacks in initial literacy instruction in an indigenous language? What does this chapter report on the choice of Setswana for literacy education in Botswana?

4. What does the author mean by "literacy for its own sake?" What does she mean by "traditional school-learning literacy?"

5. What does the issue of postliteracy planning involve? How is it related to the interviewee in Botswana who said: "We can read and write now, but we don't use these . . . skills to earn a living like you?" How is postliteracy planning tied to formal education?

Literacy and Cultural Erosion in the Pacific Islands

DONALD M. TOPPING

The penetration of literacy into an overwhelmingly oral, native culture tends to cause massive social, religious, ideological, political, economic, and cultural changes. (Graff 1987, 380)

While many ethnographers, linguists, and oral historians are busily compiling written records of vanishing cultures and languages of the world in the hope of preserving them, the literacy tools that they use in doing so may be the very instruments that are contributing to cultural erosion. Even while it is being used by social scientists as a means of cultural preservation, literacy is serving as a quiet but powerful agent of change. As it penetrates further into the societies and psyches of the traditionally oral people of the Pacific Islands, literacy poses ever greater threats to the survival of the traditional languages, customs, and social structures. Indeed, literacy in the Pacific Islands may be another instance where introduced technology intended to help has gone awry, and is serving to destroy the very things it was meant to improve. Unless current practices are modified, literacy will help sweep the island societies and their cultures into the mainstream of modernity, where they will surely be diluted beyond recognition.

This chapter will discuss how current uses of literacy in the islands may be contributing to cultural erosion, and suggest different strategies that might be employed to use literacy as a positive force to help direct the inevitable change that the island cultures are now facing.

THE PACIFIC ISLANDS

Most people outside of the region have only a vague concept of the Pacific Islands. Technically, the term includes all of the islands—and there are thousands of them—between Australia and South America in the southern hemisphere, and between mainland Asia and North America in the other half (excluding Japan and the Ryukus). The ones we will be concerned with in this chaper are the island groups of Polynesia, Micronesia, and Melanesia, all of which share a common Christian, colonial history, and are just emerging from more than a century of colonial rule. The major island groups are as follows:

Polynesia	Micronesia	Melanesia
American Samoa	Guam	Papua New Guinea
Western Samoa	N. Marianas	Solomon Islands
Tonga	Yap	New Caledonia
Niue	Belau	Vanuatu
Cook Islands	Chuuk	
Fiji	Pohnpei	
French Polynesia	Kosrae	
	Marshall Is.	
	Kiribati	

(Hawaii and New Zealand, though Polynesian, are excluded from this discussion because they represent quite different and separate histories, particularly since the late 1800s. Francophone areas—French Polynesia, New Caledonia, Wallis and Futuna—though not mentioned specifically in this chapter, share nearly identical colonial histories with their Polynesian and Melanesian neighbors.) See map (Figure 2.1) on page 34.

The total population barely exceeds 5 million, and they are spread out over nearly one-fourth of the earth's surface. The indigenous languages number well over a thousand, many of which are spoken by only a few hundred people, or less.

Until the early part of the nineteenth century, most of the people of these islands lived in relative isolation from Western influences. There were some early explorers (Magellan landed on Guam in 1521), but the pervasive influence of Western technology, and all of its implications, did not begin to take hold until the early nineteenth century through the expansion of Christian missions and colonial rule. The pervasiveness of that influence seems to correlate with the power of the technology. As will be shown in the discussion that follows, the technology that is the focus of this chapter—literacy—has proved to be more pervasive and lasting than most in the islands of the Pacific.

SOME ASPECTS OF LITERACY

In looking at the eroding forces of literacy on the cultures of the Pacific Islands, three aspects will be drawn into focus: (1) literacy as a technology; (2) the influence of literacy on cognition; and (3) literacy as autonomous authority. Since these topics are treated elsewhere in this volume (see the Introduction), as well as in numerous scholarly works (e.g., Ong, Havelock, Goody, Olson), no further definition will be offered here.

The position taken here is that these aspects of literacy have had, and are having a profound influence in the Pacific Islands on the way people believe and think, as well as on their social structures. It is a technology that has been adopted to a large extent into the daily lives of people undergoing the shift from orality to literacy. It has penetrated even the most remote island communities, spread by the institutions founded on literacy—schools and government—and has been instrumental in the colonization of the traditionally oral societies of the Pacific and the consequent cultural erosion.

EARLY CONTACT

The first purveyors of literacy in the Pacific were not the early explorers, traders, and beachcombers, even though their use of books, charts, and logs were certainly known to the islanders. Rather, it was the men, and their wives, in black suits carrying black books titled Holy Bible. When these Christian missionaries came to Polynesia, beginning in 1797 in Tahiti, their primary aim was, in missionary parlance, to "convert souls," which means changing the way people think. They soon learned that the surest route to success was through literacy.

At first, the islanders viewed literacy as another instance of Western technology, along with such things as the calendar, telescope, ship's compass, clocks, steel axes, and guns. They all came together in the same sailing ships from strange and distant lands. The islanders soon learned to their amazement (Goody and Watt 1968, 300–309) that this technology—literacy—could be used to send language across space and time. They observed that language could be made visible by use of a variety of manual implements, as well as with the technologically complex printing press, which the missionaries set up not long after their arrival for the purpose of printing biblical material in the languages of Polynesia. As with the other technological wonders—particularly nails and axes—the islanders were eager to partake of literacy. As G. S. Parsonson points out:

> The Pacific Islanders had long grasped the idea that the real difference bet-
> ween their culture and the European was that theirs was non-literate, the
> other literate. The key to the new world with all its evident power was the
> written word. (Parsonson 1967, 44)

In the beginning, the islanders sought the medium, not the message. In New
Zealand, according to Jackson:

> The desire on the part of the Maoris to become converted to Christianity
> went with a desire to be literate. Missionaries often ascribed Maori conver-
> sion to a Maori's desire to be a Christian, but the desire was to have access,
> through literacy, to the books in which reposed the lore and knowledge [i.e.,
> technology] of the Europeans. (Jackson 1967, 126)

The obvious relationship between visible language and the secrets of the
technological world provided the motivation for the islanders to become literate.
Their desire to learn was matched by the desire of the missionaries to teach.
The success rate, according to missionary reports, was very high. The Rev. Elisha
Loomis, one of the early missionaries to Hawaii, wrote in 1825 to Mr. J. Evarts
at the Mission Headquarters in Boston:

> A vast number of people have become able to read; and a vast number of
> others will be able to read by the time one of the gospels can be put into
> their hands. (Missionary letters 1819–1837)

The technology of literacy, limited though it was, spread throughout the islands
within a relatively short time. The concept of representing sound in visual, per-
mutable segments took root.

It is doubtful that this early literacy in itself caused any cognitive changes.
However, the content of the available texts undoubtedly did. From their pedagogical readers the islanders learned the dramatic concept of life after death,
either in the heavens or a place of eternal suffering somewhere deep in the bowels
of the earth. They learned of a single, omniscient, wrathful deity whose authority
and power were supreme. And, they learned that the laws of Moses were ir-
refutable because, not only were they written, they were written in stone.

To the island people these concepts were as alien as the white men who
introduced them. Because they were presented in bound volumes, each of which
said exactly the same thing, they were very persuasive. Acceptance of these ideas
demanded major changes in the traditional belief systems of the nonliterate
islanders. As more and more island souls became converted, major changes in
their ways of thinking took place.

This early stage of literacy in the islands also wrought changes in the social
structure of the islanders. For one thing, some of those who gained early mastery
of the technology emerged as a new priestly class. They became ministers of
the gospel, a position that is still held in high esteem throughout the islands.
Others became teachers, thereby establishing a new rank in the social hierar-

chy. A social dichotomy was created between the literate and illiterate, along with the social stigma that persists in nearly all parts of the world today.

The introduction of literacy under the banner of education also marked the beginning of a new social institution, the school, which was, and is still, an exclusively literate endeavor. The mission school systems were developed methodically and steadily, making the Gospel available to more and more of the multitude through the printed word. Literacy, albeit of a limited scope, was entering new minds and probably changing the thought patterns in them.

The establishment of missions and schools in Polynesia (especially Tahiti, Hawaii, Cook Islands, Tonga, and Samoa) led to the later expansion into most other parts of the Pacific. Before the end of the nineteenth century, churches, schools, and literacy were well established in all of the major island groups in the Pacific. It was the earlier converted Polynesians who brought the written word of Christianity to many parts of Melanesia where earlier European missionaries had failed.

COLONIZATION

While the covert colonization of the islanders' minds was moving apace through the efforts of the missionaries, the more overt colonization of their lands by European nations also got underway. (The United States did not enter the colonial arena until 1896, when it annexed the Hawaiian Islands. Two years later the U.S. added Puerto Rico, Guam, the Philippine Islands, and American Samoa to its colonial empire.) Again, technology played a major role. In addition to the ships, cannons, and muskets, literacy was employed as a vital instrument of colonialism. It was used to formulate and legitimize declarations, proclamations, and deeds of cession, as well as the new laws of the land. The proliferation of such documents during the nineteenth century bore witness to the complete colonization of the Pacific Islands from east to west, and from north to south.

(Ironically, the Kingdom of Tonga was the only island group in the Pacific that was never colonized, mainly because a maverick missionary, the Rev. Shirley Baker, persuaded King Tupou to let him write a constitution establishing Tonga as a sovereign state, which therefore could not be colonized. See Latukefu [1974, 171–74, 193–203] for a full account of the Rev. Baker's role in formulating Tonga's Constitution.)

As the new colonial governments became established in the islands, their appointed governors installed the necessary support systems: militias, courts of law, a small cadre of indigenous civil servants, and the schools to train them in the ways of the literate world. The impact was significant. The proliferation of the new social institutions created yet new social classes: soldiers, clerks, teachers, and students.

Those islanders—mostly males—who joined these newly created social classes rapidly became identified as the new elite. They wore watches, shirts, and shoes; sat in offices; and received money for services to the government. Many of them processed words and numbers on paper. This dramatic shift in life style from villages to schools and offices contributed to the growing alienation of this emerging class from the traditional beliefs and customs which had guided their ancestors for countless generations. As this group of select people took on more and more of the Western ways—even to the point of speaking the colonial languages to their children—early signs of cultural erosion began to appear.

Education played a prominent role. Whereas the mission schools were typically conducted in the indigenous languages of the islands, the additional schools created by the colonial governments for the children of the civil servants and settlers used the colonial languages exclusively. In most cases, there was a single government school, to which privileged children of island leaders would be admitted to matriculate alongside the children of the colonial servants. There they were trained in the ways of Western thought through the medium of print in the colonial languages. There they began to learn such fundamental Western concepts as atomism, logic, linearity, rationality, analytical reasoning, individualism, and interiorization—all the byproducts of alphabetic literacy, and all antithetical to the thought patterns of orality. The cognitive shift among the people of the Pacific was under way.

Under the colonial governments the restructuring of the island societies began. A major force in this restructuring was the written word. Customary law, traditionally adjudicated by customary chiefs and tribal councils, gave way to written documents, which were interpreted by literate judges. Ministers of the Holy Writ supplanted the diviners and traditional priests. The status conferred by birth (and in some places achievement) in the highly stratified societies of the islands became progressively overshadowed by the stigma of illiteracy during the century of colonial rule.

The shift from the authority based on oral traditions to that supported by written documents was central to these changes in law, religion, leadership, and status. The pattern that was established during the colonial era had its greatest impact in the government centers. It took a while longer and a change in circumstances for it to take firm root and be nourished by the island people themselves, which is precisely what happened in the years following World War II.

THE MODERN ERA

The Pacific war in the early 1940s ushered in the *modern era,* and in the process created conditions for the greatest social upheaval the islanders had ever known, particularly in the islands of Micronesia and Melanesia. The forces of social and cultural change were powerful ones. In addition to the hundreds of thousands of military personnel that swarmed the islands, in many cases outnumbering the indigenous populations, the war created dislocation of people and destruction on a scale never seen before, using newly developed, horrifying technologies.

The effects on the island people were profound, and somewhat varied. For example, islands such as Guam, Saipan, Tarawa, Peleliu, and Guadalcanal were virtually devastated. Homes, meeting houses, schools, landmarks, and even vegetation were obliterated by bombs and fire. The people of the Truk Lagoon witnessed the annihilation of an entire naval fleet through aerial bombardment. *Ni Vanuatu* (indigenes of Vanuatu, formerly the New Hebrides) were aghast at the massive quantities of implements of war that passed through their islands, and, for many of those employed by the military, through their hands. They were even more confounded by the wanton disposal of unused war materiel after the fighting had stopped. Even in islands that were spared the staging of troops and the ravages of armed combat, the lives of the people were touched by the war indirectly by such things as food shortages and conscripted labor. The Pacific would never be the same.

The end of World War II also marked the beginnings of the end of legitimate colonialism in the Pacific, the last stronghold of the colonial world. Compared with the rest of the newly emerging nations of the world, independence was slow in coming to the Pacific Islands. In 1962 Western Samoa became the first of the island groups to establish its sovereignty. During the following twenty years, others followed. Except for the remaining Chilean, French, and U.S. territories, the other island nations gained independence during the next twenty-three years, at least in form—written form—if not in substance.

Almost without exception, the new countries established systems of governance that were exact replicas of those of their colonial mentors, with written constitutions, laws, and education systems based upon books from the metropolitan countries from which they had sought independence. Not surprisingly, the new Pacific ministates had been cloned, and were ready to begin their journey into modernity.

THE ROLE OF LITERACY

Since the Western forms of government and commerce adopted by the new island nations were products of the literate mind, visible language was to play a major role as the fledgling microstates of the Pacific became selfgoverning. The prerequisite for the establishment of postcolonial governments was a set of documents, invariably conceived and written in the colonial language, which served as proof of sovereignty. In a world governed by literate nations, where nothing is legal unless written, the traditionally oral people of the Pacific had to offer proof through literacy in order to join the world system as self-governing states.

There were documents establishing the new political status. More documents which spelled out the constitution were laboriously created. And from these documents began the flow of the never-ending stream of documents establishing laws, departments, bureaus, portfolios . . . all of the accoutrements of a Western, literate form of government. As the governments grew in size, more and more of the islanders left the orality of the village and migrated to the urban centers, discarding the technologies of fishing and farming for those of the new era, the tools of which are pencils, paper, calculators, and typewriters. Discarded also, though not consciously, were the village ways of thinking, and governance, based on centuries of oral traditions through which complete social and belief systems were formed, which had enabled them to live in delicate balance with their environment for countless generations.

Just what were some of these "village ways of thinking" that succumbed to the advances of the Western, literate society? And how did the shift from "traditional" to "modern" among the islanders lead to cultural erosion? Let us review a few of the critical areas.

The schools, of course, played a major role. Universal education became a human right in the Pacific Islands, as in many other parts of the developing world in the 1960s. Education became big business—the biggest, in fact, throughout most of the Pacific Islands in terms of money expended and people employed. New schools were built. More native teachers were trained at local teachers' colleges, staffed by expatriates. The United Nations embarked on international literacy programs. Governments of big powers gave generously to educational development programs throughout the Third World. The U.S. government funded a Right to Read program. Literacy was on the march as never before in history, and in lockstep with the sociopolitical institutions it has spawned. Without literate operators, the expanding social institutions in the Pacific Islands—government bureaus, schools, businesses, banks—could not function.

In keeping with the new literate social and political institutions, the schools took on the responsibility to prepare people to live within those institutional frameworks. The first step was to inculcate a new style of literate learning, which Ong contrasts with oral learning as follows:

> In an oral culture, verbalized learning takes place in an atmosphere of celebration or play. . . . Only with the invention of writing and the isolation of the individual from the tribe will verbal learning and understanding itself become "work" as distinct from play, and the pleasure principle be downgraded as a principle of verbalized continuity. (Ong 1967, 30)

In the new schools of the Pacific Islands, the function of language is diffent from that in the real-life world. In the school, language is no longer used primarily as a means of interactive communication, but rather as a tool for abstract learning. In the schools, island children are taught to learn in silence, either by listening to an authority figure, or by trying to process thoughts through reading and writing rather than by the traditional oral means of direct experience and dialogue. This new approach to learning, determined by literacy, has required a drastic shift in the young minds of the island youth. Through literacy, communication becomes interiorized.

The study of language (and numbers) in the school introduced island children to the world of analysis and segmentation, where one looks for discrete units as opposed to whole systems. Coming from a world where even preschool children understand the holistic relationships of moons and tides, of seasons and fish, of weather and insects, and so on, to one of piecemeal, segmental, linear reasoning as fostered by alphabetic literacy, the children of the Pacific have become subjected to the conflict of contradictory cognitive patterns.

As Hallpike has observed:

> Language in these [nonliterate] societies is not a tool of conceptual analysis, but the basic vehicle of interaction, of conveying information, of persuading, of concerting action, and there is no awareness of "propositions" dissociated from the context of utterance or of "language" as a phenomenon distinct from "speech." (Hallpike 1979, 129)

In other words, language at home and in society was for human interaction; at school, it has become something different. Through the teaching of literacy, language is an isolating rather than an interactive experience. The young students must learn to interact with the word itself, an entity unto itself, immutable and firm.

The schools have played a contributory, if not dominant role in other important areas where traditional, orally transmitted knowledge and conceptualization is being abandoned, or rapidly displaced by the book. Even something as basic as storytelling shows the effects. For example, the oral narratives of the Pacific Islands tend to be "circular," often beginning in the middle, with many peripherals added as the story shifts back and forth, whereas literate narrative structures, such as those taught in the schools, demand a sequential beginning, middle, and end. (In this respect, the island tales are much like the epics of the preliterate Homeric tradition.)

Masao Hadley of Pohnpei (Micronesia) must have been aware of this different concept of narrative structure when he included the following caution in his oral history of his people:

> After some description of each era, we will return to the first and discuss different individual events, said to have occurred during that time. All eras will be treated this way. This arrangement may confuse some readers, but only those who are inattentive. The stories related after the main descriptions will help detail what occurred between the main events. (Hadley 1968–1969, 4)

Similarly, many of the precontact mythologies of the Pacific have no marked beginning in time nor any portended finale, while that of the West begins with an act of creation and foretells of an inevitable, sudden end.

Another striking example of the difference in manner of conceptualization between the oral cultures of the Pacific and that of the literate West can be seen in the systems of navigation. The Western man navigates linearly across the waters, measuring each segment with the sextant and recording it in the ship's log. In the Pacific Island navigator's system, all of the moving parts—clouds, birds, waves, currents, and shadows—and their relationship to each other are sensed as one, all interacting in a holistic relationship. For the navigators of central Micronesia, even islands move as part of the whole. (See Gladwin 1970, and Lewis 1972, for detailed descriptions of Micronesian navigational concepts and methods.)

As the Pacific children spend more and more of their time in the literate environment of the schools, learning from attempted interaction with the printed word rather than by the familiar oral tradition, their experience is one of increasing isolation and alienation from traditional sources and areas of knowledge. Essential repositories of the culture, such as the oral histories, genealogies, poetry, and song become submerged by the plethora of textbooks in European languages. Traditional myths, some of which get recorded and written down, are reclassified as "folk tales," and are no longer taken seriously. Oral histories become "legends," with the implication that they are based on hearsay rather than historical fact. The unwritten chants, poems, and songs are lost as the young people turn to recorded and printed forms.

Other essentials of the traditional oral societies, such as the technologies of canoe building, weaving, and navigation, are discarded as artefacts of a time gone by. Even the traditional medicines from the local flora and fauna are replaced by the injection and pill. These various types of knowledge, all of which depended on memory and oral transmission, are no match for that transmitted by the printed word, such is the power of literacy.

Aside from the changes being fostered by the schools, the most significant change leading to cultural erosion, triggered by the new paper-fueled governments, was the quiet overthrow of the traditional leaders. The new governments, legitimized by written documents, demanded new leaders who were literate in the metropolitan languages. Traditional leaders of the oral societies, for the most part, have been relegated to advisory roles, while the new elite, elected by popular vote, have become the voices of authority (see Weisbrot 1989, 81ff.). It was they who wrote the documents that became the new law of the land, usually in languages barely known by the electorate. It was they who were elected because they could write the documents, having been educated overseas in the colleges and universities of the former colonizing countries. Many of the new leaders in the Pacific Islands now carry attache cases, sit behind large desks in air-conditioned offices, and have secretaries (usually expatriate) to prepare and file documents, the major products of government. Many of the traditional leaders remained in the village, adjudicating minor disputes and reminiscing about times past and traditions lost.

Literate Societies	Nonliterate Societies
Religion: organized, salvationist, exclusionary. anthropomorphic	Belief system: pantheistic
History: documented, presented as fact, formal subject of study in school, very limited data on minority cultures, disconnected from living past through distance of print	Legend: reposed in human memory of designated individuals, rich in data, connected with living past through oral transmission
Literacy: reading, spelling, and writing skills are rewarded	Oracy: eloquence of speech, imagination, and memory are rewarded
Literature: stories are told through print; great literature is read only in school setting	Oralature: stories are told to living audiences; great epics are preserved and transmitted by popular demand
Law: rules for social organization and conduct codified by specialists in specialized jargon, written, filed, and catalogued; arbitrated by appointed specialists	Custom: rules for a social organization and conduct known and understood by all, and arbitrated by designated authority
Information storage: data books, files, archives, libraries; memory is suspect, denigrated	Memory storage: select individuals are repositories of information; memory is honored, developed
Rationality, logic, reason are supreme values; wisdom defined through intellect as defined by calculated measurement	Spiritualism, instinct, empathy, knowledge of the past and capacity to explain are indicators of wisdom
Logical, analytic conceptualization and linear thinking, taught in schools and held as the perfect model	Holistic conceptualization: less concern with analysis of constituent parts, but rather how they work together
Individualization, privacy, alienation, isolation; the *id* is a thing in itself	Communal, cooperative, familial; the *id* is part of a larger entity
Success-failure image: begins with early literacy experience in school	Each individual has an appropriate place in the system, even if a hierarchical one

Listed on page 29 in juxtaposition, is a summary of some of the major areas that have been affected in the ongoing transition from oracy to literacy in the Pacific.

Conclusion

Like many of the other aspects of modernization, literacy has become a source of confusion and doubt in the oral societies of the Pacific, and, as I have argued, is contributing significantly to cultural erosion. Like other introduced features of technology, it is causing unexpected consequences which have not been taken into account as the concerted move towards universal literacy gains momentum.

There is no doubt that literacy has come to the Pacific to stay. There is the question, however, of its proper role. Will literacy in European languages lead to their ultimate domination at all levels of society? Would increased efforts to develop literacy in Pacific languages make a difference? Will literacy be governed by well-articulated policies and planning? Or will it be allowed to continue on the course already set through the absence of policies and planning?

If the erosive impact of literacy in the Pacific is to be mitigated, steps must be taken to counter some of the practices that are already firmly entrenched, particularly those found in the major social institutions of education, politics, law, media, and government bureaus. Since the main function of the schools is preparation for the social institutions, the changes should begin there. And, they should begin by harnessing the very force that has been the focus of this chapter: literacy.

Along with increased literacy activities in the indigenous languages, the traditional oral histories, mythologies, chants, and poetry must be revitalized by all means possible. Appropriately recognized and rewarded performances and contests would help to achieve this goal.

The schools of the Pacific should consider more extensive use of the indigenous languages of the Pacific both in oral and written form. It is not enough to have three or four years of desultory reading and spelling exercises, such as those found in the bilingual education programs in the primary schools of U.S. Micronesia. Rather, what is needed are curricula that are based on and conducted in the indigenous languages throughout the school systems. Limiting the study of Pacific languages to the elementary school will guarantee that the development of those languages will be stifled at the elementary level. If the languages are going to develop along with the drastic changes that are taking place in the societies, then they must be given an appropriate place in the school system alongside the metropolitan languages.

There are major problems in such an approach. One is the lack of text materials in the Pacific languages. These must be developed. Another is the choice of languages, especially in polyglot Melanesia, where even the village elementary schools are likely to have pupils from different languages, with the teacher speaking none of them. Solutions to these problems need to be worked out at the local level, and can be accomplished if the desire to maintain the indigenous languages is strong enough. Inexpensive desktop publishing technology now makes it possible to produce attractive and affordable text material on any scale.

Throughout the Pacific the government offices and the people who run them have been innundated with documents, nearly all of them written in English or French in the pattern set during the colonial period. Governments should seriously examine this practice. They must recognize that much, if not most of internal government correspondence could be carried out in the indigenous languages. As long as governments continue to be conducted in the colonial languages, they will continue to be clones of colonial governments, while the indigenous languages and ideas of governance will be eroded.

Throughout the Pacific, entire legal systems are founded on and conducted in colonial concepts and languages. Beginning with the constitutions and other documents of political status, and continuing down to laws, rulings, and parliamentary proceedings, English or French is the dominant language in conceptualization and formulation. Only afterwards are they translated into Pacific languages. Aside from the lower courts, where indigenous languages may be used (but in most cases recorded in a European language), English or French still functions as the language of rule in countries where it is still the language of only a few. This is another area where Pacific languages must be reinstated.

Pacific countries must ask themselves if the situation just described is true, and if so, should it be changed? It is recognized by all that the colonial languages are needed in the Pacific, and are there to stay. What may not be recognized is that the spread of these languages in their written form is exerting a very powerful and subtle force on the people and cultures of the Pacific. The extent of this force and consequent erosion of the indigenous languages and cultures may not be known until it is too late to control it.

Policies that will permit and encourage the use of the Pacific languages, especially in their written form, will do more than help preserve the cultures in the museum sense. The right kinds of language policies which recognize and accord significant status to the Pacific languages can serve to keep them, and therefore the cultures, alive. There are serious dangers in having no policies.

The absence of policy is an invitation to continued cultural erosion. If, indeed, the act of literacy is as powerful as I have suggested, it should be linked as firmly as possible to the roots of Pacific cultures, to the Pacific languages themselves. Perhaps the harnessing of literacy to the languages of the Pacific will at least help to limit the effects of the alphabetized way of thought.

References

GLADWIN, T. 1970. *East is a big bird.* Cambridge: Harvard University Press.

GOODY, J. and I. WATT. 1968. The consequences of literacy. In *Literacy in traditional societies,* ed. J. Goody. Cambridge: Cambridge University Press.

———. 1977. *The domestication of the savage mind.* Cambridge: Cambridge University Press.

GRAFF, H. 1987. *The legacies of literacy: Continuities and contradictions in western culture and society.* Bloomington: Indiana University Press.

HADLEY, M., assisted by K. GALLEN 1968-1969. *Pahsonen Pohnpei.* Translated by Melody Moir. Unpublished manuscript.

HALLPIKE, C. R. 1979. *The foundations of primitive thought.* Oxford: The Clarendon Press.

HAVELOCK, E. 1963. *Preface to Plato.* Cambridge, MA: Belknap Press.

———. 1986. *They must learns to write.* New Haven: Yale University Press.

JACKSON, M. 1976. *Literacy, communication, and social change: A Maori case.* Unpublished master's thesis. University of Auckland, Auckland, New Zealand.

LATUKEFU, S. 1974. *Church and state in Tonga: The Wesleyan Methodist missionaries and political development.* Canberra: Australia National University Press.

LEWIS, D. 1972. *We, the navigators.* Honolulu: The University Press of Hawaii.

LOGAN, R. 1986. *The alphabet effect.* New York: St. Martin's Press.

LOOMIS, E. 1825. *Missionary letters, Loomis to Evarts, Oahu, 26 December 1825.* Honolulu: Hawaiian Mission Children's Society Library.

MEGGITT, M. 1968. Literacy in New Guinea and Melanesia. In *Literacy in traditional societies,* ed. J. Goody, 300-309. Cambridge: Cambridge University Press.

Missionary letters, "Typed copies" from the Sandwich Isle mission to the American Board of Commissioners for Foreign Missions, 1819-1837. Honolulu, Hawaii Mission Children's Society Library.

OLSON, D. 1977. From utterance to text: The bias of language in speech and writing. *Harvard Educational Review,* 47:257-281.

ONG, W. 1967. *The presence of the word.* New Haven: Yale University Press.

———. 1977. *Interfaces of the word.* Ithaca: Cornell University Press.

———. 1978. Literacy and orality in our time. *ADE Bulletin,* 58:17-18.

———. 1982. *Orality and literacy: The technologizing of the word.* London: Metheun.

PARSONSON, G. S. 1967. The literate revolution in Polynesia. *Journal of Pacific History,* 2:39-57.

SCRIBNER, S. and M. COLE. 1981. *The psychology of literacy.* Cambridge, MA: Harvard University Press.

STREET, B. V. 1984. *Literacy in theory and practice.* Cambridge: Cambridge University Press.

WEISBROT, D. 1989. Custom, pluralism, and realism in Vanuatu: Legal development and the role of customary law. *Pacific Studies,* 13 (1):65–97.

Discussion Questions

1. Use the map (Figure 2.1) on page 34 to locate each of the islands listed under the three headings: Polynesia, Micronesia, Melanesia. With which ones are you familiar, at least by name? What do you know about any of them?

2. In what ways does Topping present the case for literacy as an autonomous authority? What is the relationship between literacy viewed as a technology and literacy as individual achievement?

3. Topping contrasts oral and literate societies. What experiences have you had with predominantly oral cultures?

4. Do you believe any of the cultures of the South Pacific area might be able to survive in the twenty-first century as predominantly nonliterate? Are there ways that traditional leaders of oral societies can guide their people into living in both worlds, oral and literate? What are some trade-offs for Pacific island people in gaining entry into the world of Western literacy? What do they gain? What do they lose?

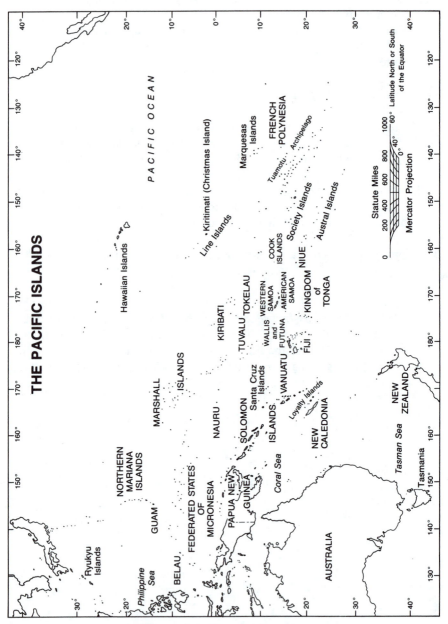

Figure 2.1 The Pacific Islands

Literacy Acquisition of Hmong Refugees in Thailand

LYNELLYN D. LONG

The war in Laos ended in May 1975, but civil strife continued for many years. Several thousand Laotian Hmong, who had been allies of the Americans, escaped to Thailand, where they established the Ban Vinai Refugee Camp in the hills of northeast Thailand with the assistance of the American CIA and Thai military. From 1975 to the present time, several waves of refugees, escaping poverty and conflict in Laos, have fled across the border. Upon reaching Ban Vinai, many have gone on to resettle in the U.S., but others, hoping to return to Laos someday, have elected to remain in camp. Although built to be temporary, a decade after its opening the camp housed more than 45,000 refugees. In 1986 the majority had lived there an average of seven years (COERR 1986).

It is well known that the lives of the Hmong who resettled in the U.S. underwent profound changes. What is less well known are the equally profound changes of those that remained in Ban Vinai. The camp began as a small village in the mountains, but over time became the largest Hmong city and one of the most densely populated places in the world. Hmong who began their lives as swidden (slash and burn) rice farmers and poppy growers in the small villages in the mountains of Laos adjusted to an urban, bureaucratic institution and welfare economy. This transformation would have major implications for how they organized their lives and what forms and kinds of knowledge became relevant.

The majority of Hmong, who arrived in the camp between 1975 and 1979, were pre- or semiliterate. By 1986, a camp survey (COERR 1986) showed that 49 percent of the adult population reported to be literate in one or more languages: Hmong, Lao, Thai, Chinese, English, and/or French. This is a dramatic increase in a very short time by any standard. What is also surprising is the variety of languages and literacies. The survey further showed that patterns of literacy acquisition varied by gender and age. Women were more likely to become literate first in Hmong, whereas men chose Lao or Thai. The young learned nonindigenous languages—French, English, or Chinese—more quickly than older people who usually did not become literate, but maintained strong oral story-telling traditions.

What hastened this literate transformation? What accounts for the gender and generational differences in patterns of literacy acquisition? Many scholars have described oral literate transformations from primitive to technological "modern" societies (Levi-Strauss [1977] 1977; Goody 1977; Ong 1982. However, as others have shown and as can be seen in Ban Vinai, societies are not simply oral or literate, but patterns and uses of literacy are related to everyday practices and embedded in particular cultural contexts (Heath 1983; Scribner and Cole 1981; Scollon and Scollon 1981).

Although as this research suggests, cultures are not static, how and on what basis do they change? Several (Freire 1970, 1980, Kozol 1980; Luria 1976) would argue that periods of social and historical transformation affect changes in human consciousness and cognition. Such transformations are described in revolutionary terms. However, the Hmong resistance was at best a counter-revolution. Yet, as in periods of revolutionary change, the forms of knowledge and everyday practices of the Hmong were transformed by the camp experience. In the *Protestant Ethic and the Spirit of Capitalism,* Weber (1976) showed that changes in institutions and material conditions affect social processes. In Ban Vinai, it could be argued that the increases in literacy rates reflected the changed material conditions and new institutional arrangements of the refugee camp.

From data based on eleven months of fieldwork in Ban Vinai during 1986, I show how camp life affected acquisition and patterns of literacy among the Hmong. The chapter begins with a brief overview of the historical evolution of Hmong oral and literary traditions. I then describe the functions and uses of literacy in the camp context and how these differ by gender and generation. In the final section, I discuss the implications of the Ban Vinai experience for literacy transformations in other contexts.

LITERATE AND ORAL TRADITIONS

Literacy for the Hmong has historically been associated with the powerful forces that they have had to resist and eventually overcome. The Hmong originated in China, but early Chinese records show that even before the second century

B.C. the Hmong resisted Chinese rule and fled south to escape oppression. Other Chinese suppression campaigns and Hmong rebellions are recorded in A.D. 47, in the fifth and sixth centuries, and again in the tenth century. Finally, major suppression campaigns occurred with the establishment of the Manchu Dynasty in the seventeenth and eighteenth centuries when the Hmong dispersed further south in several directions. The Hmong's first known writing system was borrowed from the Chinese writing system, but the transcription was not adapted to the Hmong language (Lemoine 1972, 20). As the Manchu Dynasty tried to incorporate the Hmong into their bureaucracy, the adoption of Chinese characters may have symbolized a capitulation to that more powerful force.

Western missionaries had a major impact on subsequent development of a Hmong writing system. The Hmong's first reported contacts were with Jesuit missionaries in China in 1736. Their contacts with the Protestant China Inland Mission, however, impressed the Hmong with the power of the written word. Pollard, an American evangelical missionary, translated the Bible and introduced the first widespread Hmong writing system (Lemoine 1972, 21). Pollard wrote that because the Hmong so valued the written word, they converted en masse. When translating the Lord's Prayer, the missionaries introduced the concept of "kingdom" into the Hmong language. The Christian Messianic themes resonated with the Hmong's own suppression at the hands of the Chinese. The Hmong in oral myths tell of how the "Hmong Book," their written word, was lost while fleeing the Chinese. According to Tapp:

> . . . we [nevertheless] see the clear connection between Messianic beliefs and a myth about the lack of literacy which is linked to the ideal of the fallen kingdom. (Tapp 1982:121)

In other myths, the Hmong, clearly influenced by the Biblical accounts of missionaries, incorporated aspects of the Exodus story in their own historical accounts.

In the mid-nineteenth century after two hundred years of bloody resistance to Chinese warlords, a group of Hmong fled south. They settled in the mountainous regions of Laos, Vietnam, and Thailand, where they cultivated opium and swidden rice crops. Although a minority in all three countries, the Hmong maintained their distinct ethnic identity and kinship ties across national boundaries. In the early twentieth century, the Hmong resisted French taxation much as they had earlier resisted the Chinese. The Hmong also played an important role in the Laotian independence movement in late 1940s and early 1950s.

In 1959, Shong Lue Yang, an illiterate claiming divine inspiration, created a new Hmong writing system, Pahwah Hmong. Half Khmú, he also created a writing system for the Khmú, another minority group which lived in the upland areas of Laos. Pahwah Hmong was quite complex, but had a large following among Hmong in Laos and Vietnam. According to Smalley (1990), a Protestant missionary and linguist,

... hundreds of people walked long distances through Laos and Vietnam jungles, many for several hours, a few even for days, to learn it. (Smalley 1990:6)

Over the next several years, Shong Lue simplified the writing system from 151 to 81 symbols in three revisions (Smalley 1990, 7).

Both the Vietnamese Communists and the Royal Lao government saw the growing popularity of the movement as threatening to their own political interests. The Vietnamese and Pathet Lao Communist forces claimed that the movement was part of a CIA plot and several times tried to capture and kill Shong Lue and his family (Smalley 1990). Although he escaped capture from the Communists, Shong Lue was arrested and jailed by the Royal Lao government in 1967. His followers eventually rescued him from jail, but in 1971 he was assassinated. The movement, however, continued after his death. With the support of Smalley, Hmong have revived the movement in the U.S. and to this day, Pahwah Hmong is still considered by some Hmong to be their most authentic writing system.

In Laos and Thailand, Western missionaries continued to have a major influence on the development of a Hmong writing system. In the 1960s, Catholic and Evangelical missionaries together developed a romanized Hmong writing system. William Smalley, Linwood Barney, and Yves Bertrais, three missionaries, created the system that most Hmong currently use in Ban Vinai and in the U.S. In 1964, Yves Bertrais created a French/White Hmong dictionary in Laos and in 1966; Ernest Heimbach created an English one in Chiang Mai, Thailand.

Western missionaries were strong advocates for Hmong irredentist movements. During the 1960s, missionaries sympathized with the Hmong in their uprisings against the Royal Thai government and sided with the Hmong who opposed the Communist Pathet Lao in the north. Their support, however, was a mixed blessing. The Christian beliefs allowed the Hmong to rationalize their political economic marginalization, and Hmong leaders later used these beliefs to foster utopian visions of recapturing their homelands in Laos.

In the latter half of the twentieth century, the Hmong also encountered forms of literacy that were associated with state rather than religious power. In 1956, the People's Republic of China encouraged the alphabetization of Hmong for the remaining five million Hmong living in China. The alphabetization did not improve the Hmong's marginal status in the new Communist state and subsequent generations became literate in Chinese.

Likewise, in Laos, Hmong adopted the national language and literacy of the new Laotian republic. The first Laotian formal primary schools organized during colonial times were designed to train an administrative elite and followed the French curriculum. During the 1960s, the Royal Lao government with massive U.S. foreign aid opened primary schools in rural areas. Lao rather than French was made the primary language of instruction. The government's attempts, however, to modernize and create a national educational system were subsumed by increasing conflict. As the Pathet Lao, the Communist forces, gained control of large parts of Laos, American forces resettled Hmong in refugee settlements around Vientiane. In these first refugee resettlements, many Hmong attended school for the first time. Young Hmong men, conscripted into the Royal Lao army, also learned to read and write Lao.

When the Communists seized power in 1975, the new Lao People's Democratic Republic (LPDR) continued earlier attempts to make Lao the national language. Creating "schools of the people," they, too, introduced the Lao language in their literacy programs. In contrast to the Royal Lao government, however, the new government made a more concerted effort to reach women and to open adult literacy programs.

FUNCTIONS AND USES
OF LITERACY IN BAN VINAI

At the end of the war in May 1975, many Hmong fled across the Thai border to refugee camps such as Ban Vinai. From then up to the present time, the Hmong have developed a semipermanent life in Ban Vinai. With thirty-five to forty-five thousand people crowded on less than a square mile in the camp, the life style increasingly resembles that of a large peripheral urban slum, but without a city core. The majority of the residents subsist on UN food rations. Although there is a strong informal economy, Ban Vinai is primarily a welfare state.

The Thai Ministry of Interior (MOI) runs the camp, but the United Nations High Commissioner for Refugees (UNHCR) coordinates the work of some fifteen Thai and international voluntary agencies (Volags). The Volags organize the camp's infrastructure and services. Encountering Thai and foreign workers of many nationalities, the Hmong have been exposed to multiple literacies. Hmong interact with Thai, English, French, Japanese, Chinese, and Dutch speakers and attend literacy and language classes in several of those languages.

There are also many opportunities to use literacy in the camp. Literacy is required for most Volag employment in the hospital, primary schools, and offices. Many bureaucratic requirements assume literacy. Hmong are expected to understand written camp announcements and Embassy forms, and carry UN identity cards. As in the past, religious Volags also promote literacy as they distribute Bibles and offer English and Hmong literacy classes. At a Catholic Easter service, for example, Hmong ushers handed out hymn sheets in Hmong and Lao. Although many in the crowd were barely literate, all held copies as they sang.

In the late 1970s, Pahwah Hmong regained brief popularity in Ban Vinai. A Hmong temple was built in the camp. At the height of its popularity, the temple housed some hundred monks and held several literacy classes daily. Several reasons for the sudden resurgence of Shong Lue's movement are given. According to Lemoine (1986, 338), the new religion was a Messianic reaction to the growing influence of Western religions in the camps. Others argue that the religious texts called for a stronger opposition to the Communists in Laos and that the sudden appearance in the camps represented growing Hmong disatisfaction with Vang Pao, the CIA-backed Hmong resistance leader (Yves Bertrais, personal interview, August 26, 1986.)

Regardless of whether the Hmong were resisting Vang Pao, Communism, or Christianity, the sudden revival of a Hmong writing system in the multiliterate camp context suggests that they were also affirming their uniquely Hmong identity. Hmong often spoke of how their traditional way of life was changing. Affirming their own writing system may have been one more attempt to take control of the changes in their lives.

In the mid-1980s, the movement faded in Ban Vinai. The young began studying Chinese in the Hmong temple. According to young Hmong, the Pahwah Hmong writing system was too complex. The young also seemed more interested in the local Thai culture, in reaffirming their roots to China, and in educational opportunities in the West.

For both young and old, Ban Vinai offers many different kinds of educational opportunities. Since the mid-1970s, Hmong people, at times with Volag support and at times privately, have offered English and Hmong literacy classes. In 1980 to 1981, the U.S. State Department funded an English and cultural orientation program for U.S.-bound refugees. A year later, the State Department moved the program to Phanat Nikom, a processing center, for those accepted for resettlement. Other Volags (French, British, and Thai) offer Hmong and Lao adult literacy classes. Volags also conduct ESL and Thai language classes primarily to train workers and interpreters.

A Thai Volag provides primary schooling and trains Hmong teachers. Until recently, these schools came under the Thai national educational system. MOI hired Thai supervisors, who were supplied by the Ministry of Education, to oversee the Hmong teachers. The children were taught in Lao, but also received one hour of Thai language instruction daily from the Thai teacher supervisors. In 1989, UNHCR reorganized the primary education system and eliminated Thai from the curriculum. The rational given by the UNHCR field officer was that since the Hmong would not be allowed to resettle in Thailand, the children should be prepared for eventual repatriation to Laos.

A Japanese Volag introduced a printing press, which the Hmong quickly adopted to create their own texts. The press produces children's story books, magazines, and primary education materials in Lao and Hmong. Young Hmong publish their own creative writing in the press and record traditional stories and myths. Other written materials are readily available in the camp. Many families own an English-Hmong phrasebook and a Thai or Lao dictionary. The more literate buy Thai newspapers and English primers. Thai pornographic magazines are sold in the camp market and Thai television with all the usual advertisements provides great entertainment for young and old.

The daily routines of life in Ban Vinai increasingly require greater need for literacy. While women and young girls spend the majority of their time sewing to earn income for the household, they also write or tape letters to relatives who sell their handmade products in the U.S. Aware of the importance of reading and writing for their children, women's sewing groups encourage children to recite lessons aloud after school. Parents even bribe their children to go to school with money for candy or ice cream sold on the school playground. Both women and men trade in the camp, and in local Thai and international markets. When they sell handicrafts in Thai and international markets, women who never learned to read and write, carefully record sales and purchases. Life in Ban Vinai is many years and kilometers away from the swidden farmers' life in Laos.

GENDER AND GENERATIONAL DIFFERENCES

In the complex, urban setting of the camp, generational and gender differences have developed which are reflected in different literacy choices. Within households, who is literate in which language (or languages) correlates with age and gender. In the Ly household, for example, the eldest Mrs. Ly, in her sixties, is nonliterate and speaks primarily Hmong and a little Lao. She grew up in the mountains of Laos. Her family, practicing swidden agriculture, moved short distances every two to three years and longer distances every ten years. The frequent migrations and daily struggle to survive left little time for study. Her late husband was also nonliterate, but learned Lao when he fought in the war. In the late 1960s, U.S. troops airlifted the family to the lowlands. There, her son received three years of primary education. He was taught in Lao, in an official government school. The son married at 17. His wife was 15 and had no formal schooling. The family, unable to grow enough rice to feed themselves and pay the tribute demanded by the Pathet Lao, fled to Ban Vinai in 1979.

Mr. Ly became the head of household at his father's death. As the household head, he negotiated with the Thai military the family's entry into the camp. Knowing how to read and write Lao from his three years of primary schooling, Mr. Ly easily learned to read Thai in the camp (since the two languages share common linguistic origins and characteristics). He also enrolled in ESL classes, but lost interest when he realized he was not likely to emigrate in the near future. Mrs. Ly enrolled in a six month Hmong literacy course in 1982. Following the classes, she has continued to write letters in Hmong, but her main activity is sewing. Her experience typifies that of many young women, who have studied Hmong. A survey (SAO 1986, 11) found that 73 percent of women respondents practiced their Hmong writing skills in letters to relatives. The Ly's oldest daughter, Xiong, has spent eleven of her twelve years in the camp. She studies in grade three in the camp primary schools. She knows the Thai and Lao alphabets, but "not very well," reported Mr. Ly disgustedly. Like many other Hmong parents, who have little control over their children's schooling, he is unimpressed with the quality of the camp's schools.

When I asked him why he learned to read and write Thai and English, but not Hmong, Mr. Ly replied, "I don't need Hmong." For men, the only work in the camp was employment with a Volag, black market activities, or the Resistance. The Volags prefer those who know Thai, Lao, English, and/or French. The other activities do not necessarily require literacy, although being literate in Thai is an advantage. Mr. Ly claimed that his wife learned Hmong first, because it was easier for a nonliterate person. His opinion is supported by many other literate refugees in the camp (and by educational research).

A Southeast Asian Outreach (SAO) survey (1986, 8) of forty-five women who participated in a Hmong literacy program found that 43 percent of the women went on to receive more formal education in Lao and/or other training. Women also found personal value in literacy; 98 percent of the respondents believed it was good for Hmong women to be literate and 85 percent believed that literacy skills helped a woman to help her family (SAO 1986, 10). Some women were also aware that they must become literate in Hmong before studying English in a processing center for refugees accepted by third countries (SAO 1986, 7). Women's reasons for becoming literate in Hmong, then, reflected both personal interest and increased opportunities.

For Ban Vinai as a whole, 51 percent of those over six years old reported that they were literate (COERR 1986). Those literate in one language often reported being literate in two or more (COERR 1986, 12). Males and females, however, ranked differently on various literacies. Men reported being literate in: (1) Lao; (2) Thai; (3) Hmong; (4) English; and (5) others. Women reported being literate first in Hmong and then the other languages. About three times as many men as women said that they were literate. The importance of Hmong for the women may reflect the responsibility that they are often given for maintaining Hmong culture and traditions.

Among young people, this gender difference slightly decreases, as younger people of both sexes are learning to read and write Lao and Thai in primary school. The camp population is predominantly young; 45 percent of 41,974 people recorded in 1986 (COERR 1986, 9), were reported under fifteen and 67 percent under twenty-five years of age. Many young people have spent the majority of their lives in Ban Vinai. Their primary activities had been education and recreation. In contrast to their parents and grandparents, who worked in the fields, 63 percent of Ban Vinai's school-age children are in primary school (COERR 1986, 1).

Beyond formal schooling, young people, with little else to do, take advantage of a wide variety of nonformal and informal educational opportunities in the camp. Xiong Ly reported the following daily schedule:

4:30   cook and clean

5:00   study Chinese (Hmong teacher)

6:00   breakfast and preparation for school

7:00   primary school (grade three)

12:00   lunch

1:00   English classes (Volag)

3:00   sewing and embroidery (taught by mother and older women).

Xiong finishes the evening early with homework, dinner, and housework. Since there is no electricity in the camp, she retires by nine.

Xiong is somewhat atypical. Most girls are still less well educated than boys in the camp. In the first grade, the ratio of girls to boys in primary school is fairly equal (44 versus 56 percent), but by grade six the gap widens (9 versus 91 percent) (COERR 1986). Hmong girls continue to marry younger than boys, usually between 15 and 19, and once married, leave school to help with family and sewing. Since sewing is the main source of income in Ban Vinai, there are strong economic incentives for girls, traditionally trained in these arts, to leave school sooner.

Different literacy traditions are also reflected in generational differences. Being literate in several languages carries a certain prestige among the young. Teenage girls said that the ideal husband is someone who can read and write many languages. Since Volag jobs usually require literacy, young men who can read one or more languages command these jobs. Elderly Hmong continue to conduct the majority of their affairs orally in Hmong, but their authority is also declining. Although Hmong traditionally consulted their leaders when they had a serious problem, 46 percent in 1986 reported not consulting anyone. This was twice the number reported just two years earlier (COERR 1986, 20).

In Ban Vinai, life is also increasingly differentiated by day and night activities. The young predominate in the more public, institutional world of the day, whereas the elders regain their authority in the more traditional world of the night. These two spheres of activities elaborate different oral and literate traditions. At night, the eldest, Mrs. Ly, for example, continues to tell traditional stories in Hmong to her children and grandchildren. Through these stories, she passes down the beliefs and practices of a Laotian Hmong mountain community.

Generational differences reach crisis dimensions over a new communication technology, the video. Several young girls, scolded by their parents for watching video films, have attempted suicide. For the girls, watching the video represents a form of revolt against very domesticated lives. Boys are noticeably less censured than girls for the same activity. The older generation rails against the video, perhaps because it symbolizes yet another assault on their traditional ways of life.

Differences in each generation's hopes for the future are reflected in their different literacies. Deciding to become literate in English or to remain within a strictly Hmong community implies very different states of mind. The oldest generation would prefer to return and die in Laos if they could. The elderly have made little or no effort to become literate in any language. They continue to tell stories of Laos to their grandchildren and foster dreams of returning. Most young people want to resettle in a third country. They have learned several languages to increase their options. They dream of going to China, the U.S. or Australia, and of kung fu, disco, and educational and economic opportunities. The middle generation is caught between the two. They know that they will eventually have to decide whether to resettle or repatriate. Meanwhile, they remain in Ban Vinai. Their conflicting hopes and fears are expressed in men's halfhearted attempts to maintain fluency in Lao, or women's aspirations to become literate in Hmong. Yet this generation also enrolls in yet another English class and as each day passes, they speak and read more Thai.

Conclusions

Refugee camp life has created new uses for literacy and literate practices. Ban Vinai has transformed swidden rice farmers into sedentary urban dwellers whose survival depends on their ability to manipulate bureaucracies and institutions. The few productive activities, sewing, or Volag work require more literacy. Like many urban welfare dwellers, however, the Ban Vinai residents' lives are compartmentalized and differentiated by public and private worlds, by gender, and by generation. Ben Vinai's different literacies are as varied as each generation's images, hopes, and fears for the future. There is the public world of the institution and the private world of the home and community. Men interact more in the public world than women and the young are more part of this world than their elders. Correspondingly, each has different oral and literate practices. Elders maintain their oral traditions, whereas the young try to become literate in several languages. This diversity of practices may ultimately contribute to the Hmong's ethnic survival wherever they go next.

As an institution, Ben Vinai has had a profound impact on literacy rates and on the kinds and forms of literacy. The evidence that institutional processes can have such an effect has implications for other contexts. The Ban Vinai experience suggests that as refugees and immigrants interact with schools, hospitals, work places, and welfare systems, such institutional interactions will affect their attitudes towards literacy. If these institutions provide opportunities, they may choose to get involved. Threatened by institutional assaults on a way of life, the Hmong and others may also resist by asserting alternative literate and oral traditions.

Acknowledgments

This work was supported by Wenner Gren Foundation for Anthropological Research and the Catholic Organization for Emergency Relief and Refugees (COERR) of Thailand. Ruth Hammer of SAO and Father Yves Bertrais shared their work with me and contributed greatly to my understanding of the Hmong literacy traditions. I am also indebted to Ger and Shoua Khang, Jack Wigfield, and Shirley Brice Heath for their comments and encouragement.

References

BERTRAIS, Y. 1986. Personal interview with the author.

Catholic Organization for Emergency Relief and Refugees (COERR). 1986. *Report of survey of refugee needs and problems in Ban Vinai Refugee Camp, Thailand, 1985–1986.* Thailand: Ban Vinai Refugee Camp.

FREIRE, P. 1970. *Pedagogy of the oppressed.* Trans. Myra B. Ramos. New York: Herder and Herder.

_____. 1980. The adult literacy process as cultural action for freedom. In *Thought and language/Language and reading,* Wolf, McQuillian, and Radwin eds. Cambridge, MA: Harvard Educational Review.

GOODY, J. 1977. *The domestication of the savage mind.* Cambridge: Cambridge University Press.

HEATH, S. B. 1983. *Ways with words.* Cambridge: Cambridge University Press.

KOZOL, J. 1980. A new look at the literacy campaign in Cuba. In *Thought and language/Language and reading,* Wolf, McQuillan, and Radwin, eds. Cambridge, MA: Harvard Educational Review.

LEMOINE, J. 1972. *Un village Hmong Vert du Haut Laos.* Paris, France: Centre National de la Recherch Scientific.

_____. 1986. Shamanism in the context of Hmong resettlement. In *The Hmong in transition,* G. L. Hendricks, B. T. Downing, and J. A. Dienard eds. Staten Island, NY: Center for Migration Studies of New York, Inc.

LEVI-STRAUSS, C. 1977. *Tristes Tropiques.* New York: Washington Square Press (Originally published by Librairie Plon, 1955).

LONG, L. D. 1988. *The floating world: Laotian refugee camp life in Thailand.* Unpublished dissertation. Stanford, CA: Stanford University.

LURIA, A. R. 1976. *Cognitive development: Its cultural and social foundations.* (Cole, ed.) Cambridge, MA: Harvard University Press.

ONG, W. J. 1982. *Orality and literacy: The technologizing of the word.* London: Methuen.

SCOLLON, R. and S. B. K. SCOLLON. 1981. *Narrative, literacy and face in interethnic communication.* Norwood, N.J.: Ablex.

SCRIBNER, S. and M. COLE. 1981. *The psychology of literacy.* Cambridge, MA: Harvard University Press.

SMALLEY, W. 1990. The Hmong "Mother of Writing": A messianic figure. *Southeast Asian Refugee Studies Newsleter* 10(2):5–9.

Southeast Asian Outreach (SAO). 1986. *Hmong literacy programme for women, Ban Vinai Camp, Amphur Pak Chom, Loei Province, Thailand.* Unpublished report.

TAPP, N. 1982. The relevance of telephone directories to a lineage-based society: A consideration of some messianic myths among the Hmong. *Journal of the Siam Society* 70:114–27.

WEBER, M. 1976. *The Protestant ethic and the spirit of capitalism. (Giddens, Intro.).* New York: Scribner's.

Discussion Questions

1. How have researchers described the role of literacy in different societies?

2. What has been the role of literacy in traditional Hmong society?

3. Why has literacy correlated with missionary and Messianic movements throughout Hmong history?

4. Why do different genders and generations employ different literacy skills in the refugee camps?

5. How does the camp, as an institution, affect the forms and uses of literacy?

Literacy Shifts in Rural Greece: From Family to Individual

ROSEMARY C. HENZE

"Μέ όποιον δάσκαλο θα κάτσεις, τέτοια γράμματα θα μάθεις."
(With whichever teacher you sit, such are the letters you will learn.)

Greek proverb

Introduction

As the proverb above suggests, Greeks are no strangers to a sociocultural view of learning. Folk theories such as the one represented in the proverb have long recognized that literacy and other skills are embedded deeply in social practices which play a critical role not only in the processes of knowledge and skill acquisition, but also in the cognitive shape of what is acquired. Greeks apply the proverb in a wide variety of situations, usually in order to explain the state of a person's knowledge or skill. It could refer to the way someone drives, cooks, writes, reads, speaks, and so on. It is often used sarcastically, a backhanded indictment of both the teacher and the results of the learning process. But no matter how it is used, it attests to the socially constructed nature of the learning process and of learning outcomes.

This view of cognition, known in academic circles through the Soviet psychologist Vygotsky, posits that all cognitive processes appear "first between people as an interpsychological category, and then within the child as an intrapsychological category.'' (Vygotsky 1962, 163) In keeping with this view, I will be defining literacy as "shorthand for the social practices and conceptions of reading and writing" (following Street 1984).

If learning first occurs as social interaction, then it is not surprising that informal learning processes differ across cultures, as well as across different subgroups within a heterogeneous society such as the United States. These differences have been pointed out in a number of ethnographic studies which look at the communicative processes of groups that typically underachieve in school. Scollon and Scollon, for example, studied Athabaskan communicative style in an attempt to learn how Caucasian teachers might better adapt instructional practices to create more familiar patterns of interaction in the classroom. They found a greater emphasis among Athabaskans on joint sense-making in conversation than is normally the case in mainstream U.S. classroom interaction. Athabaskan elders do not, for example, ask questions of children in order to make them elaborate on their utterances, but rather tend to repeat or gloss after the child (Scollon and Scollon 1981).

Teachers in cross-cultural situations may find research such as this informative, particularly if it addresses the communicative style of the particular group or groups with whom they are working. Language and literacy teachers in particular need to develop an awareness of the ways in which oral and literate practices are embedded in the social and family lives of their students. This may seem an impossible task, given the numbers of students in most classrooms and the cultural diversity in many. Studies of particular groups may appear on the surface to provide little guidance for teachers not working with those groups. Yet one finds in many of these ethnographic studies keys not to the specific students one works with, but rather to the *kinds* of questions one might ask in order to learn about those students. This chapter, based on an eight-month ethnographic study, focuses on the relationship between literacy practices and family life in a Greek community. Through the specifics of the Greek context, the chapter develops suggestions as to the kinds of information that could be elicited from students of any cultural background in order to better understand the influences on and consequences of their literacy acquisition.

LITERACY IN GREECE

In Greece, as in many places in the world, literacy rates have risen dramatically in the last century. Thessaly, the area where I conducted research, is no exception. In 1907, the literacy rate in the rural areas of Thessaly close to the city of Trikala was less than 20 percent (Sivignon 1976). In 1986 I found that a sample of village families in the same area showed a literacy rate of 74 percent (Henze 1988). This is only slightly lower than the national literacy rate of 75.8 percent cited in a Sept. 8, 1986 Greek National Television news broadcast.[1] As is often the case, the literacy rate was lower for women, elderly people, and people living in rural areas. These groups, in fact, comprise most of the 24 to 26 percent who are not literate in Greece.

The language situation deserves special mention here, for until recently Greece had two quite different varieties of language for different functions, a phenomenon known as "diglossia" (Ferguson 1959).[2] Katharevousa, literally "the purifying language," was until 1976 the "language of officialdom," used in education, government, the military services, and all other official functions. All school texts were written in Katharevousa and classes were conducted in it as well. Demotika, on the other hand, was and still is the language of everyday life. In 1976, two years after the colonels' junta fell, Demotika was declared to be the official language of Greece (Mackridge 1985). At the same time, the number of years of compensatory schooling was extended from six to nine years. "All in all, Katharevousa [had] served to draw the line between the educated few and the semi-literate masses, between the rulers and the followers, since it was impossible to learn it in the six years of compulsory schooling." (Dimaras 1978, 15) Those students who began school after 1976 have had the advantage of nine or more years of schooling carried out in Demotika, the language they speak at home.

Because of these educational reforms, illiteracy (the inability to carry out reading and writing functions basic to everyday life) is almost a thing of the past among the youngest generation. However, the middle generation—parents of the students now in secondary school and university—are far less uniformly literate, many having attended only six or fewer years of school in which Katharevousa, a language they did not speak at home, was the medium of instruction. The oldest generation—grandparents of those now in school—retains the even lower literacy rate of an era when schooling was not required and when Greece, still recovering from 400 years of subjugation by the Turks, was torn apart by World War II and the Greek Civil War. There was little time in these people's lives to concentrate on education.

This distribution of literacy among the three living generations is certainly not restricted to the Greek situation. What makes it particularly interesting in Greece is the dynamic relationship between literacy distribution and Greek family relations. To show how the relationship between literacy practices and family roles is changing in the wake of mass literacy, I will bring together several

[1] The survey was conducted by Giorgos Papandreas of the Ministry of Culture.
[2] A diglossic situation also exists in West Germany, Switzerland, and Austria, where *Hochdeutsch* (literally "high German") is the language of official use, and *Plattdeutsch* (literally "low German") is the everyday language, including many dialects. Similarly in the Arab countries, classical Arabic, which is reserved for official functions, exists side by side with the less formal dialects of Morocco, Egypt, and other Arab countries (Ferguson 1959).

sources of information about informal acquisition and practice of literacy across three generations of an extended family. These include interview data in which a grandmother recalls the way she learned to read and write; observations of current literacy practices across all three generations; and audio and video recordings of everyday literacy events in the family and their immediate community.

Before moving to these specifics, I want to make a few comments about the typicality or generalizability of the data which follow. The majority of information in this paper is based on thirty to forty people who are related to one another, most living in a village and some in nearby towns. While it is tempting to attribute what one sees among a few individuals to a whole culture, Greeks, like any group of compatriots, are disarmingly varied. There are gulfs between rural and urban, between male and female, among the different regions of Greece, between the educated and less educated, and of course among individuals. Western Thessaly, where this study took place, has received little attention in the anthropological literature (Friedl 1976), and the "argumentatively different historical voices of individual rural Greeks" have tended to be romanticized in descriptions of the supposedly typical peasant (Herzfeld 1987). This paper honors some of the particulars of a few people's lives, invoking their situations more than their "Greekness" in order to explain intergenerational changes in the practice of literacy.

LITERACY AND FAMILY INTERDEPENDENCE IN THE PAST: THE CASE OF KATERINA YORGAKI[3]

Born in 1920 of two farmers, Katerina Yorgaki has lived all her life in the village of Kiriakitsa, near the town of Trikala. She and her husband Grigoris have spent their working lives raising wheat, corn, cotton, watermelons, and other crops. Until she was sixty-four, she had not even been to the sea, only two hours away. Her parents were illiterate, as are both her sisters, who live nearby. However Katerina, the second in the family of three girls, became literate and maintains her literacy to this day. She can read newspapers, television subtitles, and labels on merchandise, and she occasionaly writes a brief letter or note to someone. When she does so, she often ruefully tells the reader, "Πάρε και πιρούνι να βγάζεις τα γράμματά μου!" (Better get a fork to pull my letters out!) Though clearly a bit embarassed at her uneven script and nonstandard spelling, she acknowledges that her literacy is unusual among women of her generation and economic circumstances, most of whom can neither read nor write. Today, when mass literacy is almost taken for granted, we tend to wonder why people fail to become literate, but Katerina's time and circumstances make it more appropriate to ask, Why *did* she become literate?

---

[3] The names that appear in this chapter have been fictionalized.

Katerina accounts for her acquisition of literacy by referring to family need, histoical circumstances, and order of birth. By the time she reached the third grade, she had to stop attending the village school. Her older sister, being bigger and stronger, had already quit school because she was needed in the fields. Her younger sister, still a toddler, needed to be cared for at home, and Katerina was the logical person to provide this care since her mother and father had to work in the fields every day. Her father at this time needed to correspond with serveral brothers and cousins who were away from the village. Katerina, because of her position in the family and her relatively recent experience with reading and writing in school, was chosen to fill this role. When letters would arrive from absent family members, she would be the one to read them to the rest of the family. When a letter needed to go out, she would be the one to write it. She also read, and, if necessary, responded in writing to any official papers or forms that came to her father. Thus Katerina, in a sense, managed or facilitated the literacy needs of a whole family.

Katerina is careful to point out that her three years of schooling are not in themselves sufficient explanation for her ability to read and write. Many other men and women in her generation have had between two and four years of schooling, but today they cannot read a newspaper or write more than their names, if that. Some of her peers cannot dial a telephone number. While schooling did of course facilitate Katerina's acquisition of some basic literacy skills, these skills, she notes, would most likely have diminished had she not had occasion to use them after she left school. Most of the women in her generation, if they had any schooling, soon lost whatever literacy skills they had acquired there because they did not use them on an everyday basis. It was the continued need for her skills in communicating with distant family members that led Katerina to maintain and increase her literacy.

Her family's literacy situation was not unusual for that period in rural Greece except in so far as the one who became literate was female. Had Katerina had a brother, he probably would have been chosen to be the literate one. In any case, most nuclear families at that time relied on one person—preferably a male, and preferably someone *within* the nuclear group—to carry out the literacy needs of the family. I will refer to this grouping of the literacy needs of related individuals as "collective literacy." In Katerina's youth, it was assumed and expected that family interdependence came before individual desires. The high value placed on family (documented as well by Friedl 1962 and Du Boulay 1974) made it almost unimaginable that illiterate members would be stranded. Even today, Katerina's illiterate cousin, Athanasia, does not worry about not being able to use the telephone to dial out; she simply assumes, justifiably, that there will always be someone who can do it for her, either in her own household or in the large network of neighbors, most of whom are also relatives. Nor does her illiteracy create a one-way dependency. Rather, it is one of many skills which contribute to the reciprocity among family and neighborhood members. This reciprocity, which includes the sharing of tools, food, childcare, and a variety of other goods and services, has been noted as well in a study of the social networks of illiterate adults in the northeastern United States (Fingaret 1983).

LITERACY AND FAMILY INTERDEPENDENCE IN THE PRESENT

Katerina is now a grandmother, and will perhaps soon be a great-grandmother. She and her husband Grigoris have raised four children, three of whom now have grown children of their own. As is often the case in rural communities these days, the younger people have moved to towns and cities, leaving the grandparents alone in the village. Katerina is proud that her children have a "better life" (i.e., that they do not have to work in the fields as she did), and glad that their urban life has not taken them too far away. Two of her daughters live only four kilometers away, in Trikala, and the third lives one hour away in Larisa, making visiting frequent and easy. Her son, the youngest of her children, lives in the United States.

Katerina's literacy is considered minimal now, her children and grandchildren read and write far more than she does. Her own literacy skills have changed little over the years, but the surrounding literacy context has changed greatly, and so have the functions of her literacy. Two of her daughters attended six years of school, and one attended nine years. They each run their own hairdressing businesses, thanks to Katerina's insistence (against her husband's wishes) that they go out and "μάθε μια τέχνη" (learn a trade/skill). At the time of the study, Katerina's son had recently finished a BFA in Film at a college in the U.S., and most of her grandchildren had completed twelve or more years of schooling. One was attending a university in Greece, and four were preparing to take the qualifying exams to enable them to go to a university. A fifth grandchild was attending a postsecondary technical school, and two were not yet finished with their secondary schooling.

The different functions of literacy among the three generations became clearer to me when, during fieldwork, I asked a seemingly simple question about social register in Greek. In the process of writing a thank-you letter to a Greek pediatrician whom I had met in a professional context and who had recently mailed an article to me, I realized that my Greek, learned mainly in informal contexts, was inadequate to the task of properly closing a letter to a professional woman I hardly knew. I went to Katerina and, after explaining the circumstances, asked her to suggest an appropriate closing (having in mind something like "Sincerely yours" in English). She replied, "Σε φιλώ με αγάπη" (I kiss you with love). Somewhat mystified, and almost certain that this closing would sound to intimate, I took note of her advice and then went to her oldest daughter with the same question. Anna, who had nine years of schooling, heard my description and question, thought a moment, then said, "Μέ φιλική αγαπή" (With friendly love). Though less direct than Katerina's suggestion, this still seemed too intimate, so I descended another generation to Mairi, Anna's seventeen-year-old daughter. Upon hearing the situation, Mairi immediately replied, "Μέ εκτίμηση" (With respect). Needless to say, I chose this closing for my letter.

Their different answers serve as reminders of the changing functions of letter writing in these women's lives and the audiences whom they address in writing. Katerina's and Anna's responses indicate that they have rarely had any experience writing letters to strangers or near strangers. They responded to my question with the only closings they knew, which were for personal friends and relatives. Mairi's answer, as she explained in a later interview, is appropriate to situations in which one writes to strangers or near-strangers. Though she has yet to really enter the public world, Mairi is being prepared in school for a life in which she has to communicate in writing with a wide range of people outside her own personal world.

The "collective literacy" of the earlier generations reinforced the interdependence of family members through an intimate and pragmatic bond of trust. The ability of one family member to read another's personal business placed the reader in a position of power in the family. The information gained could be quietly safeguarded, or it could be brought out and used against that person and his/her family at a time of conflict. How much someone paid for a piece of land, or the exact nature of an illness in the family—these are the kinds of knowledge that can in some instances make or break a family's standing in the community. Family information was and still is carefully guarded, and in Katerina's youth, the literate family member was responsible for much of that private information. Young people in Mairi's generation, on the other hand, are learning to read and write for communicative purposes that take them outside the family or inner circle. While they can and do still assist less literate family members, the primary function of their literacy is no longer service to the family.

INFORMAL INTERACTION IN LITERACY EVENTS

Today, though the functions of literacy in the family are more varied than before, the interdependence of family members continues to be evident in everyday life in the village and town. The following four vignettes describe some of the more typical literacy events[4] I observed, all of which involve family members interacting with printed or remembered texts[5] of some kind.

[4] Heath defines literacy events as "occasions in which written language is integral to the nature of the participants' interactions and their interpretive processes and strategies" (1986, 98).
[5] The term *text* is used here to include the object of any literacy game, as well as the more usual sense of printed discourse or words.

The vignettes move from childhood to adulthood. The first two involve children, first in a spelling game and then playing school. The third example, exam preparation, involves adolescents reciting memorized material for an exam to their mothers; and the fourth, television viewing, describes family interaction among all age groups during a foreign, subtitled show. Childhood literacy events set the stage for later interactions among adults in that the participants, regardless of their literacy skills, are all able to contribute somehow to the interpretation of texts. Instead of the dichotomy which exited in Katerina's youth between literate and nonliterate, these interactions show family members with varying degrees of literacy who take on a range of roles vis-à-vis the text.

Spelling

One of the games village children played frequently involved spelling the names of gods, goddesses, and flowers while rocking back and forth with a partner. Two children would sit on the ground facing each other, with their legs straight out in front and toes touching. Grasping hands and rocking forward and backward, one child would take the lead by spelling a name in the following manner:

closest Roman letter equivalent

Με λενε (They call me) _Π_	"P"	
Με λενε (They call me) _E_	"E"	
Με λενε (They call me) _PO_	"R"	
Με λενε (They call me) _ΣI_	"S"	
Με λενε (They call me) _E_	"E"	One rock per
Με λενε (They call me) _ΦI_	"PH"	letter
Με λενε (They call me) _O_	"O"	
Με λενε (They call me) _N_	"N"	
Με λενε (They call me) _H_	"E"	

Με λενε (They call me) ΠΕΡΣΕΦΟΝΗ (name of goddess, i.e.
"PERSEPHONE")

The leader would announce the letters until the partner recognized the name of the god, goddess, or flower, at which point both children pronounced the rest of the letters in unison, culminating with the name pronounced as a whole.

In this game, one child was responsible for the spelling of the name, while the other child participated as an interpreter. When the interpreter's interpretation merged with that of the speaker, the two children's voices literally merged and they finished the spelling in unison. In the cases I observed, both children in the pairs were literate (ranging in age from eight to twelve), but they played different roles in constructing the meaning of the letters, one taking the lead as the speller, the other taking on the role of interpreter and eventually, cospeller. Sometimes the two would switch roles, but in either case both children were mutually responsible for the final interpretation and choral ending.

This spelling game, with its marriage of body movements to letters, is reminiscent of one which black preadolescent girls play in the United States (described by Gilmore 1983). In their game, girls line up and challenge one of their peers to "Spell Mississippi [or some other word]; spell Mississippi right now!" The girl who takes the challenge goes to the front of the line and "spells" the word by imitating the shapes of the letters with her body. Thus for example the letter "S" is called "crooked letter" (often pronounced "crookaletta") and girls simulate its shape by curving their bodies in an "S" shape.

Games such as these provide valuable information about the social construction of literacy activities outside of school. The Greek game in particular points to an early separation of roles for children acquiring literacy in which one child knows the spelling of the god or goddess, and the other guesses from the first few letters and interprets which name is meant. The first child provides the "text," while the second child plays the role of "reader" of that text. When children switch roles, each gains valuable experience as both the source and the reader of texts.

Playing school

Another popular game among children in the neighborhood where I lived was "playing school." The game usually took place on the front steps of one of the neighborhood houses and involved anywhere from four to eight children, ranging in age from four to twelve. The older children were already well acquainted with real school while the youngest had not yet attended at all. Usually an older child played the role of "teacher" while the younger ones participated as "students." During the game, the children engaged in three distinct kinds of activity: (1) management; (2) transitions; and (3) "reading lessons."

Management activities were used by the teacher to regulate the behavior of the individuals in the group. This included telling other children where to sit, physically moving them if they did not comply, and directing them to read or be quiet. Transitional activity most often consisted of a group prayer. This was used in much the same way as it was used in village kindergarten classes, that is, to separate one activity from the next as well as to provide a frame for beginning and ending the kindergarten session.

The reading lesson was the content area most emphasized in playing school. During the reading lesson, the children who had brought school books would place the books on their laps and the teacher would select, one at a time, children to read. The one who was selected would read from his or her book (or a borrowed one) until the teacher told him or her to stop. Sometimes, if a child had trouble reading, another child would lean over and help. The youngest children, who did not yet know how to decode the letters, would also have a turn at reading, which they carried out by holding an open book in their laps and uttering passages of their own using intonation patterns similar to the reading intonation of the school-age children. As soon as the teacher told one child to stop, she designated the next reader.

Like the letter game, playing school shows an interdependence in which the older, more literate children are responsible for the text and its words, but the younger, less literate children still participate. There are no great gulfs between literate and nonliterate. By following the form of reading, even though they cannot yet decode the words on the page, the less literate children also interact with the text. Together, the group of children constructs an approximation of schooling and of the process of learning to read.

Studying for the Panhellenic Exams

The activities described so far involved children interacting with each other through two different kinds of literacy games—a spelling game and a game of school. In the next two activities, adolescents and adults are the participants.

The Panhellenic exams are a national test given each June to all Greek high school graduates who want to attend a Greek university or technical college. Competition is intense and many students fail. Families with children eligible to take the exams do everything they can to insure success, including spending large sums of money on "frontistiria" (private after-school classes) to give students the extra learning time needed to pass the exams. When they declare their intention to take the exams, students must state an "omada" or intended career path. The exam will cover several areas related to that path. For example, a student who declares an interest in law will be examined in history, Latin, classical Greek, a foreign language (French or English), and composition. The history exam, as well as the language exams, requires vast amounts of memorization. Whole books—hundred of pages—have to be memorized almost word for word. "What the book says" is sacred in this context, and personal interpretations or paraphrases of the text are unacceptable. This contrasts with the more open interpretations that are encouraged in informal literacy events such as playing school. However, the fact that Greek children do spend a great deal of time reciting and performing poems, songs, TV ads, and all manner of other texts serves them well at this later stage, when so much of their future depends on their memory of texts.

Preparation for the exams involves not only the individual student, but also the student's family. In the four cases I observed (two boys and two girls), the mother took on the role of monitor. She would set aside several hours a week to listen to her daughter or son recite texts, following along with the text and correcting the students as needed. The mothers also offered advice about studying—mneumonic devices, ways of prioritizing, and so on. The rest of the family would cooperate by giving the student as much time and space as they were able. Deviations from the routine, such as a relative coming to stay, were avoided if at all possible, and meals were planned with the student's schedule in mind. Unfortunately, not one of the four students I observed passed, despite the elaborate preparations and the fact that three of them were trying for the second time, having already failed once the previous year.

The older generation finds it difficult to understand why young people so often fail these exams. To them, having a text to refer to is almost a guarantee of learning the material. As Katerina pointed out, "Αφού έχουν τα βιβλία τώρα, πως να μην μαθαίνουν;" (Since they have books now, how can they not learn?). In her own early schooling, only the teacher had a book and students had to copy from the teacher's oral reading of the text. She feels that now, with books in plentiful supply, students have little excuse other than their own laziness for not learning (i.e. memorizing) the subject matter.

As can be seen, family cooperation and interdependence are deemed essential in the critical task of preparing for the exams. The exams are a "gatekeeping" event (Erickson 1982) by means of which future lives are channeled one way or another. For those who fail, the family seeks alternatives such as sending the student to a university abroad (Italy and Yugoslavia being the usual choices); setting him or her up in a small business; or if family resources are minimal, finding work for the student with family or friends.

Though the students in these cases were more literate and better schooled than their mothers, the mothers were the ones responsible for the accuracy of the student's recitation. They held the texts which were the authorities. This created an interesting reversal of what we saw in the early childhood activities, where the more literate children were responsible for correct spelling or correct reading. In exam preparation, the less literate person was responsible for the correctness of the recitation. The mother's age and position in the family no doubt contributed to this authority, making her literacy level less of an issue. Such flexibility in the roles of family members, however, is only possible in the wake of mass literacy.

Television viewing

Television has become almost ubiquitous in village homes in the last ten years, and viewing it is by far the most common evening activity among village families. In 1986 the two Greek television stations, ERT 1 and ERT 2, in addition to broadcasting Greek shows, also aired a large number of foreign shows, including such programs as *McGyver* and *Dynasty* from the U.S., as well as programs from Portugal, France, Germany, the USSR, and other countries.

Though these foreign programs were quite popular in Greece, people whose literacy skills prevented them from reading the Greek subtitles quickly enough had trouble following them. However, because families often watched television as a group, the more literate family members could provide a running oral interpretation of subtitled foreign shows for those who read less well. Participants did not seem to find this distracting, for television viewing was almost always accompanied by group dialogue about and to the characters on the screen, even when no subtitles were involved. Viewers frequently talked back to characters on the screen, contradicting or agreeing with what they said, calling them names, and offering them advice about what to do next. Different viewers would also discuss their interpretations of the actions on the screen, often disagreeing with each other. These oral interactions with other viewers and with characters on the screen did not cause them to lose track of the story line; they managed to pay attention to both scenes at once.

Family members in these interactions, with all their different degrees of literacy, actively worked together to construct the meaning of the television show. Though the most literate members had greater access to the text, and could if necessary read it word for word, they did not carry full responsibility for its subsequent interpretation. Other members with differing degrees of literacy played important roles as interpreters as well. Thus the interdependence we see here is not the reliance of the nonliterate on the literate, which we saw in Katerina's reflections on her youth, but rather a shared responsibility for interpretation of meaning among people with different literacy skills.

IMPLICATIONS FOR LANGUAGE TEACHERS

Literacy and Family Roles

The relationship between literacy acquisition and the roles of literate individuals in the family is an important one for language educators to consider, both in terms of influence and consequence. A person's acquisition of literacy may be shaped by prior experiences with literacy in family settings. In turn, changes in a person's literacy may have consequences for the social roles these individuals play in their families. In rural Greece, individual literacy and family literacy appear to have a mutually influential relationship.

As we educate students in a new language, or in the written form of an already familiar language, we make small but significant changes in the roles of those individuals in their families. The family in turn must adjust to the new situation, an adjustment that may or may not be welcome. Katerina's family has adapted well to the changes, perhaps because they occurred over a long period involving three generations. In some cases, however, literacy acquisition brings with it sudden shifts in family roles, such as those educators have observed among recent immigrants from Southeast Asia to the U.S. (see Long—Chapter 3). Among Lao and Hmong refugee families, children often acquire English more quickly than their elders. The elders then begin to rely upon the children to carry out the public language and literacy needs of the family—a role traditionally reserved for the father. Students in these situations have reported friction in their families due to the unfamiliar roles now assigned to children, and the implications of powerlessness for the father. Language teachers need to be aware of such effects on their students' families.

Such awareness can come about through learning activities in the classroom. Teachers can make it a point to find out about the literacy of students' families through ethnographic projects that involve students with each other and with their families. Students can interview family members and each other, asking questions about who is literate, what kinds of things family members do with their literacy, and which people are responsible for the literacy needs of the family. They can work cooperatively to make diagrams and tables of each other's families, showing literacy skills and patterns. This will bring the relationship of literacy and family structure into awareness and enable the teacher to talk about these issues with students.

The Individual's Relationship to the Text

When literacy becomes distributed among many family members, as is the case in the rural Greek family described here, people take on different roles not only with each other, but also vis-à-vis the text itself. Some situations call for an individual to adhere strictly to the text, while others evoke greater interpretive license. Within situations too, we see that one person may be responsible for the correctness of text, while another is responsible for its interpretation. This was the case in the children's spelling game, where one child took on the role of the speller, while the other listened to the letters until s/he was able to voice an interpretation and finish the game in choral mode. Adolescents and adults may, depending on the situation and their skills, emphasize word-for-word recitation of text, as we saw in the exam preparation, or more open interpretations, such as that which occurs during television viewing, where participants make multiple interpretations of the same text.

Teachers in cross-cultural situations may find it useful to consider the circumstances in which word-for-word recitals and fixed meanings are favored over more personal interpretations. In most cultures, the classroom is perceived as a serious place where the authority of the teacher, once established, is not questioned, and where the printed word is to be taken literally. Playfulness is not encouraged, and student interpretations are often discarded in favor of interpretations by higher authorities such as the writer, the teacher, or a literacy critic. Outside the classroom, on the other hand, a different view of texts may prevail, as illustrated in this chapter. Informal situations in which production and/or comprehension of print play a role are often seen by participants as fun and playful, as opportunities to value a variety of interpretations simultaneously. These distinctions between adherence to text and open interpretation can be explored in the classroom through projects that ask students to reflect upon and discuss the kinds of situations that require word-for-word adherence to text and those that allow more open interpretation.

Conclusion

This chapter has suggested that the consequences of literacy for families can be significant, whether in a first or other language. In the rural Greek context, changes in the distribution of literacy within the family have made it possible for individuals to be literate primarily for their own advancement, rather than to serve the needs of the family. At the same time, interdependence of family members is still a salient feature of informal literacy activities among rural Greeks, though it is now more a matter of choice than of necessity.

Language teachers play critical roles in changes such as those described here. Rather than ignoring or minimizing their powerful role as change agents, teachers can allow the classroom to become a forum in which all participants actively relate literacy to the wider social realm. This will accomplish two things: First, teachers and students will gain valuable knowledge about the meaning of literacy in other people's lives, and secondly, students will improve their literacy skills by participating in meaningful, collaborative activities.

References

DIMARAS, A. 1978. The movement for reform: A historical perspective. *Comparative Education Review,* Special issue on Greece 22 (1).

DIMEN, M., and E. FRIEDL, eds. 1976. *Regional variation in modern Greece and Cyprus: Toward a perspective on the ethnography of Greece.* Annals of the New York Academy of Sciences, 268.

DuBOULAY, J. 1974. *Portrait of a Greek mountain village.* Oxford: Clarendon Press.

ERICKSON, F.D. 1986. Tasks in time: Objects of study in a natural history of teaching. In *Improving Teaching: 1986 ASCD Yearbook,* KAREN K. ZUMWALK ed. Alexandria, VA: Association for Supervision and Curriculum Development.

_____ and J. SHULTZ. 1982. *The Counselor as gatekeeper: Social interaction in interviews.* New York: Academic Press.

FERGUSON, C.A. 1959. Diglossia. *Word* 15: 325–40.

FINGARET, A. 1983. Social network: A new perspective on independence and illiterate adults. *Adult Education Quarterly* 33(3): 133–46.

FRIEDL, E. 1976. Remarks. In M. DIMEN and E. FRIEDL eds. Regional variation in Modern Greece and Cypress: Toward a Perspective on the Ethnography of Greece. Annals of the New York Academy of Sciences 268: 286–288.

_____ 1962. *Vasilika: A village in modern Greece.* New York: Holt, Rinehart & Winston.

GEE, J.P. 1986. Orality and literacy: From *The savage mind* to *Ways with words.* TESOL *Quarterly* 20 (4): 719–46.

GILMORE, P. 1983. Spelling "Mississippi": Recontextualizing a literacy-related speech event. *Anthropology and Education Quarterly* 14 (4): 235–55.

GOFFMAN, E. 1974. *Frame analysis.* New York: Harper & Row.

HEATH, S.B. 1983. *Ways with words: Language, life, and work in communities and classrooms.* New York: Cambridge University Press.

HENZE, R. 1988. *Informal teaching and learning in a Greek community.* Doctoral Dissertation, Stanford University.

HERZFELD, M. 1980. Honour and shame: Some problems in the comparative analysis of moral systems. *Man* 15: 339–51.

―――― 1987. *Anthropology through the looking glass: Cricital ethnography in the margins of Europe.* New York: Cambridge University Press.

MACKRIDGE, P. 1985. *The modern Greek language.* Oxford: Oxford University Press.

SCOLLEN, R. and S. SCOLLON. 1981. *Narrative, literacy and face in interethnic communication.* Norwood, NJ: Ablex.

SCRIBNER, S and M. COLE. 1981. *The Psychology of literacy.* Cambridge, MA: Harvard University Press.

SIVIGNON, M. 1976. Frontier between two cultural areas: The case of Thessaly. In *Regional variation in modern Greece and Cyprus: Toward a perspective on the ethnography of Greece,* M. DIMEN and E. FRIEDL eds., 268: 43–58. Annals of the New York Academy of Sciences.

STREET, B. V. 1984. *Literacy in theory and practice.* New York: Cambridge University Press.

VYGOTSKY, L. 1962. *Thought and language.* Cambridge, MA: The MIT Press.

Discussion Questions

1. What do you know about education in general, or English language education in particular, as it takes place in some specific country outside of the United States? How might the philosophy of education in another country contribute to the attitudes students hold toward the acquisition of literacy when they come to the United States?

2. What "playing school" strategies have you observed in young children either in other cultures or in the U.S.?

3. Discuss generational changes in uses of and acquisition of literacy as discussed in this chapter. Who is the primary/secondary person responsible for family literacy?

5

Police at Work in Hawaii: A Community of Writers

JOHN MARK SUMMERS AND TED PLAISTER

Introduction

In many ways, Hawaii provides a rather typical example of the introduction of literacy into a preliterate society, that is, a traditionally oral society was, over time, radically altered by changes accompanying the spread of written language in the islands. Hawaii is somewhat unique, though, in that the events of those early years were well documented by the American missionaries who systematically set out to write the Hawaiian language; to teach the Hawaiians *palapala* (reading and writing) (Pukui and Elbert 1975); and to convert the Hawaiians to Christianity. The Hawaiians were enthusiastic about *palapala* and the efforts of the missionaries were remarkably successful.

The acquisition of literacy, however, was linked to tremendous social and cultural changes which, by the middle of the nineteenth century, presaged the decline of the Hawaiian people in their own land. As Hawaiians succumbed to disease and decreased in number, *haoles* (Caucasians, white persons) assumed control of the islands. Utlimately, Hawaii became part of the United States as its 50th state.

Today, the descendants of Hawaiians, missionaries, *haoles,* imported plantation laborers, and others who have settled in the islands form an unusual society of literate people. The language of *palapala* in Hawaii is now English, as is the language of the media, government, commerce, education, tourism, and

the law and law enforcement. The uses and functions of *palapala* in this excep-
tional part of America merit serious study.

Within the larger historical and social context of literacy in Hawaii, the
palapala of a law enforcement agency—The Kauai Police Department—was
selected for study because all of the activities of the Kauai Police Department
(hereafter KPD) today involve extensive use of written language (Stubbs 1980,
162). This is in contrast to the more informal procedures that prevailed during
the days of the Kingdom of Hawaii and the Territory of Hawaii when speech
was the primary means of communication. These days, however, what counts
is what is written down and this feeling pervades the KPD.

The writing done by the officers of the department is shaped by a lengthy
process involving two factors: formal training in the kinds of writing required
by the department, plus on-the-job training and feedback on written work. In
addition, all written work is reviewed by senior officers at critical junctures within
the department. This serves to manage the flow of written material through
the department as it strives to teach and maintain an appropriate tone, style,
and content of the writing. Thus, reports that pass muster move quickly through
the chain of command, whereas reports in need of correction and change are
returned to their authors for action. The more serious the crime that is being
reported on, the more review junctures the writing passes through to ensure
that such written records will stand up in court. The higher the rank of the officer, the more control is exercised over written language emanating from subordinates. For example, watch officers, those officers in charge during a particular
duty period, may approve and forward written reports that will then be rejected
by officers higher up in the chain of command.

Successful recruits and new officers must cope with the demands of
transformation (of oral performances), justification (of police action), and map-
ping (of events into prearranged categories) as they strive to learn to produce
acceptable writing. Both operational and administrative writing are problematic,
especially the Event/Crime Report or E/CR.

THE STUDY: SUBJECTS

Six officers in the department (two patrol officers, two sergeants, one lieutenant and one captain) were selected for close study. Each was born in a different
part of Kauai and grew up in homes where a language other than English—
Japanese, Hawaiian, Portuguese, or Ilokano—was often used or heard. None
of them became proficient users of any of those languages because the languages
were used primarily by their parents when "they didn't want us to understand
what they were talking about." In everyday life, these men and their families
spoke a variety of Hawaii Creole English (hereafter HCE) which grew out of
the early pidgin used between plantation overseers and the plantation workers,
and among the plantation workers who spoke different native languages.

The six officers studied range in age from 29 to 43, with an average age of 36.6 years. They have served on the police force an average of 11.6 years, representing a range of 3 to 19 years. (See Table 1 for specifics.)

Four of the officers went to parochial schools for their kindergarten and elementary education; all are graduates of Kauai high schools. In interviews with these officers, typical comments from them concerning their education included: "not a good student," "poor to mediocre student," "had a hard time with writing, didn't like reading." One notable case is the officer who reported that when he was a high school freshman, he was reprimanded by a teacher who accused him of copying a composition that he had devoted considerable time to and of which he was very proud. He commented: "That was the end of my writing."

In the mid-1970s a police science curriculum was introduced at Kauai Community College. All six officers subsequently enrolled in courses, and three of the six earned the associate of arts degree. Their curriculum included writing courses, but other than the name of a teacher or a course, they have no specific recollection of the training they received in writing. Seemingly, most of their knowledge about writing they have learned through their work in the KPD where they have received 80 hours of work-related writing instruction. Their grades in English courses were generally in the C and B category, with one D reported as well as some uncompleted courses. The only additional schooling of significance (for two officers) was at the Federal Bureau of Investigation Academy in Arlington, Virginia (11 weeks).

WRITING TASKS IN KPD

Event/Crime Reports

There are two important tasks involving written language in the KPD: the writing of Event/Crime Reports and the reading of administrative directives. The Event/Crime Report (E/CR) is the single most important form used in the department's work. From its initial submission to its final acceptance, it is open to considerable oral negotiation of meaning among officers as it works its way through the chain of command. It is a multipaged printed form which calls for detailed information on such crimes as burglary, theft, crime against persons, auto theft, and fraud. While much of the form consists of fill-in-the-blank items, there is a final open-ended investigator's report section which requires extensive use of written language. This section calls for straightforward descriptive writing coupled with any necessary police jargon (Cicourel 1968).

The E/CR is subject to a review process by superior officers before it is accepted in final form. This process includes rejection notices (a form completed by the watch officer and returned to the officer concerned with any inadequacies checked, e.g., not legible, signature needed, classification incorrect/needed);

TABLE 1
Officer Reading Profile

Officer/Age	Years on KPD	Ethnicity	Home language as child	Newspapers	Magazines	Novels	Other
1/43	19	Part Hawaiian	Hawaiian/English	*Honolulu* (1) "occasionally" *Kauai Times*	*Sports Illustrated* *Reader's Digest* *The Airman* *The Guardsman* *People* *Playboy*	Police	Cookbooks
2/29	3	Japanese	Japanese/English	*Honolulu* (2) "for comics"	On police work hunting fishing weapons diving		
3/35	13	Portuguese	Pidgin Portuguese /English	*Honolulu* (1) "once in awhile"	*Pro* *Reader's Digest* *Consumer Reports*	Mysteries Police Westerns Supernatural "Can't remember last book read"	
4/42	17½	Japanese	Japanese/English	*Honolulu* (1) "daily" *The Garden Island* "daily"	*National Geographic* *Work Bench* *Popular Mechanics*		
5/35	5	Filipino	Ilokano/English	*Honolulu,* Sunday only "sports and Hawaii news" *The Garden Island* *Kauai Times*	*Reader's Digest* "some" *4x4* *Motor Trend* *Mechanics Illustrated* *Handibook*		
6/36	13	Portuguese-Hawaiian-Irish-Mexican	Portuguese/English	*Honolulu* (1) "irregularly" *Kauai Times* "fairly regularly"	*Police Product News* *Stereo Review* *Consumer Reports* *National Geographic* "occasionally" *Strength & Health*		

NOTE: *The Garden Island* and *Kauai Times* are small, local island newspapers.

"call-ins" (where supervising officers handle corrections by calling in the reporting officer and suggesting corrections verbally, because of reluctance to write up a rejection notice); and "little notes" revisions (a procedure whereby short correction notes are attached to E/CRs in lieu of completing a rejection notice).

Serious vs. Less Serious Crime

Officers learn that written reports of serious crime are treated differently from written reports of less serious crime. The more serious the crime, the more the written reports are scrutinized. This causes more talk to be generated in terms of how the report has been written, its errors, its omissions of information, etc. On the other hand, reports of nonserious crime are not so carefully scrutinized nor is there as much discussion generated.

Reading Administrative Reports

The reading and understanding of administrative directives does not receive the close scrutiny that the E/CRs do, although there is considerable discussion of their meaning among the officers. Noncompliance with an administrative directive is felt to reflect a lack of comprehension rather than any negligence on the part of an officer.

Performance Appraisal

Both the reading of administrative directives and the preparation of E/CRs are linked to a system of performance appraisal conducted by superior officers. The amount of time supervising officers are required to spend providing feedback to junior officers on the quality of their E/CRs and in interpreting administrative directives to them, affects the overall evaluation of the subordinate officers' work. This ongoing supervision is a constant reminder to the subordinate officers to attend to their reading and writing tasks within the department.

Translating Verbal Data into Print

One of the most difficult tasks officers face is learning how to translate the verbal data they obtain from witnesses and crime victims into a form that will be acceptable on their E/CRs. Compounding this, victims and witnesses are more often than not speakers of HCE (which may be a variety different from that spoken by the officer) or are nonnative speakers of English with varying degrees of English language proficiency. The statements from victims and witnesses must then be filtered through the officer's own variety of HCE before being cast into print. (This linguistic barrier to effective transmittal of information is particularly difficult for those officers who are not native speakers of HCE.)

Dealing Effectively with Victims and Witnesses

Another important social factor is the ability or lack of ability on the part of the officers to deal effectively on a personal level with victims and witnesses so as to maximize the amount of accurate and factual information they can get from them, especially when this information is couched in nonstandard English (Summers 1985, 85). There is a great amount of skill involved in couching questions which are nonthreatening yet which generate the kinds of information leading to an accurate description of what has occurred in a particular situation. If officers are not successful in getting adequate and sufficient information, this will be reflected in their narratives on the E/CRs and will be cause for questioning by superior officers.

FACTORS AFFECTING WRITTEN SKILLS

Social Factors

The social interaction that shapes KPD writing—for example, the giving or not giving of rejection notices on E/CRs—is viewed as being more powerful than the other factors that are widely believed to influence a person's writing, namely educational background, cultural heritage, the literate behavior of one's parents, literacy in a second language, reading habits, and even prior experience in another police department ("Honolulu reports are different from ours.") The reality of the job is that an officer must spend considerable time reading and/or writing reports, forms, and other documents and this makes demands on an officer's time and energy which, in some cases, serves to confound and frustrate an individual officer's efforts to perform well as a police officer. The situation becomes more critical as officers learn that their ability to use written language in certain ways will inevitably influence the direction of their careers within the department.

Job Factors

Recruits desirous of becoming police officers are not made aware of these requirements involving the use of written language prior to joining the force. These six officers are representative of the community upon which the KPD draws for its personnel and as such were ill-prepared for the linguistic aspects of the job. That is, they are average or below average high school graduates, native speakers of HCE, limited in their reading agendas, and individuals who do little or no writing other than that required on the job.[1]

---

[1] In this connection, it should be noted that some recruits are now coming into the department who have various amounts of tertiary education. In some cases, they come from mainland U.S. dialect areas, which itself can constitute a problem because they are not familiar with HCE which, at first, can seem almost like a foreign language to them.

Linguistic and Cultural Factors

There are specific reasons why the six officers studied found the writing tasks of KPD to be "the most rotten part of the job." These reasons grow out of the linguistic and social backgrounds of these officers. Present day Hawaii is an amalgam of many races and tongues. A number of the residents are bilingual in their L1 (mother tongue) and some variety of English. There is also a steady stream of immigrants, primarily from the Republic of the Philippines and Korea, with fewer numbers coming from other Asian and Pacific areas. The language of daily discourse in the islands is English, but that English takes varying forms. There are a few elderly speakers of Hawaii Pidgin still living.[2] From the early Hawaii Pidgin evolved a creolized version of English which is in widespread use today (Day 1990). Hawaii Creole English (HCE) exists in many forms. Some varieties are not too different from the old pidgin, while other HCE dialects extend up to speakers of Standard Hawaii English (SHE) (Day 1981).

According to Reinecke (1969), HCE was underway by 1900 and well established by 1910. Today, true pidgin speakers—native speakers of Japanese, Ilokano, Portuguese, Hawaii, English, etc., who, in addition, speak pidgin as an auxiliary language—are rare and these survivors of an earlier linguistic era are, as noted, quite elderly. It is typical of the immigrant population of Hawaii to insist that their children use English exclusively, the result of which is that the children avoid the use of the native language of the parents, usually to their regret when they reach adulthood. This attitude applied equally in the homes where Hawaiian was spoken, and clearly the Hawaiians were not recent immigrants to the islands. Today the only place where significant numbers of native speakers of Hawaiian may be found and where the daily language of communication remains Hawaiian is the small privately owned island of Niihau.

The speech and writing of HCE users clearly distinguishes them from speakers and writers of SHE, one of the Standard Englishes of the United States. The public schools have long promoted the use of Standard English (in actuality, SHE), but in implementing this policy a significant number of teachers have denigrated speakers of HCE rather than making the effort to study the history of HCE and understand its origins as a means of helping HCE speakers learn SHE. There persists the naive assumption, reflected in the not infrequent occurrence of letters to the editor of the two main Honolulu newspapers, that if all the children of Hawaii spoke Standard English most of the island's social and economic problems would disappear.

---

[2] Note that the language is Hawaii Pidgin, and not Hawaiian Pidgin; the pidgin that developed in Hawaii was an English-based pidgin, not one based on Hawaiian.

SPEECH AS A SOCIAL FACTOR

The oral reports at every level that precede, accompany, supplement, and explain written accounts of police activities form the basis for everyday social interaction among KPD officers. Talk about what is going to be or has been written down holds the department together—and to its assigned task. Moreover, the social interaction generated by the giving or not giving rejection notices on police reports (and the attendant "call-ins," "little notes," etc.) shapes the style and content of KPD writing as it shapes the way officers understand and talk about the work of writing. However, in spite of these discussions and the ongoing feedback on writing, problems in writing persist.

Police Metalanguage

In fact, as the officers have learned to perform the writing tasks of the KPD with varying degrees of proficiency, they have acquired a metalanguage to talk about these tasks. Accordingly, they speak of "elements of crime," "investigate rather than report," "kick back the report," "call in the officer," and so on. This mode of talking about KPD writing and the production of KPD writing is in addition to the jargon one might expect to hear in conjunction with police work. The use of this special language to talk about writing cuts across persons, across ranks, and across lines of age, sex, and ethnic background. For example, "Use 'I' instead of the undersigned" was heard from every one of the six officers on a variety of occasions as an expression of the accepted way to write.

Further, the use of this special language to talk about writing identifies the user as one who is knowledgeable about the writing tasks of the KPD. That is to say, the training officer, the report-writing instructor, the new lieutenant in the Patrol Services Bureau, and others who control the writing of the KPD all speak about writing in the same way using virtually the same vocabulary. On the one hand, this conformity in talking about written language reflects the intensity of the social interaction around writing in the KPD; on the other hand, it reflects shared and tacit understandings about writing that are pervasive in the KPD.

The special language also serves as a cover for underlying anxieties about the adequacy of KPD writing, especially when a KPD officer is talking about writing to someone outside the department. The acquisition of the metalanguage by new officers is an indication that they are becoming cognizant of the importance of writing in the KPD and are becoming "members of the club." It does not ensure, however, absolute conformity to established standards of writing.

READING AGENDAS AS A FACTOR

In an attempt to look at how reading skills may relate to the writing difficulties of the KPD officers, the officers reading agendas were examined. Krashen's 1984 review of the literature on the relationships between reading agendas and writing ability clearly points out that good writers are good readers. However, not all good readers are good writers, but the evidence is clear that poor readers do not make good writers. The six officers were queried about their current reading practices to see if they would qualify as good readers. The results are summarized next. (See also Table 1.)

Clearly the term *avid reader* is not descriptive of the reading agendas of these six officers. They obviously do not read newspapers thoroughly but rather focus on local news, sports, and comics. Their other reading reflects their off-the-job interests such as crafts and mechanics. Two subscribe to the *National Geographic* and three to the *Reader's Digest*. These publications are shared with spouses and children and it is doubtful if they are read in their entirety by the officers. Thus, there is an impoverished reading base which could lend support to these officers for their primary writing tasks: preparing police reports and filling out routine police forms requiring some writing. In addition, their reading agendas are of little help to them in coping with their professional police reading (the administrative directives).

WRITING AS A FACTOR IN CAREER ADVANCEMENT

Although "written expression" is only one among fifteen Basic Performance Factors on the Performance Evaluation Report for all KPD officers, the reality of the department is that the ability to respond to the writing requirements of the KPD influences an officer's career more than the other factors on the list. Superior officers closely supervise and direct the tone, style, and content of their subordinates' written reports: they also control assignments and promotions.

Written language can be separated from an officer and evaluated on its own, whereas factors such as "grooming and dress," "work judgment," "compliance with rules," etc., cannot be evaluated independently of the officer. Moreover, the remediation of deficiencies in written expression is not thought to be easy, whereas deficiencies in grooming, compliance, and judgment are felt to be more easily remedied.

Since the rating on the writing factor is averaged in with ratings on twenty-four other factors (the fifteen Basic Performance Factors plus ten Job-Related Performance Factors), the impression is gained that the importance of writing in the performance appraisal of an officer has been reduced. Nothing could be farther from the truth. The officers in the KPD know that failure to prepare written reports appropriately will work against their careers in the department and will lead to less desirable assignments and delayed promotions. Poor writing can even lead to dismissal from the department. In the final analysis, it is the management of written language that determines the direction of an officer's KPD career.

To emphasize its importance, a look at the success/promotion record five years after the completion of this study reveals that only two of the six officers have been promoted. Officer 3 (see Table 1) has been promoted from Acting Sergeant to Sergeant, a relatively minor promotion. Officer 2 has gone from Patrol Officer to Detective, a major advancement, according to Deputy Chief of Police Kenneth O. Robinson. He noted that Officer 2 "had struggled more with his writing than the other officers." Robinson also explained that promotion is a complex civil service matter involving many factors including a written examination (Robinson 1990).

It is a reasonable assumption that Officer 2 was motivated to put forth a considerable amount of effort in order to gain promotion. His writing, according to the Deputy Chief, is still a source of worry to the officer. In this connection, the Deputy Chief remarked that writing continues to generate concern within the department and he was quick to place blame for this on the educational system in Hawaii which is "doing a poor job."

Role of the Educational System

While it is convenient for society to fault a school system for the shortcomings of its graduates in general terms, in the case of these six officers, the linguistic dimension is of paramount importance and interest. The educational system of the State of Hawaii was not and is not particularly sensitive to the linguistic diversity of its student population including native speakers of HCE as well as those who are nonnative speakers of English, despite a certain amount of lip service paid to the problems.[3] Teachers hired from the United States mainland arrive with little or no knowledge of the sociolinguistic milieu in the islands. Few take the trouble to become conversant with it and the majority tend to assume a *laissez-faire* attitude toward the linguistic and social uniqueness of their students.

The educators who are truly *akamai* (knowledgable) about the complex language situation in Hawaii are so few in number that their voice is all too often not heard when they press for a more enlightened approach to language

---

[3] A case in point: a home economics teacher was put in charge of the ESL program at one of the largest high schools in the state with a significant ESL population, despite strenuous objections from a professional ESL educator to the Superintendent of Schools.

concerns in the public schools. It is a telling commentary that prominent business, political, and educational figures tend to send their children to private schools in Hawaii. By the time individuals such as these six officers enter a profession requiring substantive amounts of written English, it may be too late for the majority of them to acquire the requisite linguistic skills necessary for career advancement.

SPECIFIC PROBLEMS

Myths About Writing in KPD

There are shared myths about KPD writing. One is that in the KPD, "we don't use big words" and "we use simple language." Not only is the use of "simple language" unrealistic given the complexities of public behavior with which the police must deal, but the belief doesn't follow when one examines the reports circulating in the department. For example, a letter from the Investigative Bureau to a crime victim speaks of "elements of solvability," in another example, an officer is asked to deliver a "Service of Legal Instrument Attempt" form, and so on.

Another myth is the assumption that police officers in the KPD are to produce writing that is sufficiently decontextualized so that a "stranger could pick it up and read it." Actually, most untrained civilians would experience some difficulty comprehending many of the everyday reports generated in the KPD.

A third myth at the time of the study was that women are more skilled at writing than men. Thus, men will have more difficulty in performing the written tasks at KPD. This assumption seems to be changing, though, as women find careers in the KPD and enter the department as patrol officers. Supervising officers find that female patrol officers experience as much difficulty with written reports as do their male counterparts.

Fossilization

The kinds and types of writing required of these officers is highly stereotyped, and under ordinary circumstances it seems reasonable to assume that they should be easily learned. By and large, these officers *have* learned the form and style of police report writing, but despite this, problems persist which strongly suggests fossilization, "a process which sometimes occurs in which incorrect linguistic features become a permanent part of the way a person speaks or writes a language" (Richard, Platt, and Weber 1985). Some examples follow, with errors italicized. (The number preceding each example identifies the officer, see Table 1.)

1. . . . and has reported to work *everyday*; Positively identified X from a *photographed*

2. Also according to the complainant the *suspect* phone is a CodeAPhone

4. Those that are to be added or deleted *has* been denoted on the schematic

5. Checked at Hale Pumehana and learned that Fujio was last seen by them *is* about 2-weeks ago

6. Also, I notice that sometimes he forgets instructions that *was* given earlier; Report writing has improved, makes *less* errors; Still has room for *improvements* in reports; Inspector X requested that Y be told that we should always try to control our tempers even if *its* hard to at times; X stated that after the vehicle stopped he was upset & his approach *on* the driver was a little harsh.

As seen in this example, the officers do not now use Standard Hawaii English nor is it likely that they ever will, so that they can hardly be expected to show significant change and improvement in their writing beyond what they have already accomplished. The two language acts of speaking and writing are, after all, two sides of the same linguistic coin. Just as the officers have plateaued in their speech, so have they in their writing. Still the implementation of carefully designed instruction conceivably could result in some improvement. (For the importance of practice in such instances, see Scribner and Cole 1981.) The amount of improvement that might accrue in light of factors already discussed is, however, questionable.

As noted previously, all six officers studied are native speakers of HCE. A case can be made that they are writers of Standard English as a Second Dialect. Yet the writing the officers do is consistent with the features of HCE so that one can argue that they are actually not producing errors in terms of their own dialect, although they will assuredly make mistakes as do all writers. But this theoretical argument for acceptance of their variety of written English will not be accepted by society because society is (as yet) quite unforgiving of written language that does not conform to its arbitrary standards of correctness. Clearly the primary function or purpose of written language is communication between and among its users, but society, rather than using logical reasons, dictates the form that language is expected to take.

Linguistic Insecurity

Clearly, these six officers function satisfactorily within their own dialect area, both in terms of speech and writing. Where they are less successful is in the use of an imposed "standard" linguistic system which is closely related to their own. Realizing that they have not mastered the standard language (and probably never will) can only result in a kind of linguistic insecurity. Clear evidence of this are the remarks the KPD officers make with respect to their written English. And yet the tongue is close to the heart, so it shouldn't be surprising if one were to discover some feelings of defensiveness on the part of these officers concerning their own linguistic usage, although none were forthcoming during the study.

DISCUSSION

The writing instruction history of these six officers consists of their primary and secondary schooling and community college coursework. They have also received on-the-job training in writing police reports. However, it is clear from reading samples of their written work that they have not mastered the skill of preparing police reports in Standard Written English.

Self-Deprecating Statements Regarding Writing

The KPD officers do show concern for their writing ability. In fact, the mere mention of writing to KPD officers usually brings forth a number of self-deprecating statements about their own writing. Equally negative statements are made about the writing in the department as a whole, as evidenced by remarks such as "KPD reports are the worst in the state." This shared concern with writing represents a common bond among members of the KPD.

Because these officers continue to produce writing which is not completely satisfactory in terms of departmental expectations, and in view of the fact that they have received considerable training in the specifics of police report writing (80 hours), it is safe to conclude that they are clear examples of the fossilization phenomenon.

The Role of Reading

Obviously there is no simple cause for such a complex behavior as poor or good writing. Nevertheless, it is tempting to name past and present reading protocols as possibly the paramount factor. By their own admission, these officers were not particularly good students in language arts and thus lack a rich background in reading and writing. Moreover, their current reading habits (see Figure 1) are not providing them with input which might be transferred to the kinds of writing they do. And, it would probably be very difficult for them to modify their reading habits given their particular life styles. Ongoing errors in syntax can be traced, in the main, to their HCE dialect and given the fact that they are not receiving input from their current reading sufficient to overcome and/or eliminate these errors, they most likely will persist.

These are very busy peace officers. They are not students. They put in long hours at their work and, in addition, have family responsibilities.

There is a social element in Hawaiian society that acts as a stabilizing influence on both language (in this case, HCE) and culture. These are the gatherings of extended family and close friends which are held on a regular basis. These events are commonly picnics, barbecues and *luaus* (Hawaiian feast) and are extremely important in the social scheme of things. Attendance at these functions is expected. For the host family, considerable preparation time is involved inasmuch as these gatherings tend to be quite large.

These occasions provide ample opportunity for the participants to "talk story" (a pidgin term) which can best be described as an amalgam of shooting the breeze, shop talk, chit chat, chewing the fat, gossiping, small talk, schmoozing, and telling tales. "Talk story" is a legacy from the days when Hawaii was primarily an oral culture. Many of the plantation workers were illiterate, and it is well known that plantation owners preferred laborers who were illiterate so as to impede any attempts at unionization. Reinecke (1969, 40) says, in writing of the early plantation worker, "He was usually ignorant not only of the native language, but of English as well."

"Talk story" plays a significant role in party-like gatherings. In addition, it is crucial for socialization in the work place in the Hawaii setting. There, it comprises an important element in the social glue that makes for harmonious working relationships in organizations such as the KPD. To "talk story" in Standard English would be almost inconceivable. Therefore, it is reasonable to assume that the frequent use of "talk story" enhances HCE dialect stabilization.

Conclusion

Written English plays a major role in the life of police officers on the island of Kauai not only in terms of communicating what transpires in daily police work, but also as a criterion for advancement through the ranks. The six officers studied come from a variety of ethnic and linguistic backgrounds and are all speakers of Hawaii Creole English of a variety very close to Standard Hawaii English.

The officers were not particularly good students in language arts and in their adult life do a minimum of reading and writing other than that required in their police work. While they have received 80 hours of instruction in writing police reports, a mostly formulaic type of writing, their written work consistently contains errors. These errors are a reflection of their HCE linguistic systems and, presumably, a lack of rigorous training in reading and writing.

There are no major problems in communication within the KPD engendered by the type of written English used, nor do serious problems in communication with the Honolulu Police Department occur. Although all of the officers within the KPD are concerned about the quality of the writing that they produce, there seems to be a lack of any concerted effort to effect significant improvement except in the case of certain individuals. This is curious given the fact that the quality of written language is claimed by all to play an important role in career improvement in the department.

The officers are seen as clear examples of fossilization in speech and writing. The one other linguistic avenue open to them which could have a positive effect on both their speech and writing, but writing in particular, is reading. If the reading agendas of these officers remain unchanged, then a case can be made that they have fossilized in their reading as well.

Finally, it seems clear that little or no change will occur in their writing abilities given their current social and work environments. The social milieu of these officers—and their fellow officers on the KPD—is not going to change. HCE will continue to be their language of daily use in, as well as outside, the work place. Dialect change can be a risky social undertaking bringing on peer scorn, as exemplified by the well-known case of students at the University of the Philippines who, though quite capable of speaking Standard English, avoid its use on the campus outside of class. A rigorous, carefully crafted course of study in police writing in addition to what is currently provided might, and only might, produce some improvements in writing quality. But, as Krashen has argued,

> . . . competence in writing does not come from the study of form directly—the rules that describe written language, or "reader-based prose," are simply too complex and numerous to be explicit taught and consciously learned. (Krashen 1984, 27)

However, there is another social factor at work which will most probably, over time, "solve" most of the writing problems of the KPD and that is that HCE is being displaced by SHE at a moderately rapid rate on all islands in the state. The influences on HCE, both overt and covert, of schooling, television, the movies, travel, and other social factors which affect dialect change will eventually see the replacement of HCE with SHE throughout Hawaii. However, the current KPD personnel will not be affected by this change and will, in all probability, continue to write as they do now. It is those children currently in elementary school who, as adults, become involved in police work, that have the greatest chance of becoming speakers of SHE and who will, with appropriate instruction, become writers of prose that will be acceptable to the needs of the KPD.

References

CICOUREL, A. V. 1968. *The social organization of juvenile justice.* New York: John Wiley.

DAY, R. R. 1981. Silence and the ESL child. *TESOL Quarterly* 15: 35–39.

_____. 1990. Personal communication.

KRASHEN, S. D. 1984. *Writing, research, theory, and applications.* New York: Pergamon Press.

PUKUI, M. K. and S. H. ELBERT. 1975. *Hawaiian dictionary.* Honolulu: University of Hawaii Press.

REINECKE, J. E. 1969. *Language and dialect in Hawaii: A sociolinguistic history to 1935.* Honolulu: University of Hawaii Press.

RICHARDS, J., J. PLATT, and H. WEBER. 1985. *Longman dictionary of applied linguistics.* New York: Longman.

ROBINSON, K. O. 1990. Personal communication.

SCRIBNER, S. and M. COLE. 1981. *The psychology of literacy.* Cambridge, MA: Harvard University Press.

STUBBS, M. 1980. *Language and literacy: The sociolinguistics of reading and writing.* London: Routledge & Kegan Paul.

SUMMERS, J. M. 1985. *Palapala in Hawaii: An ethnographic account of police literacy.* Unpublished doctoral dissertation, Columbia University, New York.

Discussion Questions

1. Some bilinguals have native control over their two phonologies and syntaxes although rarely, if ever, can bilinguals be equally fluent in all domains of two languages as adult speakers. Can there be bidialectalism of the same order within *one* language? Note that some actors are very skilled at faux bidialectalism when they perform, but they do not have to sustain their "second" dialects or foreign accents on a daily basis in ordinary communication situations. In fact, they only use their "second" dialect or foreign accent for short stretches of memorized speech.

2. What are the probable social costs to someone who is successful in changing from a nonstandard to a standard dialect? Once the switch from a nonstandard dialect to a standard dialect has been completed, can a speaker ever really "go home?"

3. Why is it the case that it is possible for speakers to retain their "less than standard" variety of a language in their phonological systems while at the same time are able to write the standard language? (Cf. nonnative speakers with pronounced foreign accents, e.g., Henry Kissinger—German—and the late Carlos Romulo—Tagalog—who write perfect English.)

4. Why can an individual both read standard written language and listen to standard speech with comprehension yet not be able to produce those kinds of language with native (standard) proficiency? Are there two different

neurological processes at work here—one for receptive language skills and one for productive language skills?

5. What kinds of activities might a teacher use to foster "linguistic togetherness" in a class containing a mix of standard and nonstandard speakers of a language?

6. The distinguished linguist Uriel Weinreich once said, "A language is a dialect with an army and a navy." In the context of pidgins, creoles, and standard languages, what was Weinreich really saying?

7. Discuss which is the easier task: for a native speaker of one language to become a fluent speaker of a pidgin, or to become a fluent speaker of another language.

6

From Oral to Literate Culture: An Australian Aboriginal Experience

WILLIAM EGGINGTON

Introduction

This chapter reports on a critical incident in the relationship between traditional, aboriginal (indigenous) and literate, Western nonaboriginal cultures of Australia. In many ways, the critical incident illustrates wider planned and unplanned social changes that have occurred in an aboriginal oral-culture community in the Northern Territory as members have assumed some elements of literate culture— and, in the process, have gained more power over their lives. The critical incident occurred at Yirrkala school in the Northern Territory where an aboriginal community acquired control of the community education program. To fully convey the significance of this event, I first review some background information about the aboriginal people and their education in the Northern Territory. Next, I trace the background for their success. Then, I analyze what I believe to be the theoretical principles underlying that success and conclude with suggestions for ways that these principles could be applied to other minority, indigenous, immigrant, and refugee communities.

The analysis of the event underscores the concept of literacy as power, supporting the hypothesis that, for a traditionally oral culture, the acquisition of higher literacy skills is more a group social issue than an individual pedagogical one. The analysis also suggests that the teaching and acquisition of survival literacy skills in a "functional literacy" paradigm allows individuals to participate in society only to the extent that the society's power structures permit.

THE NORTHERN TERRITORY
ABORIGINAL COMMUNITY

The pre-European history of aboriginal people in Australia extends approximately 40,000 years into the past. Since aboriginal people formed hunter-gatherer oral cultures, much of the history of this extensive period is intertwined with mythology and traditions.

An estimated 300,000 indigenous or aboriginal people inhabited the Australian continent at the time of initial European settlement in 1788. The history of aboriginal people since then can fall into a number of stages: namely the domesticate or exterminate period from 1788 to the 1960s; the protectionist period from the 1860s to the 1940s; the assimilationist period from the 1940s to the 1960s; and the self-determination and management period which continues up to the present time (Baldauf and Eggington 1989). Since 1983, this self-determination policy has been seen as creating a situation where

> Aboriginals have sufficient economic independence to enjoy the civil and political rights provided in our system; and where they can control basic services such as health, education, housing, so that they come in a form and of a standard that meet Aboriginal needs as defined by the Aboriginal people themselves. (House of Representatives Select Committee on Aboriginal Education 1985)

In 1788 there were between 200 and 650 aboriginal languages spoken in Australia, depending upon which definitions of the terms *language* and *dialect* are used (Senate Standing Committee on Education and the Arts 1984). The two hundred years since European settlement have seen a dramatic decline in these languages to the point that only eight languages with more than 1,000 speakers survive today (Baldauf and Eggington 1989); five of these languages are in the Northern Territory of Australia. Black (1983) estimates that, in addition to these five languages, twenty-five languages with one hundred or more speakers also survive in the Northern Territory. Thus, of the 35,000 aboriginal people living in the Northern Territory, there are 20,000 speakers of one or more aboriginal language.

In the early days of European settlement in the Northern Territory, an English-based contact language developed which has followed the contact language continuum: minimal pidgin, pidgin, extended pidgin, initial creole to extended creole (Todd 1974; Muhlhuler 1986; Romaine 1988). This creole or *Kriol* is becoming the *lingua franca* of the aboriginal people of the Northern

Territory with an estimated 20,000 speakers (Sandefur and Harris 1986).

However, the English language remains as the dominant language in almost all domains requiring interaction with the ever-present nonaboriginal society. It is the language of communication with government, health, commerce, and education programs. Unfortunately, significant communication barriers exist due to a number of factors including inadequate English language proficiency levels among the aboriginal people, cultural insensitivity among the English-speaking nonaboriginal people, and huge differences in communication strategies between the two groups (Shimpo 1985). As may be guessed, the English spoken by the aboriginal people—aboriginal English—exists as a nonstandard, low status variety of the language.

Formal Western-style education came to aboriginal people when various Christian churches established mission schools in aboriginal community settlements. These community mission schools were eventually taken over first by Federal and then Territory Education Departments. Enrollment figures for aboriginal and nonaboriginal students in the Northern Territory are given in Table 1.

TABLE 1
Northern Territory Schools
Aboriginal and Nonaboriginal Enrollments, July 1987

	Aboriginal	Nonaboriginal
Preschool	1,067	2,091
Primary	7,282	14,406
Junior Secondary	1,775	5,061
Senior Secondary	212	2,765
Ungraded	156	516
Total	10,492	24,839

Source: Northern Territory Department of Education, 1987

Note the low number of aboriginal students enrolled in secondary programs. To date, not a single aboriginal youth from a traditional background has graduated from a Northern Territory High School. These figures do not point out the considerable absenteeism in aboriginal schools, or the apparent lack of enthusiasm for Western-style education. Literacy levels are very low, with most youth leaving school with a third grade reading level.

In addition, Walton (1989) estimates that there are another 1,417 aboriginal students not enrolled in any school program. This is because many aboriginal people have chosen to return to "Homeland Centers" in order to live a traditional life style in tribal lands. However, as Walton points out,

> . . . a minimum of 12 school age children is set (as a guide) for the establishment of a homeland centre school, thereby precluding many outstation children from existing services. Non-Aboriginal families on cattle stations with one school age child do have access to School of the Air. The question seems to be put for non-Aboriginal Territorians along these lines, "How can a service be provided for all school age children?"; while for NT Aborigines it is more like, "If they request a service, what is the minimum we might provide?" (Walton 1989, 3)

In an effort to better meet the educational needs of the Northern Territory aboriginal people, the Australian government introduced a bilingual education program in 1972. This program now consists of sixteen bilingual schools and has had mixed results in achieving its stated objectives. For example, in some schools established indicators such as literacy achievement, overall scholastic abilities, attendance rates, and community involvement have risen marginally while cost effectiveness has decreased. In other schools, no success has been reported (Eggington and Baldauf 1990).

The general effectiveness of one such bilingual school program was reported in *TESOL Quarterly* in 1981 (Gale, et al. 1981). This report provided statistical evidence verifying that this bilingual program was achieving a measurable degree of success. However, in 1986 I visited that same school and found a skeleton bilingual-in-name-only program. Most of the bilingual material developed during the program's golden years, as reported in the *TESOL Quarterly* article, lay in a dusty storage area unused by the new staff at the school. The program had fallen victim to reduced funding and frequent nonaboriginal staff transfers, which replaced experienced and committed staff with staff much less experienced in, and committed to, bilingual education. Also, the community had very little interest in the program. In general, the program had declined due to a subtle and usually unconscious form of institutionalized cultural insensitivity.

Educational achievement levels in the Northern Territory for aboriginal people are well below national standards and significantly below aboriginal student standards in other Australian states (House of Representatives Select Committee on Aboriginal Education 1985). The reasons for this are numerous and frequently discussed, a general consensus being that language and cultural differences are major factors contributing to poor educational achievement (Eades 1985; Harris 1980; Christie and Harris 1985; Graham 1986).

As Walton (1989) and Wearne (1986) have shown, and as I have alluded to in the homeland center and bilingual education examples given above, there appears to be a structural inequality in many areas of Northern Territory society suggesting covert institutional racism. Using the term *institutional racism* may seem a little harsh, but I believe it can be found in many Western societies. Chambers and Pettman (1986) define it as

. . . a pattern of distribution of social goods, including power, which regularly and systematically advantages some ethnic and racial groups and disadvantages others. It operates through key institutions. . . . [for example] the
education system. (Chambers and Pettman 1986, 7)

Cummins draws attention to "disabling structures" that are built into
social access and equity systems. He states that

. . . groups that tend to experience the most pronounced education failure
are those that have historically experienced a pattern of subjugation to the
dominant group, over generations . . . the relationship between the majority
and minority group is one which historically has led to an ambivalent and
insecure identity among native minorities. (Cummins 1989)

Using Ogbu's (1988) classification system, it would appear that aboriginal
people in the Northern Territory fall into the category of a "castelike" subordinate minority. Ogbu suggests that this particular type of minority group has
been "either incorporated into a society more or less involuntarily and per-
manently or are forced to seek incorporation and then relegated to inferior
status" (Ogbu 1988, 232). He notes that social structures make it more difficult
for an individual from a subordinate minority to "advance on the basis of individual training or ability" (Ogbu 1988, 232).

Very few aboriginal people in the Northern Territory are independent of
support from the dominant culture. Many are losing their traditional values
and cultures. Alcoholism, drug abuse, gasoline sniffing, malnutrition, and poor
health are epidemic in many communities. Despite heavy government involvement, most aboriginal settlements exemplify third-world housing and health
standards. And yet people care. There are numerous nonaboriginal educators,
health workers, missionaries, government officials and politicians in the Northern Territory and throughout Australia who have devoted a significant portion
of their lives to assist aboriginal people in finding solutions to these problems.
But successes are too few and too limited in scope, while newer problems continue to develop. Every few years a new approach is tried only to be replaced
by another direction and a new hope. Government funds for ongoing support
programs such as bilingual education are beginning to be questioned, with an
attitude developing among government politicians that nonaboriginal Australians
are doing enough, that the problems and the solutions lie in, and with, the
aboriginal people (Walton, 1989).

In all this history, there has been one example that is strikingly different,
the success at Yirrkala School.

THE CASE OF YIRRKALA SCHOOL

In describing the development and nature of this success at Yirrkala, I am indebted to Greg Wearne and the master's thesis he wrote on the subject in 1986.

Greg was the assistant principal at Yirrkala from 1982. He is now deputy principal of Nhulunbuy High School which is located 23 kilometers from Yirrkala. Throughout the remainder of this paper, I will often refer to the Yirrkala people as *Yolngu*, their term for themselves. I will also refer to white Australians as *Balanda*.[1]

Yirrkala is a traditional aboriginal coastal community of about 1,000 aboriginal and 100 nonaboriginal people located 700 kilometers east of Darwin. Although there was some contact with nonaboriginal Australians or Balanda, the Yolngu or Yirrkala aborigines remained isolated from nonaboriginal culture until 1971. At that time a large mining operation commenced at Nhulunbuy, 23 kilometers away. Nhulunbuy now has a population of 4,000 nonaboriginal Australians. Generally, the Yolngu have managed to keep themselves distant from Nhulunbuy Balanda culture.

A small mission school was established at Yirrkala during the 1950s. This school was taken over by the government in 1968. In 1972, when the Federal Government introduced bilingual education into the Northern Territory, Yirrkala was chosen as one of the Bilingual Schools. Of course, bilingual education required a core of aboriginal assistant teachers, but, at that time, there were no aboriginal teachers or assistant teachers. Thus, a group of young adults, mostly female, were trained through various aboriginal teacher training programs. One particular program brought aboriginal prospective teachers into a rural aboriginal college for a number of years where they received training in Western-style advanced education.

Until 1982, Yirrkala was a typical bilingual school in which part of the curriculum was taught in English and part in *Yolngumata* (the aboriginal language) by aboriginal assistant teachers. The "core" curriculum in these bilingual programs was determined by the Northern Territory Department of Education and generally reflected Western notions of education. Initial literacy and other foundation subjects were taught through the aboriginal language following a transition bilingual model (Eggington and Baldauf 1990). Throughout the sixteen Northern Territory bilingual schools, those committed to bilingual education began to worry that the hoped-for results of bilingual education were not being seen. Students were not achieving better results using standarized tests which measured proficiency in literacy, mathematics, and English. Attendance was still much lower than at nonaboriginal schools and, in general, community adults were not involved in the education of their children (Eggington and Baldauf 1990).

---

[1]This is an interesting aboriginal word that refers to whites across the "top-end" of Australia. We didn't know its history until we realized that it is a Malay-Indonesian borrowed word. For at least 500 years before Europeans came to the far north of Australia, Indonesian fishermen were coming to the area in search of sea cucumbers. They frequently encountered aboriginal people and told them about strange white men who called themselves "Hollanders." *Hollander went through phonological assimilation processes to evolve as balanda.*

However, perhaps because of their proximity to a Balanda mining town, the Yolngu people of Yirrkala were particularly concerned that their culture not only be preserved, but be developed. They began to extend the concept of bilingual education to what they termed "both ways" education. They wanted community children not only to be taught in two languages, but to learn to function in both Yolngu and Balanda ways at school. This meant that the curriculum had to be adjusted and that significant aspects of Balanda ways and learning had to be replaced by Yolngu ways and learning as part of the school's core curriculum. The Yolngu at Yirrkala wanted to be heard. In his thesis, Wearne includes a significant statement on this subject expressed by the Aboriginal Community Development Officers:

> Yolngu want bilingual education. They also want high standards. This is not happening as children are leaving school knowing nothing. Children still don't understand how (or why it is important) to learn to a high standard. Yolngu can do this if student teachers learn hard to be good teachers (same for nurses, doctors, mechanics, plumbers, farmers, navy, airforce) so that in turn they can help children to learn.
>
> We need Yolngu and Balanda co-operating in schools. But the Balanda teacher must be one who can step back and support Yolngu, not take over. Many Balanda teachers find this hard to do. Balanda teachers should want to learn from Yolngu. Both learn, one from another. At Yirrkala there is strong community support for their own Yolngu teachers. These are the people who will help the children in homelands to develop "both ways." (Wearne, 1986, from an interview with Community Development Officers conducted by John Henry, Deakin University, November 1983)

As Yirrkala assistant teachers and community leaders began to toy with the idea of adjusting the curriculum, it became evident that they were moving into a sensitive area, one where self-determination policies were not allowed. The Northern Territory Department of Education had declared that "Aboriginal students should receive the same core curriculum as other Northern Territory students, with importance placed on centralized and standarized curricula" (Northern Territory Department of Education 1983, 17). In other words, aboriginal children could be educated only if they learned what *we* determined was best for them. Battle lines were drawn; a power struggle was inevitable. Key events in this struggle are described next.

1. In 1983, the school principal, motivated mostly by a desire to receive federal funding, established the Yirrkala Community School Council. The Council membership consisted of some aboriginal leaders and teachers and senior nonaboriginal teachers. However, since the principal shaped both the composition of the Council and the agenda of each meeting, community input was restricted to nonessential elements of the school's operation.

2. In early 1984, the Council met with a new chairman, an articulate and forceful senior clan member who had been elected to that position by fellow tribal leaders. Even though his formal Western education was minimal, he had acquired an ability to understand the system used by the dominating non-aboriginal culture. The chairman began to reflect the growing desire for the community to be involved in the school. He held a meeting with aboriginal teachers where minutes were kept and a decision made to send a letter to the principal with a request that it be sent to the Department. The letter said in part:

> During school appraisal, we were often told that Yirrkala had a Community school, and that "we would work together to make things better." We agree that this is the way it should be, but as parents and community members we must say that we are worried at the way the school is being staffed. *It is time for you to listen to our wishes, and to start "working together to make things better." We cannot agree to European teachers who are unsatisfactory or to senior teachers who do not understand our wishes.* (Wunungmurra 1984 as quoted in Wearne 1986, 58) [emphasis added]

The letter was sent to the department, but no further formal departmental action was taken. Although it is beyond the scope of this paper to investigate the department's lack of response, previous government patterns would suggest that the department was stalling in the hope that the community would find a new interest which would divert attention away from the issue. This procedure had been successful many times when dealing with aboriginal people.

3. Some time later, the principal received written notification, from the chairman, of a School Council meeting to be held the next week. He became very upset, forcefully suggesting that no meeting be held without his approval or presence. His edict was ignored. "Unofficial" meetings continued to be held, and gradually a plan of action was developed.

4. During 1984, Yolngu teachers and community leaders suggested the formation of a "School Action Group." Balanda teachers scheduled a discussion of the topic at a "cultural development meeting." In contrast to other staff meetings, all the Yolngu teaching staff arrived early. Throughout the meeting, Yolngu teachers told each other in their own language to demonstrate enthusiasm, to be involved, and not to be "tired or lazy."

5. Toward the end of 1984, staffing selections and promotion recommendations were to be submitted to the department. As usual, decisions were made by the principal, with little discussion with Yolngu staff or community members. The Yolngu staff Action Group discussed staffing and submitted their own recommendations to the Community Council in writing. The let-

ter, explaining why the Action Group felt they could make the recommendations, was well written and made public by the Community Council. The principal responded immediately—and emotionally—by suggesting that "there's white involvement here" and that the feelings contained in the letter represented youthful exuberance out of step with older aboriginal leaders. He stated that

> . . . this has put self-management back four years. The Yolngu have egg all over their faces. I've been working for self-management for 10 years. Why didn't they come to me first?" (Wearne 1986, 68).

The skirmishes continued, with the aboriginal teachers becoming more and more skilled in using nonaboriginal power structures. Eventually, they won: institutional barriers preventing "both ways" core curriculum adaptation were removed, aboriginal community members gained the power to negotiate staff selection, and an aboriginal senior teacher was promoted to become a co-principal of the school.

It now appears that a large majority of the school's teaching is done by trained aboriginal teachers. In addition, the focus of discussion has changed from issues of control to issues of curriculum, secondary education, and bilingual "both ways" education. It appears that the community is beginning to adapt Western educational values to fit their culture and, in turn, is adapting their aboriginal culture. There is cultural movement both ways and there is a sense of ownership of the school.

The concept of aboriginal people gaining control of government schools is spreading throughout the Northern Territory, but Yirrkala remains the only community school to have achieved control. Obviously, we need to ask a number of questions, for example: "Why did this happen at Yirrkala and not elsewhere?" and "What mechanisms can be put in place for this to happen elsewhere?"

There are of course many contributing factors which enabled the Yolngu of Yirrkala to gain control and become involved in the educational process. Geographical location and community values seem essential ingredients. However, I would like to highlight one major variable.

It appears that the Yirrkala aboriginal community was able to use a powerful technology in their battle—literacy. I make that assertion based on the following pieces of evidence:

1. All the influential aboriginal participants were skilled at manipulating the written word. For the most part, they were people who had been sent off to college as part of the bilingual education training program. As teachers in a Western school, they were involved in "literacy" education, and thus had gained a significant degree of power within the Yirrkala community.

2. Many of the "watershed" events in the battle were responses to letters or submissions written by the aboriginal people. These letters, in turn, were based on written minutes of meetings made by the aboriginal people. In addition, many of these letters were "published" which suggests that the aboriginal people involved knew the power of the printed and published word.

3. Of greatest significance is the fact that these aboriginal people exhibited behavior which suggests that they were part of a literate culture as well as their more traditional oral culture. I believe this is the key factor that contributed to Yirrkala's rare success in aboriginal education.

   To better understand this last point, it is necessary to review what has been labeled as the oral to literate culture continuum.

THE PRIMARY ORAL CULTURAL TO LITERATE CULTURE CONTINUUM

Havelock (1988) has observed that "human culture is a creation of human communication" (Havelock 1988, 127); that is, the nature of communication within a society will affect the culture that develops as a major part of that society. When we begin to investigate the nature of communication, we are confronted with two major classifications. Much human communication is oral and much is written.

   We have begun to understand that the invention of an easy writing system by the Greeks around 600 BC introduced a new technology into human society, one that has affected those societies that adopted the technology to the point at which specific and important components of the society changed, and have continued to change since then. These social changes allow us to make comparisons between literate cultures and oral cultures (Goody and Watt 1988; Ong 1988).

   For example, Ong (1988) contends that since, in an oral culture, one knows only that which can be recalled, communal memory is protected. Social and mystical power rests with the ones who know, the repeaters of the past, the knowers of the ancient law and those who have the right to speak of the past. Couple these values with the values generated by a hunter-gatherer culture whose main preoccupation is to hunt and to gather for today (because survival is a daily struggle), and the result is a culture that focuses, to a large extent on the past, somewhat on the present to meet immediate needs, but seldom, if at all, on the future. With this focus on the past, obviously oral cultures are conservative or, as Ong suggests, homeostatic—always returning to stable values.

   I am not suggesting that those from oral cultures, or to be more specific, aboriginal cultures, have limitations on their intellectual abilities because they have not been exposed to writing systems. What I am suggesting is that literacy can be thought of as a major technology which has so shaped some features of social interaction that a distinction between aspects of the communal behavior of those societies that have used this technology and societies that have not had access to it has evolved.

Goody and Watt state that the "world of knowledge" transcends political and temporal units with the development of literacy. They quote Spengler's proclamation that "writing is the grand symbol of the Far" (Goody and Watt 1988, 19). Thus, in literate cultures almost all the world's past and present literate knowledge is within reach of any individual. Information, thought, and philosophies are gathered from beyond the immediate society and beyond recallable time, threatening a homeostatic centralized power outlook and destroying cultural bonds. Rather than past knowledge simply dropping off the edge of recallable memory, it is preserved and layered, creating an incredibly complex society. Because it is impossible to absorb all this accumulated knowledge, one must be selective. This selectivity eventually results in individual or small group cultures experiencing the sense of alienation that is often discussed with reference to our present culture.

Literacy has become so central to Western culture that we have assigned a number of metaphors to the ability to use this technology. They are not universal truths but could be seen as part of the metaphors that we live by. Scribner (1984) labels three of these as "literacy as adaptation," "literacy as a state of grace," and "literacy as power."

The literacy-as-power metaphor, developed most significantly by Freire (1970, 1978), recognizes that the acquisition of literacy skills by a group has been used to either allow that group to dominate nonliterate groups or to free that group from oppression by another literate group. Literate communities and even literate individuals have access to the power structures of most democratic societies. In addition, becoming literate can assist nonliterate groups or individuals toward gaining more individual control over their lives as well as toward reaching full group or individual potential. The literacy-as-power metaphor in relation to the Yirrkala Yolngu will be developed throughout the remainder of the paper.

Among the contrasts that can be made concerning oral and literate cultures, I would like to concentrate on those differences evident in the Yirrkala struggle that involve power in terms of decision-making processes, negotiation, and contract making. These differences are summarized in Table 2.

Many aboriginal people are functionally literate. However, outback aboriginal culture is largely oral. Thus, an oral culture is attempting to survive in a literate culture environment. Naturally, there will be conflict as the two cultures interact.

I could provide evidence of this conflict, but one example stands out as being indicative of cultural conflict not between aboriginal and nonaboriginal people, but between aboriginal people. Among the aboriginal people there are

TABLE 2
Oral Culture and Literate Culture Power Values

Oral culture	Literate culture
Decision Making	
You only know that which can be recalled.	You have access to all information once it has been recorded.
Power discourse is spoken only by those who have the right to speak and the right to decide.	Power discourse is written by those representing power institutions. Institutions make decisions, not people.
Negotiation	
The spoken word in negotiations is considered carefully. It is the only message. It must have a high truth value.	The spoken word is not as carefully articulated as the written word. It is not the final message. It does not need to have a high truth value. The truth value of an utterance is only valid when it is in writing. Thus we say, "Get it in writing!" or "Show it to me in writing."
Issues are resolved quickly through personal, face-to-face negotiation with practical limitations on the side of the negotiating network.	Issues are resolved slowly through depersonalized committee structures with no practical limitations on the size of the negotiating network.
Contract Making	
Once agreed upon, a spoken contract between those who have the right to speak is locked in *personal* memory.	Once agreed upon, a spoken contract is only validated through the the renegotiation of a written contract. That contract, or demand, becomes more powerful when it is "published" by

	institutions and locked in *institutional* memory.
Power discourse must be stored in memory. Consequently it is structured to aid in memory retention. Thus simple additive relationships and much repetition are favored in discourse.	Power discourse is packed with complex subordinated and nominalized language where processes, qualities, logical relations, and assessments are expressed as nouns or adjectives (Martin 1990).
There is a general past or present orientation in discourse.	There is a major focus on the future in discourse.

those who have crossed over to a high literate culture. These are usually younger people who have been urbanized and "acculturated." They tend to live in the cities and try to assist aboriginal people to cope with their significant personal and group problems. These people see things through literate-culture eyes and are often seen as betraying traditional aboriginal values. One such individual began making statements about aboriginal land rights in *The Bulletin,* a current affairs weekly magazine of the *Newsweek* variety. Shortly afterwards, a group of aboriginal elders, obviously literate, but not from a literate culture, responded to his comments in a letter to the editor. They stated that

> We are four Kimberley elders touring Australia to launch our book *Raparapa*. We speak many Kimberly [sic] Aboriginal languages *Walmajarri, Nyikina, Bunapa, Guniyan, Tjuwaling*—and we understand many others. We speak at the meetings in the Kimberley to our people in our languages.
>
> We read your magazine and saw the letter from Rodney Rivers (B. March 21) claiming to be a spokesman for the Kimberley Aboriginal people. Rivers is one individual and he does not speak for any Kimberley Aboriginal people. He has not had a traditional education and he speaks only English. He lives in Toowoomba in Queensland on the other side of Australia. He is not initiated and has nothing to do with our people and has nothing to do with our law. He is not a Law man. He does not and cannot speak for the Law men of the Kimberley.
>
> We have been speaking for ourselves. Our ancestors governed this country according to our laws for many thousands of years and we are still running this country and abiding by our laws, traditions and keeping our languages. . . .
>
> The Kimberley Land Council invited Rivers to attend the council meeting to meet the representatives of all the Aboriginal groups in the Kimberley. He refused to face up to us. He did not come to the meeting at our invitation. How can he then claim to represent, somewhere in Queensland, people who he refuses to meet? (*The Bulletin,* April 11, 1989)

Notice the values attached to the message: only the elders can speak for the people; we are the elders; we have the right to speak; Rivers, although aboriginal, does not have the right to speak; Rivers did not attend a face-to-face meeting so his comments are invalid.

This minor conflict underscores a dilemma facing aboriginal culture. Aboriginal people want the power to control their own destiny. They recognize that one way to achieve that power is to become literate, to write books and other documents, as in the example just given. Or, as Martin (1990) reports, aboriginal leaders want their children to gain access to a "secret" language which, when mastered, offers power. His reference to the language being secret comes from a number of sources, including Bain (1979) who quotes an aboriginal leader's views of educational needs:

> We want them to learn. Not the kind of English you teach them in class, but your secret English. We don't understand that English, but you do. To us you seem to say one thing and do another. That's the English we want our children to learn. (Bain 1979)

In addition, von Sturmer (1984) states that

> . . . the specific complaint, then, is that balanda (nonaboriginal Australians) withhold the secret of their power, and that much of this "power" is tied up with the "big English" to which Aboriginal people are denied access. According to one interpretation, schools are failures because they fail to teach this "power." (von Sturmer 1984, 273)

Aboriginal people want "power" through literacy, but that power is interwoven with literate culture values which are in direct conflict with traditional oral culture values. And traditional aboriginal people naturally do not want to lose their culture.

As the case of Yirrkala school has illustrated, it is possible for traditional aboriginal people to adopt literate culture values while still retaining most of their oral culture. In terms of decision-making processes, the Yolngu were prepared to function in committees and action groups—their own institutions—thus depersonalizing their demands. They recorded the proceedings of their meetings by taking minutes and referred to these minutes at subsequent meetings. This enabled them to build their information store and to make progress toward their objectives. In both decision-making processes and in negotiations, the Yolngu traditional leaders were prepared to compromise their sole "right to speak" in at least this one domain. Incidentally, because many of the young Western-trained aboriginal teachers were women, a further significant shift away from traditional values was made when aboriginal female teachers became involved in discussions affecting the whole community—an area which would normally be seen as "men's business." In negotiation and contract making stages with Balanda representatives, the Yolngu used power written discourse addressed not only to individuals but also to institutions. Since the Yolngu negotiators had learned not to trust the spoken word of Balanda institutional representatives, they wanted responses to Yolngu demands in writing. Throughout the process, the Yolngu created a power network that formed a lobby which was impossible to overlook. Contracts and demands were written and "published" in a written discourse style Balanda attribute to power language. Finally, the Yolngu exhibited an obvious concern for the future during the whole episode.

Conclusion

What we have seen, then, is the inculcation of literate culture values into a predominantly oral culture. These new values helped an oppressed culture fight institutional racism and gain control over the community's educational processes. Is there anything in this that can be applied to situations outside of the aboriginal context?

It might be argued that there are few analogies except perhaps for indigenous populations in the Americas. That is true. However, there are some principles that could be applied to immigrant and refugee minority groups as well as to indigenous populations.

It is recognized that programs which attempt to raise literacy levels of individuals from predominantly oral societies can succeed to a certain extent. Individual functional literacy may be achieved. However, as has been shown in the Yirrkala example, functional literacy could be defined as attaining a degree of literacy in society which would allow one to function in that society to the extent that the society's power structures will permit. Functional literacy alone will not provide individual and group power to an oppressed people. It appears that there are many oral or oral residue nonnative English-speaking minority people who daily face examples of institutional racism and insensitivity. These people have little power over their lives, and they do not have the tools to combat the oppression they may feel. The adoption of key literate culture values would enable these people to mount a campaign that might eventually lead to those in a minority group gaining more control over their lives. As literacy teachers of many kinds, I believe we can do much more than teach basic survival or functional literacy skills. We can teach aspects of the "secret" language, the literacy of power.

References

BAIN, M. 1979. *At the interface: The implications of opposing views of reality*. M. A. thesis, Monash University, Melbourne.
BALDAUF, R. and W. EGGINGTON. 1989. Language reform in Australian languages. In *Language reform: History and future,* I. FODER and C. HAGEGE eds. Hamburg: Buske.

BLACK, P. 1983. *Aboriginal languages in the Northern Territory*. Batchelor, N.T.: School of Australian Linguistics.

Bulletin, The, 1989. Sydney: April 11; 10.

CHAMBERS, B. and J. PETTMAN. 1986. *Anti-racism: A handbook for adult educators.* (Human Rights Commission Education Series, No. 1). Canberra, ACT: Australian Government Printing Service.

CHRISTIE, M. and S. HARRIS. 1985. Communication breakdown in the Aboriginal classroom. In *Cross-cultural encounters: Communication and mis-communication,* J. PRIDE ed. Melbourne: River Seine.

CUMMINS, J. 1989. Language teaching for student empowerment and social justice. Plenary address ATESOL Conference, Sydney Australia, January 1989.

EADES, D. 1985. English as an Aboriginal language. In *Aboriginal perspectives on experience and learning: The role of language in Aboriginal education,* M. CHRISTIE ed. Geelong: Deakin University Press.

EGGINGTON, W. and R. BALDAUF. 1990. Towards evaluating the Aboriginal bilingual education program in the Northern Territory. In *Language planning and education in Australasia,* R. BALDAUF and A. LUKE eds. London: Multilingual.

FREIRE, P. 1970. *Pedagogy of the oppressed.* MYRA B. RAMOS Trans. New York: Continuum.

_____. 1978. *Pedagogy in process.* New York: Seabury.

GALE K., D. McCLAY, M. CHRISTIE and S. HARRIS. 1981. Academic achievement in the Milingimbi bilingual education program. *TESOL Quarterly* 15; 297–314.

GOODY, J. and I. WATT. 1988. The consequences of literacy. In *Perspectives on literacy,* K. KINTGEN, B. KROLL and M. ROSE eds. Carbondale: Southern Illinois University Press.

GRAHAM, B. 1986. *Language and mathematics in the Aboriginal context: A study of classroom interactions about addition in the early years.* M. A. thesis, Deakin Univesity, Geelong, Australia.

HARRIS, S. 1980. *Culture and learning: Tradition and education in NE Arnhem Land.* Darwin: Northern Territory Department of Education.

HAVELOCK, E. 1988. The coming of literate communication to Western culture. In *Perspectives on literacy,* E. KINTGEN, B. KROLL, and M. ROSE eds. Carbondale: Southern Illinois University Press.

House of Representatives Select Committee on Aboriginal Education. 1985. *Aboriginal education.* Canberra: Australian Government Publishing Service.

MARTIN, J. 1990. Language and control: Fighting with words. In *Language: Maintenance, power and education in Australian Aboriginal contexts,* WALTON C. and W. EGGINGTON eds. Northern Territory University Press.

MUHLHAUSER, P. 1986. *Pidgin and creole linguistics.* Oxford: Blackwell.

Northern Territory Department of Education. 1983. *Directions for the eighties: Northern Territory schools.* Darwin: Northern Territory Department of Education.

OGBU, J. 1988. Literacy and schooling in subordinate cultures: The case of black Americans. In *Perspectives on literacy,* E. KINTGEN, B. KROLL and M. ROSE, eds. Carbondale: Southern Illinois University Press.

ONG, WALTER, 1944. Some psychodynamics of orality. In *Perspectivees on literacy.* E. KINTGEN, B. KROLL, and M. ROSE, eds. Carbondale: Southern Illinois University Press.

ROMAINE, S 1988. *Pidgin and creole languages.* London: Longman.

SANDEFUR, J. and J. HARRIS. 1986. Variations in Australian kriol. In Fishman J. et al. (Eds.) *The Furgusonian impact, Vol. 2: sociolinguistics and the sociology of language.* Berlin: Mouton de Gruyter.

SCRIBNER, S. 1984. Literacy in three metaphors. *American Journal of Education* 93:6–21.

Senate Standing Committee on Education and the Arts. 1984. *A national language policy.* Canberra: Australian Government Publishing Service.

SHIMPO, M. 1985. *Communication processes between the Northern Territory Government and Aboriginals: Antagonistic cooperation.* Darwin: Northern Territory Government.

TODD, L. 1974. *Pidgins and creoles.* London: Routledge.

VON STURMER, J. 1984. *Interpretations and directions. Aborigines and uranium: Consolidated report on the social impact of uranium mining on the Aborigines of the Northern Territory.* Canberra, ACT: Australian Institute of Aboriginal Studies.

WALTON, C. 1989. Aboriginal education in the NT: Access, equity and pedagogy issues. Paper presented at the Australian Reading Association Conference, Darwin, Australia, July 1989.

WEARNE, G. 1986. *Towards 'bothways' schooling: An exploration of the role of non-Aboriginal educators in Aboriginal schools in the context of self-determination and management.* M. A. thesis, Deakin University, Geelong, Australia.

WUNUNGMURRA, 1984. Community Council Minutes. Yirrkala.

Discussion questions

1. Eggington suggests that many aspects of the social behavior of oral societies are different from the social behavior of highly literate societies. What would some of these differences be? Are these differences sufficiently large to justify the classification of societies as "oral" or "literate?"

2. Eggington links literacy with individual and group power in a highly literate society. Is this linkage justified? Are there language domains where orality is more valued than literacy? Do these domains have "power?"

3. Eggington emphasizes that differences between oral and literate people are sociolinguistic rather than psycholinguistic. Is such a distinction valid?

4. Eggington claims that literacy was one of the factors that contributed to the Yirrkala community gaining control over their school. What other factors may have contributed to this outcome?

5. Is it legitimate to conclude that what happened at outback Yirrkala, and what Freire (1978) has described happening in South America, is relevant to the literacy education in inner city Western society?

7

The Yakudoku Tradition of Foreign Language Literacy in Japan

NOBUYUKI HINO

Introduction

In the analysis of literacy in foreign languages, it is important to take socio-linguistic factors into account. Approaches to the reading of foreign languages used in a particular country are often under the influence of its indigenous socio-linguistic factors.

Hino (1982) briefly described the tradition of foreign language learning in Japan called *yakudoku*. Its sociolinguistic aspects were further discussed in Hino (1988). The present paper makes an attempt to review the yakudoku tradition in Japan in terms of cross-cultural literacy with special reference to the reading of English as a foreign language.

WHAT IS YAKUDOKU?

Yaku means "translation," and *doku* means "reading." Yakudoku is defined as a technique or a mental process for reading a foreign language in which the target language sentence is first translated word by word, and the resulting translation reordered to match Japanese word order as part of the process of reading comprehension (Kawasumi 1975). An illustration of the yakudoku process might be as follows:

[Target language sentence] She has a nice table in her room.

Stage 1 [The reader mentally makes word-by-word translation]

She	has	a	nice	table	in	her	room
kanojo	motteiru	hitotsu-no	sutekina	teburu	naka	kanojo-no	heya

Stage 2 [Translation reordered to match Japanese syntax]

Kanojo   kanojo-no   heya   naka   hitotsu-no   sutekina   teburu motteiru

Stage 3 [Recoding in Japanese syntax]

Kanojo-wa kanojo-no heya-no naka-ni hitotsu-no sutekina teburu-wo motteiru.

At stages 2 and 3, very complex operations are required of the Japanese reader of foreign languages, except when s/he reads a language such as Korean whose linguistic structure is comparatively similar to Japanese. The Japanese language has SOV word order, inflections of verbs and adjectives, and most importantly, particles to indicate grammatical functions. It is linguistically quite remote from many of the major languages in the world.

There are two aspects to yakudoku. One is the regressive eye movement resulting from the word-by-word translation. The other is the fact that the meaning is not understood directly in the target language, but only via translation (Ueda 1979). These two features distinguish yakudoku from normal reading.

In teaching students how to read English, teachers introduce students to the yakudoku technique. This is a method used by the majority of Japanese teachers of English from junior high to college level. The Yakudoku method aims to teach the yakudoku technique to a point where the student is able to use it without help from the teacher. The teacher's job in class is to explain the word-by-word translation technique, to provide a model translation, and to correct the student's translation (Kakita 1978; Tajima 1978).

Two nationwide surveys administered by the Japan Association of College English Teachers (Koike et al. 1983, 1985) showed that from 70 percent to 80 percent of Japanese teachers of English in high schools and universities resorted to the Yakudoku Method. Hino (1987a) also found that 70 percent of his university students had been taught to read English solely with this method. Yakudoku is "the" method in the teaching of foreign languages in Japan.

It should be explained here that under the yakudoku tradition, reading a language is essentially the same as learning the language. Foreign language education in Japan traditionally places a heavy emphasis on reading. Or, at least, yakudoku is used as a foundation for the learning and teaching of the other three language skills. In this sense, the Yakudoku Method is not only a pedagogy but it is the basis of foreign language literacy itself.

DISADVANTAGES OF THE YAKUDOKU METHOD

For many Japanese students, reading English and yakudoku are the same thing (Matsumoto 1965; Tazaki 1978). They are not aware that it is much more natural to read English in the original word order, nor that it is desirable to read directly in English without recourse to a Japanese translation. Hino (1987a) observed that Japanese students of English tend to use the word *yakusu* (translate) synonymously with *yomu* (read). Having been trained to read English via translation, they have come to identify this with the process of reading in a foreign language itself. It may even be that the goal of reading a foreign language text is regarded as simply to render it into a possible Japanese equivalent, without consideration of the value of the translation in understanding the contents of the original. Once the English is transformed into Japanese, it is considered read. Conversely, if an English text has not been recoded into Japanese, "reading" is not considered to have taken place (Ueda 1979; Kakita 1978).

The yakudoku habit clearly is a severe handicap to the Japanese student. It limits the speed at which the student reads, induces fatigue, and reduces the efficiency with which s/he is able to comprehend. The meaning of a text is obtained via Japanese translation, and is only an approximation to the original.

In terms of reading strategy, yakudoku is ineffective in that it puts an undue emphasis on each word. Meaning is dealt with at the word level only, or at best at the sentence level. The yakudoku reader usually does not recognize the importance of discourse as a semantic unit.

Yakudoku also has detrimental effects on the other aspect of literacy, that is, writing. In writing English, the yakudoku process is applied in reverse. A Japanese sentence is composed, translated into English word by word, and then the words are reordered according to English syntax (Matsumoto 1965). The result is seldom idiomatic English sentences, which are produced very slowly.

In spite of these serious disadvantages, why is the Yakudoku Method so prevalent? It is important to note that the Course of Study for English prescribed by the Ministry of Education, which defines and controls the contents of English teaching in junior and senior high schools, makes no mention of the skill of translating English into Japanese (cf. Mombusho 1978a, 1979a). In other words, the Education Ministry by no means encourages yakudoku. The Yakudoku Method of teaching English is not necessarily something that is politically imposed upon the teachers by the administration, but is a long established tradition which exists at a deeper level of the sociolinguistic structure of Japan.

HISTORY OF YAKUDOKU

Yakudoku originally comes from the reading of classical Chinese by ancient Japanese. It is believed that Chinese texts were first brought to Japan around the year 400. As Japanese had had no letters to transcribe their language until then, this was their initial contact with a writing system. For the aim of the present paper, our attention should be given to the fact that Chinese was the first foreign language studied in Japan.

Chinese, an SVO language, does not have particles nor inflections, but has a strict word order to indicate grammatical functions. Chinese and Japanese are linguistically so remote from each other that reading Chinese must have been a rather difficult task for the Japanese of those days. However, they gradually developed a method of reading Chinese by translating it word by word into Japanese. This process is basically the same as the current yakudoku practice. For example:

[Target language sentence]
毎 見 秋 瓜 憶 故 丘
(Every time I see an autumn melon, I remember the hill at my home.)

Stage 1 [Word-by-word translation]

毎	見	秋 瓜	憶	故 丘
goto	miru	shu ka	omou	ko kyu
(every time)	(see)	(autumn melon)	(remember)	(hill at home)

Stage 2 [Reordering]

shuka	miru	goto	kokyu	omou
(autumn melon)	(see)	(every time)	(hill at home)	(remember)

Stage 3 [Recoding in Japanese syntax]

Shuka-wo	miru	goto-ni	kokyu-wo	omou
(an autumn melon)	(I see)	(every time)	(the hill at my home)	(remember)

However, there is an important difference between the original form of yakudoku and the current yakudoku practice in reading English. Today, yakudoku is usually an implicit mental process. Yakudoku in reading Chinese, on the other hand, was an explicit process. At Stage 2, some symbols are added to indicate the Japanese word order:

毎　見　秋　瓜　憶　故　丘
レ　　二　　　　　一　　二　　　　　　一

The symbol レ , for example, indicates the reversal of the adjoining two characters. The symbols 一 and 二 come from Chinese numerals, but are used here as signs which direct the reordering according to a set of rules. At Stage 3, Japanese particles and inflectional suffixes are written in *kana,* a phonetic writing system developed in Japan by simplifying Chinese characters, beside the Chinese words:

二　ル　　　　ヲ　フ　　　　　ヲ
毎　見　秋　瓜　憶　故　丘
レ　二　　　　一　　二　　　　　　一

Even today, this method of reading classical Chinese is taught in senior high schools in Japan as part of the instruction in the Japanese language, following the Course of Study for the National Language issued by the Ministry of Education (cf. Hombusho 1978b, 1979b).

It should be noted that it was none other than yakudoku that gave birth to the system of writing the Japanese language which is still used today basically in its original form. That is, the Japanese began to transcribe their native language according to the yakudoku practice. Nouns, verb stems, and adjective stems are normally written in Chinese characters, which are described as ideographic, logographic, or morphemic. In fact, many words that are written with Chinese characters came to be pronounced in Japan in accordance with their Japanese translations. Although the present paper focuses on the influence of yakudoku on foreign language literacy, the reader should be aware that yakudoku has also been a key factor in first language literacy in Japan.

Having perfected the yakudoku technique in later years, it came to be applied to the study of other foreign languages. In the nineteenth century, the Japanese produced textbooks for the study of Dutch in which the yakudoku technique was used. *Kunten Oranda bunten* (1857) is a typical example of the application of yakudoku to Dutch, with the word *kunten* in the title meaning the symbols used for the reordering. For each Dutch sentence in this text, the Japanese equivalents of the Dutch words are written out in Chinese characters with particles and inflectional suffixes added in *kana*, which are to be reordered according to the same symbols as the onces used in reading Chinese. For example:

(all)	(original names)	(of)	(women)
諸 ／	本名 ガ	之	婦人
Alle-eigennamen		van	vrouwen
二	上	一	
		レ	(Reprinted in Sogo 1970)

After Dutch, yakudoku was applied to the study of English. The following is an excerpt from *Eibei taiwa shokei* (A shortcut to English conversation, 1859), an English textbook written by Manjiro Nakahama (1827–1898) toward the end of the *Shogun* period. Japanese translations for each English word are written in Chinese characters and *kana* in the top row, which are to be reordered into the Japanese word order in accordance with the reordering symbols. (The *kana* letters above the English words are the transcriptions of the English prounuunciation.)

幾　　許　　字数 カ　　在 ル　　其処 ニ
　　　　　　　　　　　　レ

ハヲ	メニ	ラタシ	アー	ザヤ
How	many	lettrs [sic]	are	there

其処 ニ　　有 リ　　二十 ニ　　六字　　於 テハ　　英国 ニ
　二　　　五　　　三　　　四　　　一　　　　　　　　　　
　　　　　　　　　　　　　　　　　　　　レ

ザヤ	アー	ツーエンテ	セキス	イン	エンゲレス
There	are	twenty-	six	in	English

(Reprinted in Sogo 1983)

Later, the reordering symbols were replaced by numerals, a simpler way of indicating the Japanese word order. Still, the process of word-by-word translation and reordering itself remained the same. Below is an excerpt from *Soyaku rigaku shoho (First Lessons on Natural Philosophy with Japanese Translations,* 1871), an English text which, in modern terms, would fall into the category of content-based language instruction. The Japanese equivalents for each English word written in Chinese characters and *kana* are numbered.

What	hemisphere	is	America	in ?
ドノ	半球 ニ	有 カ	アメリカ ガ	於 テ
一	二	五	四	三
1	2	5	4	3

The explicit writing of numerals also gradually came to be less frequently used in the reading and teaching of foreign languages. However, the essential process of yakudoku, though more implicitly, continued to be widely practiced. Yakudoku is a strong educational or sociolinguistic tradition in Japan, which enjoys a history of over a thousand years. But that is not to say that it has been without its critics.

CRITICISMS OF YAKUDOKU

An early critic of yakudoku was the Confucianist Sorai Ogyu (1666–1728) with his disciple Shundai Dazai (1680–1747) (Suzuki 1975). Ogyu voiced objections to yakudoku in his book *Gakusoku (Rules of Learning)* written in 1727. His main point may be summarized as follows:

> The traditional method of reading Chinese is a misleading one, which should be avoided. You cannot truly understand Chinese in this way. Chinese should be read as Chinese. (Kawasumi 1975)

Ogyu warned that the spirit of the Chinese people could not be grasped through yakudoku, which is merely a literal translation that ignores the linguistic and cultural differences between the two languages.

Gentaku Otsuki (1757-1827), scholar of the Dutch language and culture, criticized the application of yakudoku to Dutch in his book *Rangaku kaitei (Steps in Dutch studies)* written in 1788. His main argument is similar to Ogyu's criticism:

> In reading Dutch, beginners may use the method used for reading Chinese, but it is desirable for advanced readers to read directly in the original word order. You can understand the contents more clearly this way. Dutch often loses its meaning if rendered into Japanese.   (Kawasumi 1975, 1978)

It is recorded that some people, though very few, were able to read directly in Dutch. The nineteenth century scholar Genichiro Fukuchi was one of them. He describes his experience and that of two other nonyakudoku readers:

> In those days, most people read Dutch in the same way as they did with Chinese. Mr. Seikyo Sugita read, however, directly in Dutch without translation. Others achieved understanding only via word-by-word translation. I also read directly in Dutch, though I may sound arrogant . . . I insisted that Dutch should not be read via such forward and backward translation . . . Rinsho was just fourteen years old, but he read Dutch in my way. He was able to read three times as fast as other students. (Reprinted in Kawasumi 1978. Translation the present writer's)

Though Fukuchi said "in those days," the situation actually remains unchanged even today. A large number of Japanese believe yakudoku to be the normal way to read a foreign language.

In 1911, Yoshizaburo Okakura of Tokyo Koto Shihan Gakko (presently the University of Tsukuba) published a book entitled *Eigo kyoiku (English Language Education)*. This was the first systematic study of the teaching of English in Japan. Here, we find a thorough criticism of yakudoku:

In the teaching of English in our country, students are taught to translate word by word, with forward and regressive eye movement. This is a strongly established convention. I think this comes from our traditional method of reading Chinese, in which Chinese words are reordered to match Japanese word order . . . This is a wrong method, which treats Chinese not as a foreign language, but as a kind of Japanese. We should not use this method in studying English . . . It is a pity that everyone considers this to be the only way of reading foreign languages.

In reading Chinese, it is best if you understand the meaning of a text in the original word order. The contents are understood well enough in this way. As a matter of fact, this is the best way to achieve understanding. Likewise, direct reading is the best way of reading English in terms of time, energy, and efficiency. (Reprinted in Kawasumi 1978. Translation the present writer's)

Today, criticism of yakudoku is frequently found in Japanese TEFL journals as well as in books and magazines for the general public. In spite of these criticisms, yakudoku still dominates the way Japanese read foreign languages. It dies hard.

WHY IS YAKUDOKU SO PERSISTENT?

Why is yakudoku persistently practiced? As a cause of the widespread practice of yakudoku, many analysts refer to its easiness for the teacher (Tazaki 1978; Ozeki et al. 1983; Ito 1984). That is, the use of the Yakudoku Method requires little professional training, and also little preparation is needed for each class. Anyone who has studied English through yakudoku is able to teach it in the same way without much effort. The inadequate training system of EFL teachers in Japan enhances this tendency (Ozeki et al. 1983; Hino 1987a). Not having been exposed to alternative approaches, many teachers are liable to depend on the same old method with which they have been taught.

Mental discipline is also often cited as a major function of yakudoku (cf. Hiraizumi and Watanabe 1975). The decoding and deciphering activities involved in the yakudoku process provide the learner with opportunities for mental training, and thus make the Yakudoku Method worthwhile.[1]

Though these analyses explain some aspects of the tanacity of yakudoku, they are not necessarily considered to be crucial from the standpoint of the present paper. The fundamental nature of the yakudoku phenomenon is more sociocultural than pedagogical.

Once a practice is accepted as a tradition, it becomes a norm. No one is

---

[1] The Yakudoku Method also gives the student useful training for university entrance examinations in which word-by-word translations are so often required. However, the existence of those translation questions in the exams should be viewed as a result of the prevalence of yakudoku rather than as a cause of it.

accused as long as s/he follows this norm. On the other hand, those who do not observe the norm are treated as deviants. And the longer history the tradition has, the stronger the norm is. The society keeps the tradition rolling in accordance with the law of inertia. This tendency is especially conspicuous in a rigidly structured society such as Japan. This is the sociocultural view of the survival of yakudoku that the present article is based upon.

Yakudoku was an effective method when Japanese first faced classical Chinese. The unfortunate fact is that yakudoku has become such a strong convention that Japanese find it very difficult to free themselves from this tradition even in the 1990's when English needs to be learned as a means of communication rather than as a dead language.

IS YAKUDOKU PECULIAR TO JAPAN?

Is yakudoku practiced only in Japan? Or can we find similar phenomena in other countries?

Yakudoku in Japan in fact presents a close resemblance to the Grammar-Translation Method used in the West. As in yakudoku, word-by-word translation is a basic component of the G-T Method. And as yakudoku comes from the method of reading classical Chinese, G-T in Europe is also an application of the method of reading classical languages, notably Latin (Kelly 1969; Richards and Rodgers 1986). This implies that yakudoku is essentially a universal strategy, though a primitive one, which is employed when the purpose of learning the foreign language is the reading of literary texts rather than practical communication.

In the East, the example of Korea is suggestive, as it has a linguistic environment similar to Japan. Both Koreans and Japanese began to learn the Chinese language in ancient times, to the extent that they adopted Chinese characters as the first writing system known in each country. Moreover, the Korean language has a relatively similar structure to the Japanese language, both of them being classified as agglutinative languages. Do they have yakudoku in Korea?

In Korea, words that are written in Chinese characters are read according to their original Chinese pronunciations. That is, unlike in Japan where those words are often pronounced in accordance with their Japanese translations, they are normally not pronounced with their Korean translations. From this, it had been generally believed until recently that yakudoku of Chinese never existed in Korea. However, archaeological studies have lately revealed that ancient Koreans actually did read classical Chinese by translating it word by word into Korean, using some reordering symbols of their own (Kanno 1986; Yoshino 1988). In other words, yakudoku of classical Chinese was existent also in Korea. This is actually not surprising if we consider the universality of the word-by-word translation strategy mentioned at the beginning of this section.

In the teaching of English in Korea, grammar-translation has been the most dominant method, though some efforts are being made to modernize the pedagogy (Pei 1988). Deyama (1988) has observed that EFL classrooms in Korea, where translation is the focus of teaching, look exactly the same as the ones in Japan. Though it is difficult to determine if the word-by-word translation practice in ancient Korea is directly responsible for the current grammar-translation practice in the teaching of English in this country, it is clear that Korea has the yakudoku problem, to some extent, as in Japan.

Yakudoku is not necessarily a phenomenon peculiar to Japan. Still, the yakudoku tradition in Japan is so explicit and conspicuous that it can be seen as a significant example of the impact of sociolinguistic inheritance on foreign language literacy today.

Conclusions

In examining the nature of literacy in English in an EFL country, it is essential to investigage its indigenous sociolinguistic tradition. In the case of Japan, it is the yakudoku tradition of learning foreign languages, which has survived over a thousand years and is still alive and well. Yakudoku may even be viewed as the solid infrastructure of foreign language literacy in Japan.

In the past, yakudoku may have had its own value as one possible method of studying foreign cultures (Ito 1978, 1984; Ozeki et al. 1983). However, in terms of the teaching of English for communication needed today, it is undoubtedly a serious handicap for Japanese students of English.

For years, many foreign teachers have been trying to introduce innovative new methods to the teaching of English in Japan, but few of them have met with significant success. It is easy to imagine that those teachers from abroad were not adequately informed about the yakudoku tradition. In fact, it may be argued that no new method could succeed in Japan unless it penetrates into this deeply rooted convention which governs the Japanese student as well as the Japanese teacher.

How can EFL teachers build on yakudoku, inasmuch as it is the prevailing mode of reading/learning/teaching foreign languages in Japan? It is possible to capitalize on the positive aspects of this method. Yakudoku, which requires the rearranging of English words into Japanese word order, is in fact fairly good syntactical training. In other words, yakudoku can be a useful tool for getting students to acquire the basic grammar of English. It is a good idea to make use of yakudoku where possible.

However, yakudoku as a means should not be confused as the end. It is imperative that teachers should gradually lead their students away from yakudoku. In fact, a growing number of EFL teachers are making such efforts in Japan. Kasajima (1987) presents several techniques to achieve direct understanding in English, including sense-group reading which discourages the regressive eye movement caused by word-by-word translation. Sagawa and

Furuya (1984) make extensive use of timed reading, using materials with limited vocabulary and comprehensive contents. Hino (1987b) suggests that comprehension practice in listening to English spoken at a normal speed should be effective for eliminating the yakudoku habit. Based on their experience, some successful Japanese learners of English claim repeated reading aloud to be a good way to achieve direct understanding in English (Kunihiro 1970, among others). Software for personal computers has also been developed which integrates timed reading and word-group reading. Taniguchi (1987) proposes the use of top-down strategy, which requires active reading through predictions, in Japanese EFL classrooms where yakudoku so often generates passive readers. However, the use of these various approaches is still restricted to the minority of Japanese teachers of English.

This paper has presented a case study of the impact of an indigenous sociolinguistic tradition on foreign language literacy. It is hoped that this type of study would contribute to the understanding of cross-cultural literacy in a global context.

Acknowledgments

This paper is a much revised version of "Yakudoku: Japan's dominant tradition in foreign language learning" (*JALT Journal*, 1 & 2, 1988). I am indebted to many scholars for their useful comments and suggestions, including Professors Fraida Dubin, Barry Duell, Charles Guyotte, Lynn Henrichsen, Kenneth Jackson, Natalie Kuhlman, Eric Morrison, Madoka Ogiwara, Ted Plaister, and Jack Richards.

References

DEYAMA, K. 1988. Kankoku no eigojijo. *The Chunichi Shimbun*. Jan. 20, evening edition.
HINO, N. 1982. Yakudoku: The Japanese approach to foreign language study. *Working Papers* 2:45-53 (Department of English as a Second Language, University of Hawaii at Manoa). Also in *The Journal of the International College of Commerce and Economics, Department of Commerce* 32 (1985):85-90.
_____. 1987a. *TOEFL de 650-ten: Watashi no eigoshugyo* Tokyo: Nanundo.
_____. 1987b. Eigo wo dou manabuka. *Kokusai Keizaijin* 55:20-23.
_____. 1988. Yakudoku: Japan's dominant tradition in foreign language learning. *JALT Journal* 1&2:45-55.
HIRAIZUMI, W., and S. WATANABE. 1975. *Eigokyoiku daironso*. Tokyo: Bungeishunju.

ITO, K. 1978. Traditional methods and new methods: A study on the methods suited for the Japanese. In *The teaching of English in Japan,* I. Koike, M. Matsuyama, Y. Igarashi, and K. Suzuki eds. 204–19. Tokyo: Eichosha.

_____. 1984. *Eigokyojuho no subete.* Tokyo: Taishukan.

KAKITA, N. 1978. Yakudokushiki kyojuho. In *Eigokyojuho kakuron,* 116–33. Tokyo: Kenkyusha.

KANNO, H. 1986. Nihongo to chosengo no kankei saguru. Interview by *The Asahi Shimbun,* Sept. 6, evening edition.

KASAJIMA, J. 1987. *Eibun sokudokusokkaiho.* Tokyo: Eikyo.

KAWASUMI, T. 1975. Yakudoku no rekishi. *The English teachers' magazine,* July special issue, 14–19.

_____. with T. SUZUKI. 1978. *Eigokyoiku ronsoshi.* Tokyo: Taishukan.

KELLY, L. G. 1969. *25 centuries of language teaching.* Rowley, MA: Newbury House.

KOIKE, I., et al. 1983. *General survey of English language teaching at colleges and universities in Japan: Teacher's view.* Tokyo: Research Group for College English Teaching in Japan.

_____. et al. 1985. *General survey of English language teaching at colleges and universities in Japan: students' view.* Tokyo: Research Group for College English Teaching in Japan.

KUNIHIRO, M. 1970. *Eigo no hanashikata.* Tokyo: Simul Press.

MATSUMOTO, T. 1965. *Eigo no atarashii manabikata.* Tokyo: Kodansha.

MOMBUSHO. 1978a. *Chugakko shidosho: gaikokugohen.* Tokyo: Kairyudo.

_____. 1978b. *Chugakko shidosho: kokugohen.* Tokyo: Tokyo Shoseki.

_____. 1979a. *Kotogakko gakushushidoyoryo kaisetsu: gaikokugohen-eigohen.* Tokyo: Hitotsubashi Shuppan.

_____. 1979b. *Kotogakko gakushushidoyoryo kaisetsu: kokugohen.* Tokyo: Gyosei.

OSAWA, S., S. ANDO, K. KURODA, and Y. NARITA. 1978. *More successful teaching of English.* Tokyo: Nanundo.

OZEKI, A., M. TAKANASHI, and M. TAKAHASHI. 1983. *Eigoka kyoikuho.* Tokyo: Kinseido.

PEI, RHOTAN. 1988. Teaching of English in Korea: Past, present and future. Paper presented at the 27th National Convention of Japan Association of College English Teachers, Sept. 25, Zentsuji Shimin Kaikan, Kagawa, Japan.

RICHARDS, J. C., and T. S. RODGERS. 1986. *Approaches and methods in language teaching.* Cambridge: Cambridge University Press.

SAGAWA, K., and C. FURUYA. 1984. *Surasura eigo sokudokujutsu.* Tokyo: Sogensha.

SOGO, M. 1970. *Zusetsu Nihon no yogaku*. Tokyo: Tsukiji Shokan.
_____. 1983. *Eigo manabi kotohajime*. Tokyo: Asahi Evening News.
SUZUKI, N. 1975. *Chugokugo to kambun*. Tokyo: Koseikan.
TAJIMA, K. 1978. The grammar-translation method: Its historical and
social background. In *The teaching of English in Japan*, I. Koike, M.
Matsuyama, Y. Igarashi, and K. Suzuki eds. 220–27. Tokyo: Eichosha.
TANIGUCHI, K. 1987. Schema-riron wo oyo-shita reading no shido.
Modern English Teaching (May):11–15.
TAZAKI, K. 1978. *Theories of English teaching*. Tokyo: Taishukan.
UEDA, A. 1979. Chokudoku chokkai. In *Yomu eigo*, 78–103. Tokyo:
Kenkyusha.
YOSHINO, M. 1988. *Kanji no fukken. Tokyo: Nicchu Shuppan.*

Discussion Questions

1. Is there any indigenous sociolinguistic tradition in your country which has
a major impact on foreign language literacy? If there is, is it a positive factor or a negative factor for the development of foreign language literacy?

2. What is the relationship between your first language literacy and your sec-
ond/foreign language literacy? What influence does the first language literacy
have on the second/foreign language literacy?

3. For someone taught English under the yakudoku tradition, what kinds of
problems might that individual encounter if s/he were to study in the United
States? What changes in reading strategies might need to be developed?

4. Models of teaching foreign language, such as yakudoku, also make social
statements about how people learn. What other methods are you familiar
with that might be culture or nation specific, and how successful have they
been within the society in which they are used? What are the advantages
and disadvantages of such systems?

8

Literacy Strategies for Chinese University Learners

JAMES KOHN

Introduction

American teachers of English in Chinese universities usually report that their students are hard working, highly motivated, and literate in English. Although there are few opportunities for meaningful use of English, their teachers use methods more traditional than practical, and although these students have little motivation to become members of an English-speaking community, Chinese students develop an impressive ability to read English. Nevertheless, newly-arrived Chinese students in the U.S. are often unprepared to complete academic tasks in English that U.S. university teachers expect. What can account for their partial success, and what can Western teachers do to help Chinese students learn to improve their college-level literacy skills?

I taught English and TEFL methodology to both teachers and students at Shandong Teachers University in Jinan, Shandong from 1984 to 1985. That year I noticed that Chinese students' ability to read English was remarkable, given their isolation from adequate sources of written English. Although many had difficulty understanding and reacting to longer reading passages, most could cope with short paragraphs, and could speak and write at an intermediate level of English proficiency. From my experience with Chinese students in the U.S., I know that many of these students are not yet prepared to cope with the longer reading assignments required in American classrooms, and will participate equally with American students only after a period of learning Western reading skills.

It is the purpose of this paper to explore the literacy strategies of Chinese students, and to speculate about how the differences between those strategies and those used by American students may account for Chinese students' successes and problems studying in American classrooms.

TRADITIONS AND LITERACY IN CHINA

The Chinese system of education, and in particular the learning of foreign languages in schools, emerges from three traditions: the Confucian tradition of filial piety and social stratification, the Buddhist tradition of learning by rote, and the pre–World War II British tradition of foreign language instruction. Confucian values of the supremacy of the teacher as spiritual leader and of filial piety reflected in students' respect and submission to the teacher's authority are still reflected in modern Chinese classrooms. From the Han Dynasty forward to the revolutions of the twentieth century, a thorough knowledge of Confucian tradition became allied to Chinese government civil service through a complex system of examinations.

One sees the survival of the Confucian tradition in the universities in several ways. Chinese students must pass college entry tests in both Chinese literature and political theory, as well as in foreign-language literature. These students are assigned to teaching positions or to graduate school as a result of examinations they must take. Once installed in positions, Chinese teachers are promoted when they have passed tests or otherwise attained degrees, which certify their knowledge of the subject area. Formal student evaluations of a teacher's effectiveness play no major role. Thus, Chinese teachers and students tend to regard the passing of tests as the one clear indication of achievement, and the gateway to a career. Since passing the test is a prerequisite to entering a university or finding a career, Chinese students work hard to learn the answers to test questions. Western teachers, who may view the goal of language teaching as the development of communicative competence, may be frustrated to discover that their students are more interested in passing the exams than in learning ways of applying English skills in a meaningful or communicative context.

The Mahayana school of Buddhism, and the Ch´an tradition in China, in which simple faith is emphasized over logic, has also had its impact on language teaching in China. The memorizing of texts as a way of demonstrating one's knowledge of the language is a reminder of this tradition. In my experience in China, it was not unusual to find crowds of students preparing for the upcoming day's lessons in English by walking along the sports fields reciting the texts of the day's lesson to themselves, in order to memorize them completely. I observed in my students' other classes that their Chinese teachers would require them to show that they knew the words of a text by rote. These students told me that they did not expect teachers to ask them to analyze the texts, nor to draw conclusions from what they had memorized, but merely to repeat what had been studied.

The influence of the British tradition of foreign language education is harder to trace than the influences just described. According to those teachers whom I interviewed in China, most contemporary foreign language teaching began in the 1950s, when the predominant foreign language taught in Chinese schools was Russian. Russian language teachers were trained by Soviets, who, in turn, modeled their foreign language methods on the British traditions of the 1920s and 1930s, methods which emphasized grammar rules, close reading of texts, and the use of translation exercises. These methods continue to predominate in the teaching of English in modern, foreign language classrooms in China.

Chinese language educators tended to favor a rigorous knowledge of the vicissitudes of grammar, and a division of the study of language into categories that applied to a comparative study of language. As a "foreign expert" in Jinan, I was asked by my Chinese hosts to teach a course in "lexicology," the text for which had been written by a Russian-teacher-turned-EFL-teacher. The course was expected to concern the etymology of English words, and their historical relation to modern-day usages, just as the teachers of Russian were doing in their classes. Such a course might well have served a comparative linguist well, but was of doubtful use to students who could barely read the high-intermediate level texts they were assigned.

Modern language teaching methods, British or American, were not widely used by Chinese teachers, even though those methods appeared through the media and in textbooks. The popular instructional English-language program, "Follow Me" was a great favorite all over China in 1984 to 1985. "Follow Me" had been produced for West German television by the BBC, and had been converted into a Chinese series for Chinese state television. Its hostess, a Ms. Catherine Flower, was so popular that she became almost a cult figure among students of English. "Follow Me" provided an attractive and intelligent presentation of English in various meaningful contexts. Its Chinese viewers set great store by it, and were very interested in its content, since it also provided a nearly nonpolitical window to the West. Yet the Chinese producers of the program did not respond to the program's goal of teaching communicative competence in English. Instead, they spliced into the show grammatical explanations and translations of the individual words in Chinese.

Although the English teachers at my school were very familiar with "Follow Me," watched it regularly, and encouraged their own children to watch it, there was never any attempt to follow it up in any formal way in the University, or in any of the public schools I visited. There were no reading passages drawn from the program, nor even copies of the dialogues available for students to read. It was as if the English of "Follow Me" were an interesting but irrelevant addition to the "true" study of the language, which could only come from translation assignments in state-approved texts, and the memorized teachers' lectures. This form of Western language teaching seemed to be regarded mainly as entertainment, and an exposure to the spoken English of genuine speakers of English.

Among some of the younger English teachers, however, there seemed to be a growing awareness of recent American TEFL methodology, although in 1984 it was still in its infancy. The text *English for Today,* assembled by the National Council of Teachers of English (NCTE), and published first in 1965, had begun to be used in China. *English for Today* had gone through a major revision in 1972, and has been used widely overseas since then. When I was teaching in China, the 1965 edition, with its short reading passages, brief grammar points, structural syllabus, and exercises in usage, was frequently mentioned as a new, progressive text. But, however popular the text may have been with younger teachers, I saw little or no training of English teachers in the principles of audio-lingualism, which is the basis for *English for Today.* Teachers who used the text might still assign their students to recite memorized portions of it in English reading classes. There was very little pattern practice, or manipulation of sentences to learn syntactic patterns. The Western influence on Chinese teaching of EFL was thus limited to the use of this outmoded American text, with a few others, which were taught through the traditional ways. Close reading, grammatical explanations, and memorization remained the methods of choice in teaching reading in English.

REGIONALISM IN EFL TEACHING IN CHINA

One cannot always generalize about language teaching methods in China, particularly because of the great differences that exist between schools and universities in large cities, compared with those in smaller cities. Faculty members from large cities, such as those in East China Normal University in Shanghai, have had much greater access to foreigners, and to foreign teaching methods, than teachers at Shandong Teachers University in Jinan, where I taught. Before June, 1989, for example, many of the East China Normal teachers observed Western teaching methods on trips abroad, whereas only a very few teachers in Jinan had had the same opportunity. Students who entered East China Normal had to survive very tough competition on the basis of high school grades and governmental standardized tests in order to be admitted. The level of student and faculty preparation at that university was high, compared with that of Shandong Teachers University.

In contrast, students in regional teachers universities, such as that in Jinan, may have come from the second rank of students. Students at regional universities are usually expected to return to their villages to become English teachers in secondary schools, or to serve as civil servants. In contrast, the students at large universities in Shanghai and Beijing might expect to remain in the cities to find important positions in government and industry.

Because of the great differences between national universities, called "key universities," and regional universities, there is quite a discrepancy in the level of student potential, and of teacher preparation. Better trained, better prepared, and more highly motivated teachers in national universities are apt to use more up-to-date methods to teach their students. Thus, the "foreign expert" like myself, whose experience is limited to either a big-city university, or a regional university, is likely to observe only the partial truth of the language teaching situation in China. I personally have had the opportunity both to teach at a regional university, and to lecture at several large universities, and to meet a wide variety of English students from such varied backgrounds as small villages in rural Shandong, to Beijing, Shanghai and Chungjing. My generalities are based on this experience.

RECENT U.S. WRITING ON TEACHING EFL IN CHINA

Before the events of June 1989, Americans were becoming more and more interested in teaching in China. After the relaxation of barriers between the U.S. and China in the early 1970s, increasing numbers of Americans spent a year or more teaching in English in China. Indeed, in the early years of the opening to the West, Chinese universities accepted many foreign teachers, even those with no experience in TEFL, and little teaching experience at all.

Since the events of June 4, 1989, much has changed concerning the numbers of Americans teaching in China, and the numbers of Chinese permitted to study in the U.S. Today, it is more difficult for an American to teach in a Chinese university than was the case before June 1989, and it is much more difficult for Chinese students to come to the U.S. to study. My own university has suspended the exchange arrangement by which I was able to teach in Jinan. I have noticed that American teachers are far more reticent to commit themselves to spending a full year in China, perhaps because of the continuing repressive political climate they perceive. The situation may change in the next few years, as government policies change, as we can only hope.

One of the more comprehensive summaries of the English language teaching situation in China, viewed from the American perspective, appears in Cowan, Light, Mathews and Tucker, "English Teaching in China: A Recent Survey," (Cowan et al. 1979). They report that English is viewed as a tool to gain access to Western advances in science and technology, and secondarily as a means of fostering broader relations with other nations. My experience in Jinan bears out that claim. In conversations I had with my Chinese students, the motivation to overtake the West in technology, which seemed to be the national Communist Party line in 1984, turned up in many conversations. The fact that the country was still quite in arrears in technology in comparison with other countries seemed quite clear to these students. What seemed less obvious to them was how the Chinese system would allow the students to gain this technology.

Many students knew that their best chance to learn Western technology lay in studying abroad, and that a knowledge of English was their key to success. I saw evidence of this new determination to become fluent in English in the rapid development of "English corners," in many cities in China: once or twice a week, students and nonstudents alike would gather in a public area to talk in English, and to trade news and views on English-related subjects. During the visits I made to these English corners, I was swamped with questions about English, ranging from the answers to grammar questions which might appear on an entrance examination, to comments on American writers, like Emily Dickinson, then in vogue.[1]

FACTORS HAMPERING THE SUCCESS OF CHINESE STUDENTS

Chinese students, both English majors and non-English majors, are limited in their access to English by insufficient exposure to well-trained English teachers, by an inappropriate curriculum, and by the intrusion of political philosophy in all courses of study. For nonmajors, whose goal is to "overtake the West," the situation is unfavorable. Cowan et al. point out that whereas Chinese students majoring in English have fourteen hours of English class each week, nonmajors taking English have only four hours each week. English skills or proficiencies are not diagnosed and dealt with through any needs assessment. Instead, reading lessons are often selected to emphasize grammatical structures, rather than the use of language of the content areas. The readings are therefore stilted and inappropriate: for example, university-level reading, copied from a high school science reader published in India, and assigned to biology majors, recounted Copernicus' discovery of the solar system. What might be termed "English for specific purposes" in classes outside China are, for Chinese students, simply different versions of traditional close-reading classes in the

---

[1]My favorite conversation of this sort developed when one student asked my opinion of "Jackson." Thinking that I would get into a rare political discussion about the political campaign that Jesse Jackson had just waged in 1984, I encouraged my new conversation partner to exercise his limited oral English. In the end, after much tea and polite conversation, it turned out that he was interested not in Jesse Jackson, the new "radical," but in Andrew Jackson, the old radical, who must have seemed to a Chinese historian like an early forerunner of Mao, in his land-reform policies.

English department, even when all the students are studying a specific content area, like technological engineering. For such students studying English, there appeared to be scant attention paid to preparation to understand English technical writing, and more attention to proper grammatical translation of basic introductory material.

Not only is the English curriculum offered to nonmajors inadequate to prepare them to "overtake the West" in science and technology, but the curriculum offered to English majors contains little to help these future teachers overcome the disadvantages of the current system. Several young teachers told me they would like very much to begin reforms of the traditional system of teaching English, but find that they cannot, given current political conditions. In every university in China in 1984, there was a separate political organization that matched the academic one. Decisions about which courses would be offered, which texts would be used, and which teachers would teach, all needed to be approved by the Communist Party leader for each department. Such an arrangement does not easily allow for the modernization of traditional methods. Young teachers had to wait until they were given the signal by their superiors to change their teaching methods. Some of these young teachers were far better trained than their older superiors. But there was reluctance to change long-held traditions. Since young people are assigned jobs by their elders, protest has little effect at the local level.

There is another reason that modern language teaching methodology has not yet caught on in China. James Patrie and David Daum (1980) point out that students prefer courses about English language and literature, not about methodology, and that students' readiness in English is inappropriate for courses in methodology. I also observed this attitude in my own experience in China. Even young teachers in Jinan appeared little interested in taking on the challenges of teaching according to principles of language teaching favored in the West. English majors assigned to teach science majors still preferred to teach literary texts, rather than science readings; indeed, the notion of being ready to answer questions about science in English was daunting to many.

The availability of Western textbooks is another problem hampering Chinese students' abilities to adopt Western styles of language teaching. In response to the Cowan *et al.* article in the *TESOL Quarterly,* Jie Tao, a lecturer at Beijing University (one of the "key" universities), wrote a letter to explain that English books are so popular in the bookstore that they sell out, and are thus unavailable. At Jinan, not a "key" university, current books in English were available only in faculty reading rooms, not usually in the main library; very few of them ever appeared in the campus bookstore.

As I have previously stated, there is a sizable difference in the experience of students and faculty at a large university in Beijing from that of students and faculty in a regional city. My host college's collection of books in the departmental reading room was impressive, I thought, considering the size of the university. There were copies, not only of classics from the British and American literary canon, but even some modern best sellers, donated to the reading room by visiting American teachers, or sent to the department by American teachers and students (including my home university). Unfortunately, these books were apparently off-limits to the students, but available only to the teachers, who seldom went there. Thus, even if students were interested in reading more, they were uninformed about the presence of the books. Students at larger universities in Beijing and Shanghai may well have access to many more books than their colleagues at smaller regional universities.

The main library at my host university provided me with an insight into the difficulties my students faced. As a classroom assignment, I had told my students to find out information about an author by checking a book out of the main library. But it seemed that the English books in the main library were stacked unmarked on the floor and shelves, and that the library monitors, the only people authorized to take these books off the shelf for the students, were not literate enough in English, let alone library classification, to find the books. Teachers who definitely wanted their students to read certain books needed personally to take them off the shelf, and place them in the reserve section of the library. Thus, independent research for papers was indeed difficult for my students to do.

Teaching materials were also subject to the inspection of the Party, whose functionaries could remove them if they were considered inappropriate. A colleague from my home university thought it would be a good idea to start a debate about the treatment of a political protest during the democracy movement in China. He made photocopies of the story printed in a Western newspaper, for distribution in his class. He was politely told that such materials were inappropriate for class discussion, and was not allowed to distribute them. He later complained that such administrative interference was an infringement on his academic freedom. What counts as an issue of academic freedom in the U.S. is sometimes not permitted to emerge in Chinese classrooms.

THE TEACHING OF READING IN CHINA

There is a close connection between the attitudes and limitations of students studying English in China, and the methods used to teach reading there. In her paper, Fischer-Kohn (1986) describes the system of English reading instruction in use in universities and pubic schools in China. There are two types of reading classes, "intensive" and "extensive" reading. In intensive reading classes, students are expected to make a very close scrutiny of texts, learning the meaning of each word and phrase, and learning alternate phrases with equivalent meaning. The traditional method of *explication de texte* in use in French language classes is reminiscent of this style of reading instruction. According to Fischer-Kohn, Chinese teachers of intensive reading would encourage students to

1. read slowly and take care that they know each word as they go;

2. vocalize or voice the material, either aloud or silently;

3. reread difficult sentences until they are understood;

4. look up definitions for all unknown words in a dictionary;

5. analyze complex structures carefully.

At first glance, it would appear that these strategies are in direct opposition to those used in the West. Following the precepts of contemporary reading theorists, such as Kenneth Goodman (1967) and Frank Smith (1971), Fischer-Kohn suggests that American teachers of reading might teach students to

1. read rapidly;

2. take care to avoid vocalization or regression;

3. use prior background knowledge to predict what a reading may be about;

4. focus on the main ideas rather than treating evey phrase as equally important;

5. guess the meaning of the words from the context wherever possible, avoiding frequent use of a dictionary.

The very patterns of reading behavior that American teachers are training their students to avoid are the ones that Chinese teachers expect their students to use. In current terms, Americans favor top-down strategies of cognitive awareness in reading, while the Chinese are following bottom-up strategies.

Certainly there was ample evidence of this pattern in my own experience in China. Even in my class of senior English majors studying contemporary American fiction, seen as an "extensive" reading class, the students studied the material following the intensive pattern—detailed concentration on the words and phrases used in the text, with little or no attention to the overall structure of the short story. When asked to write a brief essay analyzing the plot or characterization in a chapter taken from Nabokov's *Pnin* (included in their China-produced English reader), my students preferred either to copy the introduction from the textbook, or to copy excerpted passages from the story. It seemed to me that in their experience, analyzing a story independently of the teacher's interpretation given in class was a very novel concept. Indeed, as I discovered later from observing other Chinese faculty members teaching the same students, extensive reading classes consisted of lectures on a literary subject by the teacher, from which lecture the students took verbatim notes, and repeated those notes on examinations. It was just the kind of behavior which might earn those students a reprimand, were they studying in an American university instead of a Chinese one.

Another way in which reading strategies employed by Chinese students and their teachers differs from Western ways has to do with the use of meaningful context as a background for reading. As previously mentioned, one of the suggestions that American reading teachers make to their students is that they try to guess the meaning of unfamiliar words from the context in the passage. Students are encouraged to think about the overall meaning of a passage and to consider what they already know about the topic. To that end, reading teachers often ask students to imagine a possible scenario before introducing a reading passage, in order to set up the cognitive schema which will enable students to interpret the passage properly.

Some Chinese teachers, however, educated in an era when the only allowable subjects in universities were the writings of Chairman Mao, or other political writings, felt at a great disadvantage in explaining the meaningful context to their students. Thus, when teaching reading to a group of teachers whose students were science majors, I found myself having to explain some basic facts about the solar system, which these teachers would need to know, in order to make the concepts clear. I felt that they would copy my words, and use the same language in preparing an explanation for their students. When I asked the teachers to reflect on what they were reading, and to supply their own explanations, some of the more experienced ones became frustrated and restless; they felt the exlanations were not for them to discover, any more than for their students. They wanted me to tell them the "answers" outright, and clearly, so that they could transmit them to their students.

It is often quite difficult to supply a meaningful context for the interpretation of a reading passage from Jane Austen, in which the expression "drawing room" appeared. The students had dutifully looked up "draw" and "drawing" in their dictionaries, but were puzzled about why there should be a room set aside for "tugging," or for "designing." When I explained that the expression came from *withdrawing* and meant a place to have a private conversation, I next had to explain that many middle-class houses in England had enough rooms that one could be set aside simply for private conversations. This expanation met with much doubt from my students, whose families lived in apartments consisting of only two small bedrooms and a toilet.

American teachers who travel to China to teach English should reconsider certain widely accepted beliefs about the teaching of reading. That students can rely on their knowledge of a familiar context, that they will guess meanings from that context, and that they will then volunteer those meanings aloud as part of a classroom discussion are all expectations quite alien to Chinese classrooms.

THE GOOD SIDE OF "INTENSIVE" READING

As I mentioned at the start of this paper, Americans are often quite impressed with the degree to which Chinese teachers and students have learned English, given the physical and social circumstances in which they must study. If the methods used to teach English reading in China are roughly as I have described them, the students' facility with English is all the more surprising. Mark Clarke (1988) suggests that the slower rate of reading in a second language may "short-circuit" the reading strategies a learner uses with his first language (Clark 1988). Although they read more slowly, the fact remains that the Chinese university students learn English comparatively well in spite of antiquated methods. In ESL classes in American universities, students coming from China often fare better than their ESL classmates who may have attended American high schools. This comparative success is partly attributable to higher motivation to succeed, and to a more limited selection process: only the brightest, most qualified students from China are apt to be allowed to study overseas.

A good part of the Chinese students' success may be attributable to their habits of study in "intensive" reading classes. Close attention to detail, mastering the vagaries of grammatical explanations, the memorizing of grammer rules and exceptions, all of these may give Chinese students greater accuracy in interpreting meaning from texts than their American counterparts. The bottom-up process these students follow seems in direct contrast to the top-down strategies advocated by Patricia Carrell and others (Carrell 1988). Yet the same Confucian devotion to the task assigned by the teacher, and to the preparation for the examination, may result in greater success for these students in doing academic work in Chinese universities.

However, these same Chinese students in American universities need to learn to use the tools of scaffolding, schema recognition, and independent critical thinking, just as American students do. In order to cope with the extensive reading expected of them in American universities, these students must greatly enhance their reading speed, while improving their overall comprehension of texts. Once these skills are mastered, their attention to accuracy in the use of English will serve them well in completing academic assignments in U.S. universities.

Conclusions

An awareness of the literacy experience of Chinese learners gives EFL/ESL teachers several insights. First, it is important to note that in China, English is learned in an environment of very limited input, involving very little interaction and meaningful exchange of conversation. Chinese students learn by listening to their teachers' explanations (often in Chinese), by memorizing rules and definitions, and by mastering translation. Second, in the Chinese context students are not primarily expected to think for themselves, so critical analysis and hypothesis formation are not relevant goals in Chinese classes. Third, many Chinese students find that a broad, general education is *not* rewarded in their academic system, whereas close reading of passages *is*; thus top-down processing of reading passages is foreign to their experience. Fourth, having acquired the skill of intense scrutiny of words and phrases, Chinese students need to be guided through the transition to thinking about the overall organization of a text.

Chinese students in the U.S. should be increasingly challenged to look for the broader implications of what they are reading. Teachers should emphasize the meaningful context of the reading passage, and be prepared to supply background information which their students may lack. In addition, Chinese students need to be taught fundamental skills of information gathering, such as the use of libraries and of reference materials. They need to learn how to draw conclusions from their reading of a text, and to find support for their conclusions using evidence from texts.

It may be quite some time before a Western-style approach to the teaching of reading becomes widespread in China, particularly since the events of June 1989. In the meantime, we Western teachers would do well to see the positive side of the Chinese students' preparation, and to help them supplement their ability to read the details by training them to recognize the schemata that provide a key to understanding in Western culture.

References

CARRELL, P. L. and J. C. EISTERHOLD. 1987. Schema theory and ESL reading pedagogy. In *Methodology in TESOL: a set of readings,* M. Long and J. Richards, eds. New York: Newbury House.

_____, J. DEVINE, and D. ESKEY. 1988. *Interactive approaches to second language reading.* Cambridge: Cambridge University Press.

CLARKE, M. A. 1988. The short circuit hypothesis of ESL reading—or when language competence interferes with reading performance. In *Interactive approaches to second language reading,* P. Carrell, J. Devine, and D. Eskey, eds. Cambridge: Cambridge University Press.

COWAN, J. R., R. LIGHT, B. MATHEWS, and R. TUCKER. 1979. English teaching in China: A recent survey, *TESOL Quarterly* 13 (4): 465–82.

FEITELSON, D. 1978. *Cross-cultural perspectives on reading and reading research.* Newark, Delaware: International Reading Association.

FISCHER-KOHN, E. 1986. Teaching close-reading for ESL/EFL: Uses and abuses. *TECFORS* 9.

GOODMAN, K. S. 1967. Reading: A psycholinguistic guessing game. *Journal of the Reading Specialist* 6 (1): 126–35.

JIE, T. 1980. Comments on Cowan et al., The Forum, *TESOL Quarterly* 14 (1): 257–60.

LEONG, C. K. 1978. Decoding and comprehension in reading Chinese. In *Cross-cultural perspectives on reading and reading research,* D. Feitelson, ed. 157–73.

LIU, S. F. 1978. Decoding and comprehension in reading Chinese. In *Cross-cultural perspectives on reading and reading research,* D. Feitelson. 144–55.

PATRIE, J. and D. DAUM. 1980. Comments on Cowan et al., The Forum, *TESOL Quarterly* 14 (2): 391–94.

SMITH, F. 1982. *Understanding reading.* 3rd ed. New York: Holt, Rinehart, & Winston.

Discussion Questions

1. How does the Chinese style of reading instruction differ from current ideas about top-down and bottom-up processing?

2. What problems in American university subject-area classes will students have, who have been taught to read according to Chinese methods?

3. What is the relationship between the use of a writing system with characters (i.e., Chinese) and the strategy of close reading?

4. How might Western teachers of Chinese-trained students improve their students' reading speed and comprehension?

5. What advantages might Chinese students from China studying in the U.S. have over other students in finding information in reading assignments?

6. How will the introduction of Western-style schemata help Chinese-trained students improve their reading in English?

9

Literacy Acquisition in Poland: University Students' Perceptions[1]

NATALIE A. KUHLMAN

Introduction

> . . . He was not allowed to speak about it openly. All actions, protests, were illegal, censors didn't allow any articles on the problem. Scientific reports . . . were not allowed to be published.
> —from the 1986 journal of a Polish university student

This quote represents what literacy could *not* be used for publicly in the mid-1980s in Poland. Since the student was able to write it to me in his journal, it also reiterates what I was told upon arriving there in October 1986: Anything

[1] This paper is the result of my two visits to Poland, first as a Fulbright scholar at the Jagiellonian University in Krakow, Poland, where I taught in the English Institute during the school year, 1986 to 1987, and second when I returned in the summer of 1989 to collaborate with Dr. Anna Nizegorodcew, an associate professor at the English Institute of the Jagiellonian University in Krakow and the director of the new English Teachers College there. I wish to thank her for all of her help and support in this project. I also wish to thank Dr. Anna Dyduchowa for the time she spent with me and information and ideas she shared.

was possible and nothing was possible and everything was a contradiction.

The focus of this paper is on the literacy acquisition experiences of the students I had as a Fulbright Lecturer in Poland, and how the ways in which they perceived their schooling, particularly in the area of Polish and English writing acquisition, later affected their ways of relating to me, an American university writing teacher. The discussion includes (1) the climate for literacy in Poland; and (2) aspects of the national model for teaching literacy (particularly writing as was current in the 1980s), as perceived by the students from their past school experiences, and how that reflected the climate in the Polish classroom during the Communist regime.

The educational curriculum in 1986 to 1987 was dictated by the state and used rote learning as its primary method. That school year was near the end of forty years of Communist rule and education was still totally under Communist influence. Just two years later, in 1989, Poland voted to have Solidarity, the union party which surfaced in the early 1980s (and was quickly banned) form their government. Future students will face a different reality than my university students did then.

THE STUDENTS

Background

As an American teaching English writing to Polish university students, at the beginning, I found it very difficult to get my students to interact with me, to question me, or to ask questions at all. I thought this may have been due to their shyness in front of a native American English speaker, or to their previous schooling, which I had been told by colleagues did not encourage such interactions with professors. While for several students (including the one quoted at the beginning of this chapter), this changed during the school year, even toward the end I found students more willing to quote or summarize their readings than to criticize them. Usually, if I asked why, they would respond that they just agreed and could not rephrase the readings better. That they had been trained to approach classroom assignments this way, prior to attending the university, did not occur to them. In order to better understand this situation, I decided to become more familiar with their educational backgrounds.

The Study

The writings of my third year Polish students attending the English Institute (i.e., school or large department) of the Jagiellonian University in Krakow during the 1986 to 1987 school year were my primary source of information.[2] These

---

[2] I wish to thank the students who provided for me their written perceptions about how they were educated and about life experiences they had had. Their names have been changed to protect their privacy, but each one of them will always be with me.

students, who will be quoted throughout the chapter, are part of the educated elite in Poland since they have gone far beyond the required eight years of schooling. The students' perceptions, however, are based on their own memory of what they had experienced, and may not reflect actual practice. Their schooling was unaffected by the political and social changes of the late 1980s, although many were in secondary school in 1980 when the Solidarity union was briefly legalized and then banned.

I gave my students two assignments, each followed by classroom discussion. The first was to recall and write down how they were taught to write in Polish, beginning with primary school and continuing through the secondary school. In the second assignment they were asked to write down how they learned to write in English, and how that experience may have differed from their initial writing instruction. They also wrote essays on why they decided to study English (and what specialization), and on convincing a friend or relative for or against becoming an English teacher. Other data came from their journal entries such as the one at the beginning of this chapter.

The students' perceptions are paralleled by a description of how teacher cadets at the Pedagogy Institute and the English Institute of the Jagiellonian University in Poland were prepared to teach. The source for information about the Pedagogy Institute was an interview conducted in June 1989 with Professor Anna Dyduchowa and translated by Dr. Anna Nizegorodcew. Dr. Dyduchowa was the director responsible for training prospective teachers how to teach writing in the public schools in Krakow.

THE CLIMATE FOR LITERACY

Some of the busiest stores in Poland are bookstores. Stores that sell books in English are particularly popular because people see English as the language of opportunity. Many American and English novels are translated into Polish and are sold out quickly. After the return to power of Gomulka in 1956, cultural censorship was greatly reduced, and with it, more opportunities for exposure to the West (Nelson 1984). Books by Carroll, Faulkner, Steinbeck, and Hemmingway, among others, were translated into Polish (Heine 1975). More recently, authors such as Fay Weldon, John Barth, and Kurt Vonnegut have become available. In the first twenty-five years after World War II, one publishing house alone distributed 30,000 titles with three million total books (Kelly 1972). After the political changes in 1989 to 1990, there has been a further reduction of censorship, and a corresponding rise from the underground of clandestine publishing houses.

Polish citizens who lived in cities at this time, tended to be more literate than those living in the country, where secondary schools (called lyceums) were less available (Wedel 1986). However, access to books anywhere in Poland was (and still is) difficult. Paper was hard to obtain, and when an edition was sold out, it was rarely reprinted (Wedel 1986). Children's books in Polish were particularly sought after. On Sunday mornings in major cities, many people went to open book markets where new and used editions, including some from around the world, were sold at higher than average prices. English as a foreign language (EFL) texts were often the first to go. In university libraries, there were frequently only one or two texts for a class of twenty-five students. All required reading had to be done in two-hour intervals in the library itself. As Alina, one of my students, wrote,

> Studying in Poland is a very tiresome task. The main reason is that there are not enough books. People queue for a long time in book-shops and in libraries only to find that the book they want was sold or lent to somebody else. The quality of books is bad too. Students of medicine . . . have to read from grey letters from yellow pages; students of politics and economy can acquire only some books with accepted views; students of foreign philologies have to fight for original texts and books.

THE POLISH EDUCATIONAL SYSTEM

Education in Poland in the mid-1980s was still controlled at the national level and used rote learning extensively. In practice, however, public schools, universities, and technological colleges took liberties with the prescribed curriculum (Nelson 1984). Probably the most flexibility existed in higher education. Public education in Poland went through several changes after the Communists took over, many of these positive ones. By the 1980's, however, approximately only one in eighty children of the lowest economic classes went on to education above the required eighth grade, while 20 percent to 30 percent of the children of educated parents continued (Nelson 1984). Hopefuly with the new Solidarity government, these numbers will increase in the future.

In 1986 to 1987, schooling in Poland was divided into a required eight-year primary school (the eighth year was added by the Communist Regime), an optional two- to five-year secondary school, and higher education consisting of technical and academic institutions. Access to secondary schools, university, pedagogy institutes, and technical schools was limited by examinations.

Primary School

Pupils had one teacher for all subject areas in the first three forms, when the children were between the ages of seven and ten. Some of the teachers of these students were graduates of secondary schools where they may have received some teacher training. Due to teacher shortages, many did not even complete secondary school.[3] Current methodologies in teaching (e.g., of writing) would probably not have been known by the average classroom teacher of these young children, nor would the teachers have the skills to use and adapt new textbooks.

According to Dyduchowa (1989) of the Pedagogy Institute in Krakow, Poland, a specific syllabus (i.e., curriculum) was adopted in Poland for the teaching of Polish writing in 1985. For the seven- to ten-year-olds in the first three forms of primary school, the syllabus emphasized mechanics and content, rather than structure. In the second and third forms, children were asked to produce narrative and descriptive writing, but no special techniques for doing this were taught. The teacher was expected to correct what was there, but the children were often allowed free writing. Grammar, however, was the focus. Knowledge about language and how to apply rules creatively, was emphasized. For example, students were taught about adjectives and their creative use in description. However, due to differences in the actual training teachers received (teacher trainers may emphasize different skills, e.g., mechanics), the syllabus in practice may not have been carefully followed.

What my Polish students remembered in general about learning to write in Polish in primary school may appear similar to what Americans may remember of similar experiences in the United States. However, Polish world views and modes of being educated differed and this too was reflected in their comments. As Agnieszka wrote, structure and not critical thought was always foremost:

> Two things I associate already with the primary school are that (1) we were told to write a plan which was to be followed in the text. It was to consist of three main pairts (an introduction, body of the essay, conclusion) with further subdivisions. (2) that we should not repeat the same words too often in the essay.

It should not be surprising to U.S. teachers that students didn't like writing outlines, and many, in fact, extracted them from finished essays. Another student remembered learning to write according to the Ministry guidelines that Dyduchowa (1989), said were in place at that time:

> As far as I remember in the first three years of the primary school I wasn't taught to write at all. We were told to describe a picture or some event but no rules concerning composition were given. Teachers were quite satisfied if we were writing at all. Only our grammar and spelling were corrected, as well as the handwriting.

---

[3] Now, there are a few experimental "social schools" where teachers are better paid and usually fully qualified university graduates with special training for young students, but my third-year students didn't have these opportunities.

A few students acknowledged that

> At the very beginning the teacher told us to write sentences on the basis
> of the given words or rather the expressions. . . . We were also told to copy
> some precis from a book. We were always advised to read a lot in order
> to learn how to build sentences, how to improve our style.

This is consistent with models that do not encourage inventions or inquiry, but
instead proper structure. As Alina remembered,

> The first thing we were force(d) to write were dictations, but these were not
> creative writing.

A reference to the use of rote learning in Polish education came from Beata:

> I shouldn't judge but I think it was a fault because we recalled them [the
> expressions] and used them without trying to create something else,
> something more original.

Fourth through Eighth Form

In the fourth through eighth forms (ages eleven to fifteen), pupils had different
teachers for different subjects. Beginning in the fourth form of the primary
school, more structured writing was expected. Sentence combining skills were
taught; functional uses of writing, rather than theory, was promoted. While
more simplified models were used in the fifth and sixth forms, by the eighth
form, argumentation was taught.

A new syllabus adopted in 1985 focused on literature. It was very detailed
and Dyduchowa (1989), suggested that it might have been too much to cover.
Teachers themselves were to decide what to leave out which might result in no
writing at all. In addition, there were no specific techniques for implementing
the syllabus. Teachers could just go straight to the children's text and not make
use of the curriculum model at all. Teachers could also choose to teach their
own way, going back to the traditional rote method, and using a homework
and grades method of teaching (as was used with my students) as opposed to
the more holistic approach in the 1985 syllabus. Also, students were taught to
listen and accept, not to question. Given this situation in the upper grades, one
may expect that the classroom was often teacher-oriented, rather than the
student-oriented approach that was recommended in the earlier forms and that
is now appearing in whole language models in the United States (Johnson and
Roen 1989).

In these upper forms, students were expected to write formal essays in
Polish which, as Dyduchowa explained in her interview (1989), followed the
official syllabus. As one student commented:

The situation changed in the 4th form [primary school], I think. Now we were supposed to write in a more organized way, yet nobody provided us with a theory. It was just: "Make a plan, points of your composition before you start writing. Be logical. Write according to the points. Introduction, amplification, conclusion." Full stop. Nothing more. No detailed hints.

Methods of correction in primary school were equivocal at best. One student complained:

We were often getting bad marks for the composition, "Contents—very good, composition poor." But why poor? What was wrong? Red arrows and crossings out the teacher made didn't clarify the situation. To improve our writings we often had to use our imagination.

One student did acknowledge,

The mistakes were corrected by a teacher and some of them were eradicated very quickly.

And, in Piotr's experience,

Only our grammar and spelling were corrected, as well as the handwriting.

Not until the seventh form was English taught as an elective, usually for two hours per week, although at some schools it was offered for as many as six hours per week in intensive sessions. Teachers in these schools frequently would not have had formal English teacher training (such as at the English Institute at the Jagiellonian), but rather were trained at the Pedagogy Institute in general teaching methods.

Topics in Lower Primary School (First through Sixth Forms)

One might expect that the topics teachers in Poland might have their children write about at this level would differ from those in the United States, due to such things as a different world view and different life experiences. However, the topics given in the early grades in Poland didn't differ seriously from what one might expect in the U.S. For example, one student recalled being asked to write about the following: "How did you spend your holidays?" and "Have you a pet?" Another student added "How do you help your mother in the housework?" and "Who would you like to be in the future?" Not surprisingly, "The older we grew the more sophisticated topics we had to write about."

Seventh and Eighth Forms and Secondary Schools

Polish secondary schools were divided into general secondary (college preparation) and vocational (called technicums). There were also two-year vocational schools which prepared skilled workers. Students at technicums studied for up to five years in one of the following areas: technology (industrial), agriculture, forestry, economics, health service or the arts (Nelson 1984). For entrance into the four-year general secondary schools, potential students were usually examined in Polish and an academic area of their choosing, which could be English or another foreign language. Teachers at these schools were usually trained either at the Pedagogy Institute or at a university.

The writing demands changed for the fourteen- and fifteen-year-old students when they reached the last two years (seventh to eighth forms) of primary school and began secondary school. According to the official syllabus, in the secondary school, more formal writing was expected to be taught, including theoretical constructs for essays. However, since the focus remained on reading and interpreting literature, writing might be required, but only a few teachers might have taught students how to write. In fact, in a recent mini-study conducted by Dyduchowa (unpublished), she found that students wrote little, if any, after entrance to the secondary school.

Dorota viewed the differences between the primary and secondary school as follows:

> I think that during my primary school we made use of our intuition in the sense we put down the things which seemed to us worth putting down without bothering about a structure. When I was in the 8th form our teachers required (us) to write strictly to the point and gave us fails for not following the rule.

Attention to different types of texts also was acknowledged by another student during the seventh and eighth forms:

> Then we were taught how to use different forms of expression, e.g., a description of a person, a room, a view. We were taught how to write summaries, letters, paragraphs and other forms. Eventually we learned how to write a thesis. We discussed each form, found characteristic features of them.

According to another student:

> Now we had lessons on composition: what are characteristics of a good description, narration, how to defend or attack a certain idea, what arguments to use. At classes we used to organize "trials" of the characters from a book we had read. Those trials also taught us to be more precise in our writings.

This type of practice would hopefully lead to a questioning of the student's readings and other events in their lives, but there was little indication that this occurred. However, Piotr recalled:

> In the 7th and 8th form . . . there was also writing in class apart from home assignments. The most popular and most often used form was what we call in Polish "rozprawka" which is a sort of argument. You are given a thesis to which you give reasons for and against and finally write a conclusion.

Dyduchowa (1989) felt that teaching such writing skills to students was effective training against manipulation by the system.

While argumentative writing is also a goal in the U.S., it is usually approached as a skill to be used so that we can be more persuasive with others and not be easily influenced by others, for example, advertisers (in a sense similar to Polish propaganda appeals). In Poland, previous to the current political structure, it was perhaps meant only as a way to interpret what others had written. As can be seen from the previous comments, the ability to influence others was not evident in my students recollections, nor in their own writing for my class. Writing persuasively continued to be difficult for them.

Secondary School: English

The methods of teaching writing in English to students in the secondary school did not seem to differ dramatically from the teaching of writing in a traditional ESL classroom in the United States. However, a few of the Polish students felt that their English writing instruction was more useful than their Polish writing instruction. Piotr commented:

> On the other hand, on my English lessons I was taught very practical things connected with writing, such as phrases useful for starting or ending a paragraph, transition words, etc. We were analyzing English texts, trying to find a framework in the text and writing summaries. We didn't like it but I think it was profitable.

However, Irena's experiences were more common:

> We were also expected to write compositions in English in the secondary school. They were very simple at the beginning (e.g., "Describe your room.") Teachers at the beginning at least, paid attention to grammatical and spelling correctness. The content itself was less important.

Beata adds:

> We did not write essays at first (in secondary school) but just answered or filled in the blanks in various texts. Then we wrote something like miniature essays which had trivial topics and they were corrected by the teacher who took practically only grammar into consideration, then the content was corrected but hardly ever the style.

As will be discussed later, by the time my students reached the university, they felt emotionally freer to express themselves in English rather than in Polish but their earlier training still did not encourage such expression, such as through journal writing. Also, perhaps because they were in elective foreign language English classes in the secondary school, some of my Polish students found that their teachers assumed they already knew how to write from primary school. As Piotr wrote,

> Surely the level was higher [in secondary school], but there were no "revelations." It was assumed that we already had some knowledge.

Urszula even claimed,

> . . . so almost not knowing how to write essays I passed the entrance examination to this university. [No essay examination was required for entrance until 1989.]

Higher Education

Following graduation from the secondary school (general or technicum), students may take examinations to enter technological or academic universities. Polish universities are divided into institutes, which are larger than a U.S. university department, but less encompassing than, say, a college of arts and letters. For example, the Jagiellonian University includes, among others, a Social Science Institute, a Chemistry Institute, and the English Institute. The technology schools tend to attract children of farm workers and laborers. Academic jobs requiring higher education (particularly teaching), typically don't pay well in Poland, while more practical or industrial jobs (such as mining) do (Nelson 1984). For example, in 1989 when the Solidarity political regime brought with it severe economic sanctions, it was the miners who were first able to obtain raises. Consequently, there was little financial incentive to attend an academic university. The incentive was prestige.

In 1986, the academic university offered a five-year "magistrar" degree, (no bachelor's, as in the United States). At the completion of the magistrar degree, a few select students were accepted, usually at the same university, to both teach and prepare for a doctorate. Due to the difficulties of finding accommodations, moving between universities for teaching positions was rare. As a result, many of the students' professors were students of the same institute at one time. Married couples might be separated if one person was attending a university, while the other lived with his or her family in another town.

TEACHER TRAINING AT THE PEDAGOGY INSTITUTE

Students intending to teach the fourth through eighth forms of primary school and secondary school were usually trained at pedagogy institutes. They would have attended the Pedagogy Institute for five years after secondary school, where EFL courses, if taken, were provided at a much lower level than at the university. Teacher cadets chose subjects (for example, Polish, physics, or biology) and when they graduated were qualified to teach in those areas.

At these institutes students were given very limited, if any, instruction in techniques for teaching writing. In their second year, students took two hours a week of practical stylistics which included theories and models of writing. This was the total time alloted to prepare them to teach writing and to improve their own skills. However, there was not enough time to prepare these students to teach other subject areas, and in reality, some professors used the two hours to focus on subjects other than stylistics. Consequently, some students might have received no such training at all.

THE ENGLISH INSTITUTE AT THE JAGIELLONIAN UNIVERSITY[4]

The English Institute required a rigorous entrance examination in English which, until 1989, did not include an essay. For those who were admitted, all course work was conducted from the first year in English, and included ten hours per week of English as a Foreign Language for the first three years (called "Practical English"). This instruction included conversation classes as well as writing classes. Outside of the Institute, year-long General Education courses in Political Science, Economics, and Psychology, among others, were required. As well, the study of another language (usually German) was mandated. Until 1990, three years of Russian were also required, but that, along with a required year of military training for both men and women, has now been eliminated. Says Alina of the university experience in English philology:

> The other thing that does not make studying in Poland nice is that students are overworked.. They simply have too many courses (30-40 hours per week). It is of course connected with the lack of books—the teachers want to tell their students as much as possible during the classes, but the effect is that students are overworked and that they learn about things rather than study things themselves.

So many contact hours left little time to digest, analyze or challenge the curriculum. It was also almost impossible to hold a job, so sacrifices were made by many parents to keep their children at the university, although many also were on scholarships.

Class hours were substantially reduced in the last two years when students

---

[4] These practices were in effect in 1986 to 1987. Some of them may have changed since that time, although the majority are still in effect.

were completing their theses. Specializations in these last two years included theoretical and applied linguistics; British, American, and Medieval Literature; Translation; and Methods of Teaching (intended for prospective secondary English teachers).

Instruction at the English Institute was British in model and orientation. Many of the English Institute professors studied for various periods of time in the United Kingdom; their accent was Polish-British. Access to Britain, by faculty and students alike, was much easier than to the United States. There were many exchanges with British universities, and a British Council lecturer was provided in most locations. Polish students were encouraged to take the Cambridge Proficiency Test, another incentive to conform to British standards and methods. In the fourth and fifth years, students often had one or more classes taken from American Fulbrighters and/or British Council lecturers.

While a few of the students at the English Institute would become translators or interpreters, most of them, regardless of their specializations, were preparing to become secondary teachers of English. As mentioned previously, they would have begun their own English instruction formally in the seventh or eighth form, although many received private instruction beginning as early as eight or nine years of age (often from students of the English Institute). To pay for this training, parents often sacrificed financially to ensure opportunities for their children.

Student perceptions

My students' perceptions of the first three years at the university varied. In general, when my Polish students reached the university they felt, not surprisingly, that more knowledge of English was expected of them than had been in previous schooling. As mentioned, they had taken special English examinations to enter the Institute and only sixty students were admitted each year.

Unlike ESL classes in the United States, each year at the Jagiellonian a different type of writing was taught. Précis writing (a kind of summary) was taught in the first year (this is the model many would use later in attempting to write literature reviews for their theses in the fifth year, without critical comment). A course in composition writing was required the second year, followed in the third year by essay writing. The fourth and fifth years were devoted to the writing of the thesis. In addition, all English Institute students faced final examinations in the first three years in Practical English (EFL), which included these three types of writing. As Piotr stated:

> Only now, during the university studies, have I understood how little I knew about writing. The classes in précis, reading comprehension, composition and essay writing has shown it to me. I think my knowledge is now more systematic, as if more rationalized which doesn't necessarily mean I write excellent writings.

But many felt it wasn't until the second year that their writing skills changed. Said Basia:

> During the second year I think a good job was done. We were reading various texts: descriptions, explanations, definitions, compositions; we were discussing them. Before it we were given a kind of theoretical background from handbooks, and while discussing those texts we discovered what are the differences between them and what devices were used to achieve various results, and of course we were writing all those compositions and descriptions ourselves.

Impact of Using English on Student Writing

I also asked the students which language (Polish or English) they preferred for writing. All but one preferred to write in English (that student had no preference). There was one major reason that they all expressed: They felt freer when writing in English, not linguistically freer, but psychologically freer to say what they wanted. Somehow the rules and regulations that applied to their daily Polish lives seemed to be eliminated through the new language. Writing in English provided these students a relief from limitations which were evident in the media.[5] Janusz reflected on how he felt the English Institute provided this freedom, and how it differed from other Institutes at the Jagiellonian:

> I like the atmosphere here. I mean you can be very direct to your teacher, discuss things in class; pupils and teachers are as though one community. It is very different than in some other departments.

The quote at the beginning of this chapter is one example of the freedom these students felt in English. While Piotr was writing about an ecologist's lack of freedom to publish his ideas, Piotr himself felt comfortable writing about the situation to me in English, also in 1986. Another student wrote in his journal to me about his experience as a sixteen-year-old in 1980 when his secondary teacher was taken away in the middle of the night as a supporter of Solidarity. Another student's journal concerned the difficulties of becoming an adult in Poland where, routinely, young married couples would live with one or the other's parents for six to ten years, until housing became available to them. Their journals revealed to me much about their daily lives, which they said they didn't feel free to write about in Polish.

---

[5] However, the BBC and Radio-Free Europe were available in English and many people, including my students listened to them regularly.

DISCUSSION

English literacy has provided these Polish university students with options. Since most of them are now English teachers, how they felt about their English experiences, the extent to which they formed a literacy community and a love of English literacy, and the extent to which that became part of their identity will impact on the future of English and hence English literacy in Poland.

In fact, these students did form a special literacy community even within the university, as evidenced by Janusz' statement. The cultural climate of their classrooms was probably more open and flexible then that of students who were studying in other fields. My students were the intellectually privileged and had access to literacy skills in a foreign language which exposed them to a broader world of ideas. Outside of the university, many of their contemporaries received only eight years of schooling. The experiences of those receiving less education differed even more.

These Polish students' remembrances of how they learned to write in both Polish and English may differ from what actually occurred (Dyduchowa 1989), but their attitudes towards their experiences were framed by their culture. What was a given was that the majority of their schooling was based on rote learning. Many of their early teachers used précis, controlled composition, copying, and fill-in-the-blank as a way to teach writing in both Polish and English, rather than having students discuss and argue.

What characterized these Polish students' writing then is perhaps more embedded in different political systems, which would affect the way in which they viewed the world. The Polish governmental structure did not encourage one to question the system; students did not challenge the professor; they did not ask questions nor take risks in their writing. The Polish students in this study had creative and innovative ideas, in spite of the system, but that was a reflection of their intelligence and innate curiosity, not the education which the system provided for them. Interestingly, Solidarity, which was the strongest statement of questioning of the political system, began in the shipyards of Gdansk where the workers probably only had eight years of education (or less). They were not university students, although much of their support came from the intelligentsia.

Even within the governmental structure, my students' individual experiences varied, as with students elsewhere. Some of their experiences paralleled the official curriculum of Poland, while other students' instruction in writing, if it existed, was minimal. Some students had very structured experiences in the organization of an essay, while others were able to write somewhat creatively, but with little instruction in models. Some felt confident about their skills, others clearly did not. For these future foreign language teachers their most consistently structured encounter with learning to write came at the English Institute of the Jagiellonian where three years were devoted to different aspects of the skill, followed by two years of writing a formal thesis. Their idiosyncracies (some wrote well, some didn't) may be tied, as with the findings described in the Murray and Nichols article (this volume), to early attitudes towards print. Dorota, not a strong writer, didn't remember reading as a child; Piotr, an excellent writer, began writing as a young child and used this tool to ease the pain of the banishing of his teacher in 1980. Each of my students was an individual. But collectively, they experienced a schooling system that affected them all.

The teachers of Polish and EFL that my students had had in the primary grades, probably had little or no training in the teaching of writing; current approaches would not have reached them. Even for those with training, teaching inquiry skills in a repressed atmosphere would have been difficult. Dyduchowa (1989) reported that this atmosphere was reinforced in the past in the training of primary school teachers. Consequently, they did not teach the writing process to their students in the early grades. Rather, they focused on grammar, punctuation, and spelling, specific skills that were easier and safer to grade than were the development of ideas and negotiation of meaning, which might cause difficulties with the authorities.

Polish university professors, however, were more exposed to global views on literacy, through travels to England, and from reference and textbooks brought by British Council and U.S. Fulbrighters. Their broader exposure was shown through the students' reflections on how the English Institute impacted their writing skills.

CONCLUSION

With the recent changes in the Polish government, and many new freedoms occurring in the media, the way in which children are educated, and how critical thinking skills are taught will most likely also change. These changes may be reflected in the writing skills and styles of Poland's future generations. New studies might focus on how the democratization of Poland changed the way in which the people are educated, what they read and write and for what purposes. That may also eventually change the cultural context of the classroom.

Opportunities for change are already taking place. In the fall of 1990, the United States Peace Corps began providing sixty EFL teachers to Poland. As well, foreign language teachers' colleges were organized in the same year wherever there was enough staff. With the fall of the communist state, students are no longer obliged to study Russian, but must take a foreign language, and English is the most popular one. This is one of the first visible results in the area of education of the Solidarity government.

A byproduct of these changes is that more openness would be allowed in classrooms and less public censorship and control. In addition, the influx of foreigners, including Americans, will impact the cultural climate for literacy in classrooms, how reading and writing are acqured, and for what purposes. Even in the last two years, articles about pollution, such as were banned in 1986, are now appearing in the Polish press. The freedom now exists to express ideas and opinions in written publications. What used to be underground newspapers and journals are now published freely. These visible signs of change in how literacy is used are bound to affect the future of Poland.

REFERENCES

DYDUCHOWA, A. June 1989. Personal interview, translated by A. NIZEGORODCEW.
JOHNSON, D., and D. ROEN, eds. 1989 Introduction to *Richness in writing,* 1–14. New York: Longman.
KELLY, E. 1972. *The land and people of Poland.* Philadelphia: Lippincott.
NELSON, H. 1984. *Poland: A country study.* Washington, DC: American University.
WEDEL, J. 1986. *The private Poland: An anthropologist's look at everyday life.* New York: Facts on file.

Discussion Questions

1. For these Polish university students, writing in English provided a sense of freedom lacking in most aspects of their lives. Think about situations in your own life that allow you to take risks, for example in your own writing or forms of expression.

2. Examine your own memory regarding how you learned to read and write in your first and/or second language. Can you compare that experience to how you now make decisions and solve problems (e.g., what critical thinking skills have resulted)?

3. Do you think there should be a national or state (province, etc.) policy on how literacy is acquired within a country? What should that be? Can there or should there ever be consensus?

4. Models of education, such as rote learning, are ways to impact how individuals view the world around them. How can acquiring literacy in a second language change that view?

10

Building Upon Korean Writing Practices: Genres, Values, and Beliefs

CHUNOK LEE AND ROBIN SCARCELLA

Korean-Americans are among the fastest growing of the Asian groups in the United States; numerically, the Korean-American population already surpasses Chinese communities in Los Angeles and San Francisco (Kitano and Daniels 1988; see also Choy 1979). Korean-American college students have, for the most part, lived in the United States less than ten years, and are in various stages of acculturation and language development (Kim 1988). Kim (1977) reports that almost 50 percent of all Korean-American students feel that they are prevented from obtaining academic success in the United States because of language difficulties. Writing is one of their most serious problems.

One factor contributing to the failure of Korean-American students to acquire English writing proficiency is that teachers often ignore their previous literacy experiences. Research has repeatedly demonstrated that dramatic improvement in English writing development can take place when teachers incorporate the experiences of their students into their instruction (Cummins 1979, 1981, 1989; see also Ada 1986, 1988). In order to develop literacy, students need to draw upon their culture and past experiences. Most teachers, probably unwittingly, discount the full range of literacy abilities of their Korean-American students. As a result, one frequently hears teachers report that Korean students are basic, unskilled writers. Rather than constantly criticizing their students about what they cannot do, teachers need to take a more global look at what their Korean-American students can do. We argue that teachers need to help their students increase their already rich repertoire of ways of using language. As Johnson and Roen (1989) argue, if we are to do this, we need to learn "as much as possible about their backgrounds and interests so that we can build on these to expand their options for making meaning and having an impact on their writing" (Johnson and Roen, 1989, 5). To accomplish this objective, the study reported here examines the written genres, values, and beliefs that Koreans bring with them when they come to the United States. Three questions are examined.

1. What types of genres do Koreans value?

2. What Korean traditions and values are tied to these genres?

3. How are these types of genres acquired inside and outside of Korean institutes of education?

Before turning directly to these questions, it is important to clarify terms at the onset. In our study, the term *Korean* is used to refer to individuals who reside in South Korea. The term *Korean-American* is used in reference to Korean immigrants who have lived in the United States from one to three years and who intend to become citizens of the United States, are already citizens or are in the process of becoming so. It also refers to recently arrived people who fit none of the above categories.

While we attempt to draw a composite of what is Korean, readers should be aware that not everyone fits neatly into such a composite. Koreans are divided into various regional and socioeconomic groups. Also, it is important that readers realize that all values are abstract, generalized principles. Individuals adhere to these principles to varying degrees. Cultural values and behaviors change across time, across individuals, and within individuals from situation to situation. Concepts such as *Korean culture* imply an unchanging, monolithic culture which is misleading. Moreover, each person's experience with writing in specific situations varies from both personal and social experience. A Korean who is adept at writing one kind of genre may be unable to write another, not necessarily because the genre is more difficult, but because he or she simply lacks experience reading and writing the genre. Keeping these concerns in mind, we turn to a discussion of Korean writing genres, values, and beliefs.

THE DEVELOPMENT OF THE KOREAN LANGUAGE

Before turning to a discussion of the results, it might be useful first to consider the origins and development of the Korean language.

The origin of the Korean language is still unknown. Research suggests that Korean is probably related to both Altaic (Turtic, Mongolian, and Manchu-Tungus) and to Japanese. The grammar of Korean resembles that of Japanese, but spoken Korean does not.

The political and cultural influences of China upon Korea over the centuries have had a profound influence on both the written and spoken Korean language.

> Chinese has had a special kind of influence on Korean; although the two belong to different language families, Korean has borrowed extensively from the Chinese vocabulary. Of the more than 160,000 entries in Kun Sajeon (The Grand Korean Dictionary), more than 50% are words of Chinese origin. Most of these words deal with abstract intellectual subjects, whereas native Korean words express most concrete or affective meanings. Koreans devised a method of writing their own language with Chinese characters, and they passed this idea on to Japan, where it was taken up enthusiastically. Writing in Chinese was simpler, and it gave them all the benefits of sharing in the Chinese cultural traditions. (Kim 1988, 260)

For centuries, there was no Korean alphabet, and Korean could only be written using an awkward system of Chinese characters which was so difficult to learn that only a few educated scholars were able to write the language.

Before the fifteenth century, what was actually thought to be worth writing down and preserving was overwhelmingly written in Chinese. King Sejong the Great (the fourth monarch of the Yi Dynasty and the Chosun Kingdom) ordered his scholars to devise a simple method of writing down spoken Korean so that even the common people would be able to express their thoughts in writing. The scholars who worked for King Sejong successfully produced a set of symbols consisting of eleven vowels and seventeen consonants. The alphabet, called *han'gul*, was introduced to Koreans in December 1443. (Later, in 1933, han'gul symbols were standardized to ten vowels and fourteen consonants.) Today it is considered a great literacy achievement and one of the most comprehensible phonetic alphabets (see, for example, Hyun 1987).

WHAT TYPES OF WRITTEN GENRES DO KOREANS VALUE?

This summary of the development of the Korean language provides a suitable background for a discussion of those genres which many Koreans value in their daily lives. Information for this discussion is derived from the existing literature as well as questionnaire and interview data collected from Koreans living in Seoul and Korean-Americans residing in Irvine, California. The available data indicates the most Koreans and Korean-Americans value poetry, short novels, and expository writing. We will discuss each of these genres. Our intent is not to give literary analyses of these genres, but rather to provide teachers with an overview of their prevalence, backgrounds, and role in the everyday lives of Koreans in South Korea and the United States.

Korean Poetry

Poetry is a popular genre in Korea. Today, most Koreans will confess to having composed a poem at one time to express personal feelings. Even the relatively less educated Korean is able to enjoy and compose poetry. Koreans from rural, as well as urban, areas write poems. For example, one of Korea's most famous poets, Yang, Sung Woo, is the son of an agrarian poet in the province of Chollanam. Yang's celebrity was initiated when he won first prize at a local outdoor poetry contest at the age of ten.

Most Koreans grow up with the experience of constructing poems on the spur of the moment. Poems are sometimes composed at the dinner table as a family pastime. According to the *Los Angeles Times* (December 16, 1988):

> . . . a radio talk show host took to the streets one cold November evening and zeroed in on a topic that seemingly was on the minds of all South Koreans: *Fifth Republic corruption* a catch phrase referring to the wrongdoings of former President Chun Doo Hwan. But the announcer did not ask the people their opinions—instead he challenged pedestrians to compose a poem about it, on the spot. And not just any poem. It had to have four lines, and the first word of each line had to begin with one of the syllables from the vernacular of the Fifth Republic corruption O-Kong-Pi-Ri in that order.

It is not an overstatement to say that poetry is everywhere.

> Serious poems are printed on chewing gum wrappers, scrawled on graffitti-covered walls, mounted in frames in the subway, published in newspapers and recited with much aspiration in coffee shops and theatres. (Schoenberger 1988, 37)

Highly philosophical verses show up on Korean university walls. There is even a twenty-four-hour-a-day dial-a-poem telephone service available.

Reading poetry is an art form in its own right, pursued enthusiastically by numerous poetry appreciation societies. "One such group met at a tiny theatre on a recent Saturday afternoon and explored the theme, homesickness, by reciting the work of several contemporary poets with the aid of colored lights and a sound track of violin music" (Schoenberger 1988, 37). Unlike other countries, where poets are often ignored, Korean poets are frequently regarded as national heroes (Hyun 1987).

Traditional Korean poetry developed in the eighth century when the kings of Shilla modelled their kingdom after the T'ang Dynasty of China (Rutt 1987). Chinese verse was also introduced at that time. After the fourteenth century,

Confucianism replaced Buddhism as a political and cultural force in Korea. As a consequence of Confuciansim and the heavy emphasis it placed on education, being able to produce good Chinese verse on civil service examinations was a determining factor for Korean scholar-statesmen. At that time, Korean vernacular folk poetry was also abundant. However, even after the invention of native script in the fifteenth century, very little was printed in Korean. From the eighteenth century onwards, care has been taken to preserve vernacular poetry, which was usually sung, in Korean. The typical form of these vernacular poems was the *shijo*, usually three or four lines of about fifteen syllables to the line. Shijo were usually recited by professional singers. Some of them were love poems, while others were philosphical or political in nature. As Koreans came to use han'gul (Korean script) more freely, writers found that they could not fully express their complex feelings in such a short poetic form as shijo. They developed the form into a more lengthy one and called it *kasa* (lengthy verse). Although formally governed by a style with a rhythmic structure related to that of the shijo, the content of kasa is more like that of the essay. Modern poetry emerged in the early part of the twentieth century from the shijo and kasa.

Much modern Korean poetry reflects the poets' preoccupation with the Korean language, which has symbolized nationalistic pride ever since Japanese authorities tried to abolish it. Hyun explains:

> The thought police tried to control the thoughts and feelings of every Korean; many of the Korean thinkers were sent to prison or executed for having dangerous ideas and ideals; and for a while the use of the Korean language was prohibited. (Hyun 1987, 77. See also, Oggins and Kwon 1989).

Indeed, it was under thirty-five years of Japanese occupation (from August 29, 1910 to August 15, 1945) that a poetry of anger was born. When an entire generation of Koreans was denied formal study of their own language, poetry served as a clandestine vehicle enabling Koreans to express their desire for freedom.

> Following the liberation of Korea in 1945, the reinstitution and promulgation of the Korean language became matters of intense nationalistic pride among Koreans. Thus, although the use of one's own native language is almost always an important symbol of ethnic identity, historical circumstances make this particularly true for Koreans today. (Kim 1988, 261)

The fact that Korea has been divided in two, the North and the South, for nearly forty years also deserves special attention. Almost all Koreans desire the unification of North and South Korea and this is reflected in Korean poetry.

> Because of their identical heritage, it is natural that North and South Koreans are deeply conscious of the bonds which transcend boundaries. The responsibility of keeping race consciousness awake in order not to lose identity and linguistic oneness is assigned to Korean poets. (Kim, Y.-S. 1985, 44)

The Short Novel

Along with poetry, Koreans attach considerable importance to the short novel, which in U.S. terms might be defined as a lengthy short story. An excellent short novel is well received, while longer novels are often overlooked. The importance of the short novel is almost entirely due to the uniqueness of the Korean literary market.

In the United States, those who wish to become novelists send their manuscripts to publishers. Their manuscripts are either accepted or rejected. This is not the case in Korea. It is difficult to have one's work published in Korea unless one is already a recognized writer. Recognition comes from publishing short novels in literary periodicals, monthly or quarterly, which promote novice writers by publishing their works. Periodicals prefer shorter novels because of limited space.

Korea is one of the few countries which publishes short novels as newspaper serials. As a result of this practice, the novels appeal to a wide audience and popular taste. The primary characteristics of this genre appear to include sentimentalism and exaggeration.

Expository Essays

Although expository essays are neither as prevalent nor as popular as short novels, they are generally appreciated. Essays appear in newspapers, magazines, and textbooks. Most Koreans feel that only intellectuals who are experts in their subject areas are capable of composing expository essays (Scarcella and Lee 1989). Thus, not every Korean is expected to have the writing proficiency needed to compose expository essays.

It is worth mentioning that most Koreans approach expository essay writing differently than U.S. Americans. Like others who have examined contrastive rhetoric (see for example, Kaplan 1966, 1987; Purves 1988, Land and Whitley 1989), we find that "the topics [Korean] students choose to write about, the ways they develop these topics, the kinds of information they include, the ways they organize the information, and the kinds of inferences they leave for the reader to make are all related to their own rich cultural experiences" (McKay 1989, 10). In producing good essays, Korean writers do not generally follow the same Western writing process suggestsed by Graves (1983) and Murray (1982, 1985) and their followers (Scarcella and Lee, 1989). For example, in a good Korean expository essay, writers do not usually state their thesis directly. Rather, they often allow the reader to interpret the thesis from hints within the text. One Korean university student we interviewed told us that good Korean writers take considerable time gathering their thoughts before they begin writing. It may take several months before they put their words in writing. On the other hand, once they compose their essay, they do not revise it again and again.

Students are rarely, if ever, asked to write expository essays in element-ary and secondary schools. There are several reasons for this. First, classroom size (usually about sixty students) makes the correction of such essays difficult. Second, teachers do not have the time to teach their students to write expository essays because they must prepare their students for the College Entrance Examination. Students must do well on this standardized government examina-tion at the end of their senior year of high school in order to be admitted to Korean universities. In 1985, when many Korean educators were concerned that college graduates were unable to produce expository essays, a writing section (in which students were asked to compose an expository essay) was included in the College Entrance Exam. However, today this essay requirement is op-tional in most major Korean universities. Third, many teachers do not feel qualified to teach this genre themselves since they lack experience writing ex-pository essays.

WHAT KOREAN VALUES ARE TIED TO KOREAN POETRY, SHORT NOVELS, AND EXPOSITORY ESSAYS?

Underlying the popularity of poetry, short novels, and expository essays are the values to which they are tied. These values include sentimentalism, the reluc-tance to state an opinion strongly, the desire to maintain face, and indirectness.

Rutt (1987) points out a common stereotype pertaining to Koreans: "Koreans might be considered the most friendly in Asia. They have a keen sense of humor, are quick to laugh but also quick to show anger in a somewhat Irish manner" (Rutt 1987, 33). Building on this stereotype, Freeman (1987) suggests that there is a sensitive, lyrical nature underlying the fiery pathos of the so-called Irish of Asia. Both aspects are demonstrated in the poetry, which as discussed previously, thrives.

The reluctance to state one's opinion seems closely tied to Korean social values. Stating one's own opinion too strongly is usually considered arrogant to Koreans (Romaine 1984). Also, by mitigating personal opinions, Koreans save others' face as well as their own. It might also be pointed out that Koreans have not grown up with the traditions of verbal play and debate. Within the home, many Asian children are expected to listen and obey rather than express their personal opinions freely (Cheng 1987). The reluctance to state a personal opinion and the emphasis on face-saving may explain the popularity of poetry and the short novel over the more explicit expository essay. (See Oggins and Kwon 1989 for further discussion.)

Kaplan observes that Korean discourse is "marked by what may be called an approach of indirection." (1966, 46) According to Kaplan, Korean writers show the subject

. . . from a variety of tangential views, but the subject is never looked at directly. Things are developed in terms of what they are not, rather than in terms of what they are. (Kaplan 1966, 16; see also Eggington 1987)

In a similar vein, Hinds (1987) proposes a related explanation for indirectness. He states:

In Japan, perhaps in Korea, and certainly in ancient China, there is a different way of looking at the communication process. In Japan it is the responsibility of the listener/reader to understand what it is that the speaker or author intended to say. (144)

Hinds also points out that in a reader-responsible language (such as Japanese),

. . . there is greater tolerance for ambiguity, imprecision of statement, an entirely different attitude toward the writer such that English-speaking writers go through draft after draft to come up with a final product, while Japanese authors frequently compose exactly one draft which becomes the finished product. (1987, 145)

Like Japanese, Korean is also a *reader-responsible* language (Scarcella and Lee 1989) since Korean writers expect readers to be responsible for actively interpreting texts. (Note that in writer-based languages such as English, writers make their intentions explicit so that their readers do not need to actively interpret their texts in the same way.) Good Korean writers do not tend to edit and revise extensively and, like good Japanese writers, good Korean writers are capable of composing a finished product the first time around. (See also Hinds 1983, 1987.)

HOW ARE THESE TYPES OF GENRES ACQUIRED?

As in many cultures, Korean schools play a major role in teaching the genres previously discussed and the values associated with these genres. (Spindler and Spindler 1987). As Hyun (1987) puts it, one of the goals of schools is "to cultivate values consistent with Korean traditions . . . " (68). Before discussing the role of schools further, it will be helpful first to provide some relevant background information about education in Korea.

KOREAN EDUCATION

Throughout history, Koreans have placed a high value on education, which was initially motivated by the old Confucian system of learning. In fact, in ancient times success in the government exams (which included knowing poetry and literature) determined appointments and government positions. Formal education in Korea dates back to the Three Kingdoms era (first century B.C. through the seventh century A.D.) when state-operated institutes called *t'aehak* began in 372 A.D. During the Chosun Kingdom (1392–1910), education was limited to reciting and writing the lessons described in *The Analects of Confucius, The Teaching of Mencious,* and *The Seven Chinese Classics* which were taught in schools, called *sowon* or *sodang,* or by tutors at home. Women received no formal education. The development of modern education was interrupted by Japanese colonialism (1910–1945). Under the Japanese occupation, only 30 percent of all elementary students went to school and one out of 30 high school-age students attended classes. Korean students were forced to adopt Japanese names, follow a Japanese curriculum, and speak Japanese in school. During the thirty-five years following the liberation of Korea from Japan, the number of Korean schools rose from 3,000 to nearly 10,000. After the Korean War, concerted efforts were made to improve education. These efforts culminated in 1968 with the creation of a National Charter of Education.[1]

The Korean educational system is divided into six-year elementary schools, three-year middle schools, and three-year high schools. Undergraduate programs in colleges are four years. Graduate programs normally include three to five years of study.

Elementary and Middle Schools

In Korea, only six years of elementary school education is compulsory. Nevertheless, almost all students who graduate from the sixth grade continue their education. Because of the strong influence of Confucianism, most Koreans value education greatly, and parents make great sacrifices to permit their children to continue in school and often pressure their children to do well academically. At home, children are often scolded for their poor academic performance and low scores on tests elicit negative remarks from parents. Parents might respond to a child who receives a 90 percent score on a test with such remarks as, "You did okay, but next time, try to get a perfect score." In the extended Korean family, not only parents take responsbility for tutoring young children, but often older siblings, aunts, and uncles as well.

Emphasis in the primary and middle grades is on both reading and writing. Until recently, students in the lower grades learned mechanical rules of writing such as spelling and punctuation by rote memory, but rarely did any creative writing in the classroom. However, beginning in 1990, a major change in the curriculum was implemented such that there are separate classes for reading and writing at the elementary school level.

Currently, Korean children are only asked to write when there is a special occasion. In the lower grades, students are instructed to write in a given genre to commemorate a specific occasion. In upper grades, however, students are given the freedom to choose the writing genre they prefer (essay, poem or story). For example, elementary children are asked to write about the Korean War on

[1]For a concise review of the history of Korean education, refer to Hyun 1987.

June 25, the day the Korean War began. Often, they are asked to construct posters. They might write a single sentence or catch phrase such as *"Let's beat the Communists"* and then draw a picture illustrating their sentence in the center of their poster paper. On Mother's Day, students write thank-you letters to their mothers, and on Teacher's Day, they write essays or poems honoring a favorite teacher. At biannual school picnics, students are asked to write or draw in a more natural setting and awards are given for the best writing or picture produced.

Outside of School

Considerable homework is given to children. This includes daily journal writing and reading. In addition to this homework, parents often encourage, or perhaps better said, force their children to complete daily worksheets and to read a special daily newspaper designed for school children.

Currently, students are not instructed specifically how to write, but they are strongly encouraged to write a daily journal. Journals are collected approximately once a week, but they are neither corrected nor graded.

Most Koreans believe that Korean writing is best taught through reading. Many middle-class urban families keep series of world literature books for their children's pleasure reading. During winter and summer vacations, teachers encourage students to read books by well-known authors. The Ministry of Education publishes lists of recommended books for different levels of students. Students are given these lists and asked to read as many books as possible. They are then required to complete a specific number of reports. Awards are frequently made for good reports.

Daily worksheets are especially popular among families with preschoolers and elementary children. Almost every urban family with children, whether wealthy or poor, pays to have daily worksheets delivered to their homes. Children usually complete these worksheets after they finish their homework. The worksheets are picked up the following day, corrected, and returned. Families subscribe to these worksheets much as they would to daily newspapers. These worksheets provide children with additional opportunities to review or preview their school subjects. In addition, they provide a daily means for parents to teach their children at home. This is important to many Korean parents since competition among parents for the academic achievement of their children is usually great, and today no one is allowed to have private tutors while attending school. (In 1989, the regulations were changed so that any student who can afford to pay for a private tutor can have one when school is not in session.)

Nearly all urban Koreans with school-aged children subscribe to a special daily newspaper for children. (Two such newspapers are the *Sonyun Dong-A* and *Sonyun ChoSun*.) This newspaper has a summary of world and national news, a review of local school events, and a special section for literary works such as poems or essays written by its subscribers. In addition, it includes cartoons and a special column reviewing the school material of the different elementary grades. Since Korean newspapers are now available in the United States, Korean-Americans often purchase these newspapers for their children.

High School Education

Although high school education is not compulsory in Korea, most middle-school graduates attend high school, and the dropout rate is extremely low (Kim 1988). The school day is very long because the first period generally begins at 8:00 A.M and the last class generally ends at 5:00 P.M. Saturday, students have a shorter schedule. The schools permit students to stay after school to study in special rooms. Hyun states:

> There are also private study halls and libraries in the cities for students to study in the evenings. Most students take this opportunity to study harder and usually do not return home until late evening. Even during the summer and winter vacations, many students spend most of their time at these study halls. (Hyun 1987, 67)

Students take a wide variety of courses. English is required throughout junior high and high school. In high school, there is a separate class for ancient Korean literature, which is generally introduced through shijo and kasa. Emphasis in the upper grades is on diverse genres including poetry, essays and novels.

Colleges and Universities

Because colleges and universities operate under strict enrollment limitations set by the Korean Ministry of Education, the competition to enter Korean universities is one of the highest in the world (Olsen 1987). There are few writing requirements in most college courses. Although some professors require end-of-the-semester term papers, the primary piece of writing college students produce as a requirement of graduation is a major essay resembling a thesis. Today, more and more university students are participating in reading circles which meet to discuss various issues. Whereas in the past, these groups were unable to discuss political topics freely, today these groups enjoy more freedom in that they are able to choose whatever discussion topics they like.

Korean Society

Korean society also encourages Koreans to practice different literary genres through local contests, literary journals, tearooms, letter writing, and game shows. There are many local contests where awards are given for well-written short novels, essays, and poems. These contests help establish novice writers. When awards are given, local newspapers feature columns about the winners as well as critiques of their works by well-known authors or literary critics.

Many different literary journals play critical roles in discovering talented novice writers and in supporting those already established ones. Newspapers also recognize amateur writers in semiannual writing contests held in spring and fall in which awards are given for different genres. Separate newspaper columns are devoted to traditional poems such as the shijo. Also, monthly magazines for housewives and teenagers reserve space for the writing of nonprofessional writers.

Activities which foster Korean writing practices also take place in tearooms, particularly prevalent in Seoul and other large cities (Hyun 1987; see also Wade 1987). There are tearooms for almost every function. In social-oriented tearooms, groups of friends and colleagues may discuss recent books, concerts, and films. In academic-oriented tearooms, writing circles are held. Many college students who major in Korean literature meet in these writing circles regularly, where they have the oopportunity to introduce their original essays, poems, and novels.

The Korean government led a letter-writing drive to encourage people to write letters more frequently and still encourages Koreans to write at least one letter each month. However, our interviews suggest that Koreans in general do not seem to write many letters.

Sometimes game shows on radio and television programs ask participants to compose poems using specific sets of characters. In this way, Koreans indirectly express their opinions about domestic problems. On *"Scholarship Quiz,"* a television game show designed for high school students, contestants often compose witty, cynical poems. The winners of this show earn scholarship funds.

IMPLICATIONS

Dramatic improvements in Korean-American ESL students' English writing development can take place when teachers incorporate their students' rich cultural knowledge into the writing curriculum. Building upon the students' existing knowledge of Korean written genres and values increases the students' writing repertoires, develops the students' self-confidence, and leads to the students' strong cultural identities. As Cummins (1979, 1981, 1989a) has repeatedly argued, first language literacy aids the development of second language literacy. (See also Heath 1986).

Suggestions for incorporating Korean literacy traditions into our schools are outlined in Table 1.

Clearly, some of the information outlined in Table 1 will be more helpful in some teaching contexts than in others. Yet it provides useful data for teachers who instruct Korean students who are recent arrivals to the United States.

Perhaps most important, as suggested by Table 1, teachers should encourage interaction in their classrooms so that their students' experiences are validated. Such interaction can enrich all cultural groups. As Cummins (1989b) forcefully argues:

TABLE 1
Incorporating Korean Literacy Traditions

Pedagogical Suggestions	Korean Literacy Practices
Interaction	
• Encourage students to share their literary traditions.	Koreans have rich literary traditions.
Reading	
• Encourage students to read poems to one another.	Reading poetry is an art in its own right.
• Provide students with lists of recommended reading.	
• Urge students to read Korean novels; make them available to students.	Short novels are very popular.
• Ask students to read extensively and report on their reading.	Students are encouraged to read extensively.
Writing	
• Encourage students to write on special occasions.	Students are often asked to write on special occasions.
• Ask students to provide a special calendar of events from their own culture for the class; use this calendar for a reference for additional writing topics for those students who prefer writing about them.	
• Encourage students to write about field trips.	Students are accustomed to writing about field trips.
• Encourage daily journal writing and reading.	Students keep daily journals.
• Ask students to share news from their daily newspapers in class.	Most Koreans and many Korean-Americans subscribe to daily newspapers.

Pedagogical Suggestions	Korean Literacy Practices
• Initiate writing contents in which awards are given for well-written poems, short stories or essays.	Students are accustomed to such contests.
Parental Involvement (For children)	
• Involve the students' parents and family in their children's literacy assignments.	Korean families want to be involved in their children's literacy development.

> . . . pedagogical approaches that empower students encourage them to assume greater control over setting their own learning goals and to use written and oral language for active collaboration with each other in achieving these goals. The instruction is automatically culture-fair in that all students are actively involved in expressing, sharing, and amplifying their experience within the classroom. (Cummins 1989b, 34)

Often teachers hesitate to allow their less proficient English students to interact. This effectively excludes participation by the newly arrived Korean students.

In addition, teachers should narrow the cultural gap between writing practices in the United States and in Korea by utilizing some of the same practices used in their students' homeland. For instance, they should encourage their students to keep daily journals (a well-documented activity used to improve writing development; see, for example, Flores and Garcia 1984; Hayes, Bahruth, and Kessler 1986; Hughes 1986, Kreeft et al. 1984; Johnson 1989). As Johnson explains, interactive journals, in which students and teachers interact with one another in journals, ". . . create a channel for communication that can accomodate personality differences among children who are just beginning to learn English" (Johnson 1989, 145). In fact, according to Johnson, for some children, ". . . journals may provide the only means by which they initiate communicative interactions in English" (45).

Teachers should capitalize on their students' previous experiences with poetry and diary writing while simultaneously providing students with additional guidance and practice in those genres with which they have less experience. Students who are adept at writing poetry may not be able to write expository essays, not necessarily because these essays are inherently more difficult or demanding than poetry, but because they simply lack experience reading and writing such essays (Halliday and Hasan 1985; Rose 1983). Teachers need to provide models of the genres students are expected to produce.

Teachers should also be aware of the different approaches U.S. students and Koreans take in writing expository essays. For example, they should realize that their Korean students may not understand the need for peer-editing sessions and may become very frustrated when asked to produce essays under the pressure of time.

Similarly, we must select topics which are within the realm of the experiences of our students. As McKay points out, "we must be certain that the topics we assign do not require students to relate experiences they do not have" (McKay 1989, 260). Every act of writing demands that the writer possess the background knowledge called for by the topic. Students may need to be given information about certain topics. A topic that is motivating for most U.S. students may pose difficulties for Koreans. Topics specific to the United States may motivate long-term residents, but not the recent arrival.

With respect to values and beliefs, it might be useful to point out that many Korean-Americans have taken on U.S. values while also maintaining traditional Korean ones (Huhr and Kim 1984). In Huhr and Kim's terms, these Korean-Americans are undergoing adhesive acculturation. Huhr and Kim state:

> . . . adhesive adaptation is one of the major types of ethnic adaptation in which certain aspects of the new culture and social relations with members of the host society are added on to the immigrants' traditional culture and social networks, without replacing or modifying any significant part of the old. . . . For example, Korean immigrants' progressive Americanization and their strong ethnic attachment are not mutually exclusive. (164)

Given this, effective teachers will respect traditional Korean values and build upon them. For instance, while respecting their students' value of face-saving, they will also teach their students the new values of stating personal opinions in English expository essays.

In short, to amplify the literacy development of Korean-American students, teachers will need to become familiar with the rhetorical traditions and cultural experiences of their students (Reid 1989; Land and Whitley 1989). In this way, Korean-American students can contribute to our classrooms from "their own storehouses of experiences" (Land and Whitley 1989, 286). They can be encouraged to demonstrate their expertise rather than their inadequacies.

References

ADA, A.F. 1986. Creative education for bilingual teachers. *Harvard Educational Review* 56: 386–94.

———. 1988. The Pajaro Valley experience: Working with Spanish-speaking parents to develop children's reading and writing skills in the home through the use of children's literature. In *Minority education: From shame to struggle,* eds. T. Skutnabb-Kangas and J. Cummins. Clevedon, England: Multilingual Matters.

BRIDGES, B. 1986. *Korea and the West.* London: Routledge & Kegan Paul.

BUCK, P. 1987. A noble people. In *Introducing Korea,* ed. P. Hyun. Republic of Korea: Jungwoo-sa, originally published in 1967.

CHANG, S. J. 1983. English and Korean. In *Annual Review of Applied Linguistics,* ed. R. Kaplan, 85–98. Rowley, Mass.: Newbury House Publishers.

CHENG, L. -R. 1987. *Assessing Asian language performance: Guidelines for evaluating limited-English-proficient students.* Rockville, Maryland: An Aspen Production.

CHOY, B. -Y. 1979. *Koreans in America.* Chicago: Nelson-Hall.

CHUNG, C. -S. 1979. In *Religions in Korea,* eds. E. Phillips and E. -Y. Yu. Los Angeles: Center for Korean Studies, California State University.

CUMMINS, J. 1979. Linguistic interdependence and the educational development of bilingual children. *Review of Educational Research* 49:222–51.

_____. 1981. The role of primary language development in promoting educational success for language minority students. In *Schooling and Language Minority Students: A Theoretical Framework,* ed. California State Department of Education. Los Angeles: Evaluation, Dissemination, and Assessment Center, California State University.

_____. 1989a. *Empowering minority students.* Sacramento: California Association for Bilingual Education.

_____. 1989b. The sanitized curriculum. In *Richness in writing: Empowering ESL Students,* D. M. Johnson and D. H. Roen. eds. New York: Longman.

EGGINGTON, W. 1987. Written academic discourse in Korean: Implication for effective communication. In *Writing across languages: Analysis of L2 text,* U. Connor and R. Kaplan, eds. 153–68. Reading, Mass.: Addison Wesley.

FLORES, B. and E. H. GARCIA. 1984. A collaborative learning and teaching experience using journal writing. *NABE Journal* 8(2):67–83.

FREEMAN, A. 1987. The Irish of Asia—full of song and laughter. In *Introducing Korea,* P. Hyun, ed. Republic of Korea: Jungwoo-sa, originally published in 1967.

GRAVES, D. 1983. *Writing: Children and Teachers at work.* Exeter, N.H.: Heinemann.

HALLIDAY, M. A. K. and R. HASAN. 1985. *Language, context, and text: Aspects of language in a social-semiotic perspective.* Victoria, Australia: Deakin University.

HAYES, C. W., R. BAHRUTH, and C. KESSLER. 1986. The dialogue journal and migrant education. *Dialogue* 3 (3):3–5.

HEATH, S. B. 1986. Sociocultural Contexts of Language Development. In *Beyond Language,* California State Dept. of Ed. Sacramento.

HINDS, J. 1987. Linguistics and written discourse in particular languages:

Contrastive studies: English and Japanese. In *Annual Review of Applied Linguistics* (Vol. 3), R. B. Kaplan, et al, eds. 78–84. Rowley, Mass.: Newbury House Publishers.

_____. 1987. Japanese and English. In *Annual Review of Applied Linguistics,* R. Kaplan, ed. 141–152. Rowley, Mass.: Newbury House Publishers.

HUGHES, L. 1987. Making language connections: Writing in ESL pull-out classes. *Dialogue* 3(2):6–7.

HUHR, W. M. and K. C. Kim. 1984. *Korean immigrants in America: A structural analysis of ethnic confinement and adhesive adaptation.* London, Toronto: Associated University Press.

HYUN, P., ed. 1987. *Introducing Korea.* Republic of Korea: Jungwoo-sa, originally published in 1967.

JOHNSON, D. M. 1989. Task contexts for second language. In *Richness in writing: Empowering ESL students,* D. M. Johnson and D. H. Roen, eds. New York: Longman.

_____. and D. H. ROEN, eds. 1989. *Richness in writing: Empowering ESL students.* New York: Longman.

KALTON, M. C. 1985. *Korean ideas and values.* Elkins Park, Penn.: Philip Jaison Memorial Foundation.

KAPLAN, R. B. 1966. Cultural thought patterns in intercultural education. *Language Learning* 16:1–20.

_____. 1987. Cultural thought patterns revisited. In *Writing across languages: Analysis of L2 text,* U. Connor and R. B. Kaplan, eds. 9–21. Reading, Mass.: Addison-Wesley.

KIM, B. -L. 1988. The language situation of Korean Americans. In *Language diversity: Problem or resource?* S. L. McKay and S.-L. Wong, eds. New York: Newbury House/Harper Row, 252–76.

KIM, S. S. 1977. How they fared in American homes: A follow-up of adopted Korean children. *Children Today* 6:2–6.

KITANO, H. and R. DANIELS. 1988. *Asian Americans: Emerging minorities.* Englewood Cliffs, New Jersey: Prentice Hall.

KOREAN OVERSEAS INFORMATION SERVICE. 1986. *Focus on Korea: This is Korea.* Seoul: Samsung Moonwha Printing Company.

KREEFT, J., R. W. SHUY, J. STATON, L. REED, and R. MORROY. 1984. *Dialogue writing: Analysis of student-teacher interactive writing in the learning of English as a second language.* (Report No. 83-0030). Washington, D.C.: National Institute of Education. (ERIC Document Reproduction Service No. ED 252 097.)

LAND, R. and C. WHITLEY. 1989. Evaluating second language essays in regular composition classes: Toward a pluralistic U.S. rhetoric. In *Richness in writing: Empowering ESL students,* D. M. Johnson and D. H. Roen, eds. New York: Longman.

LEE, C. and R. SCARCELLA, forthcoming. An investigation of Korean writing practices. Unpublished manuscript, University of California, Irvine.

LEE, K. 1982. Students from Korea. In *Asian Bilingual Education*. Cambridge, MA: Evaluation, Dissemination and Assessment Center.

LEE, K. -B. 1984. *A new history of Korea*. Trans. E. W. Wagner and E. J. Shultz, Seoul, Korea: Ilchokak Publishers.

MCKAY, S. 1989. Topic development and written discourse accent. In *Richness in writing: Empowering ESL students,* D. M. Johnson and D. H. Roen, eds. New York: Longman.

MURRAY, D. 1982. *Learning by teaching: Selected articles on writing and teaching*. Upper Montclair, New Jersey: Boynton Cook.

––––––. 1985. *A writer teaches writing*. Boston: Houghton Mifflin.

OGGINS, J. and S. -W. KWON. 1989. Cultural factors affecting Korean students and their study of English. *TESOL Newsletter, English for Foreign Students in English-Speaking Countries Interest Section* vol. 7, (1): 5–8.

OLSON, L. 1987. *Crossing the schoolhouse border*. San Francisco: California Today.

PURVES, A. (ed.) 1988. *Writing across languages and cultures: Issues in contrastive rhetoric*. Newbury Park, Calif: Sage Publishers.

REID, J. 1989. English as a second language composition in higher education: The expectations of academic audience. In *Richness in writing: Empowering ESL students,* D. M. Johnson and D. H. Roen, eds. New York: Longman.

ROMAINE, S. 1984. *The language of children and adolescents: The acquisition of communicative competence*. New York: Basil Blackwell.

ROSE, M. 1983. Remedial writing courses: A critique and a proposal. *College English* 45:109–128.

RUTT, R. 1987. Traditional literature. In *Introducing Korea,* P. Hyun, ed. 72–76. Republic of Korea: Jungwoo-sa, originally published in 1967.

SCARCELLA, R. and C. LEE. 1989. Different paths to writing proficiency in a second language. In *The Dynamics of Interlanguage: Empirical studies in second language variation,* M. Eisenstein, ed. New York: Plenum.

SCHOENBERGER, K. 1988. South Koreans just love to wax lyrical. *Los Angeles Times,* (December 16, 1988): 1, 36, 37.

SKILLEND, W. E. 1987. In Korea Today, *Introducing Korea,* P. Hyun, ed. Republic of Korea: Jungwoo-sa, originally published in 1967.

SPINDLER, G. and L. SPINDLER. 1987. *Interpretive ethnography of education: At home and abroad*. Hillsdale, New Jersey: Lawrence Eribaum Associates.

WADE, J. 1987. Korean tearooms. In *Introducing Korea,* P. Hyun, ed. Republic of Korea: Jungwoo-sa, (originally pubished in 1967).

Discussion Questions

1. In what specific ways do you think students' previous cultural experiences affect their literacy development in a second language? How does acculturation affect this development?

2. Why should teachers build upon the already rich literacy experiences of their ESL students? How does this practice help their students to acquire English literacy skills?

3. Although many Korean-American students in the United States hold the values and beliefs outlined in this paper, many others do not. Why is this the case? In answering this question, it may be helpful for you to consider such variables as acculturation, input, and interaction.

4. Should teachers in U.S. schools attempt to build upon all the literacy practices of their ESL students? Is this desirable and/or possible?

5. In what specific ways, if any, can American students benefit from learning Korean literacy traditions?

6. How is composing in Korean similar or dissimilar to composing in English?

7. What are some specific techniques and/or activities teachers can use to encourage their Korean students to state personal opinions?

8. To what extent is it possible to acquire literacy skills in one's second language while maintaining literacy skills in one's first language?

9. What advantages are to be gained by developing strong literacy skills in one's first and second languages?

11

Beating Hirsch With His Own Game: Reading For Cross-Cultural Literacy

MARY LEE FIELD

Introduction

Cultural literacy has become a much discussed and widely debated topic, in good part due to the publication of E. D. Hirsch, Jr.'s *Cultural Literacy: What Every American Needs to Know* (1986) and the subsequent appearance of *The Dictionary of Cultural Literacy* by E. D. Hirsch, Jr., Joseph Kett, and James Trefil (1988). These books appeared for many months on the best seller lists, strong testimony to the public's need to know what it takes to be culturally literate. Hirsch's argument, sometimes labeled elitist and ethnocentric, and the compilation of more than 6,000 names and items in the *Dictionary,* provide one definition of what cultural literacy means to many Americans. Nevertheless, the books drew sharp criticism—some from educators who feared that such lists create superficial exercises in memorization, some from critics who provide detailed analyses of the sexist-racist-Western bias of the list, some from reading specialists who question whether or not using such a list will actually enhance background schema for readers. Teachers of English as a second and foreign language (ESL/EFL), and teachers of nontraditional students, struggling to find ways to give students the cultural background which they need in order to read well in English, turned to Hirsch to see what these texts could offer, but they were also faced with the controversy over the Hirsch material that seriously challenged its usefulness.

Rather than become embroiled in the Hirsch controversy, I propose here to focus on the broader issues of cultural knowledge and cross-cultural literacy which were raised in the controversy. Those who wish to follow the intricacies of the academic world's debate over Hirsch's description of cultural literacy will find Smith (1988) and Swearingen (1988) good starting points. However, teachers who want to enhance student learning without compromising their own values and sensibilities will find more fertile ground in considering two general applications of the Hirsch material: (1) as a way both to make conscious the concepts of cultural and cross-cultural literacy, using Hirsch as a starting point to explore the issues raised by cross-cultural literacy; and (2) as a specific tool for building cross-cultural literacy. These applications are predicated on the assumption that the Hirsch material is, indeed, of some use in the classroom. The type and extent of that use, however, is considerably different from what Hirsch argues for in *Cultural Literacy* and the *Dictionary*, and the applications which I argue for here essentially constitute a way to use Hirsch to undermine the elitism and ethnocentricity of his own argument: to beat him with his own game.

CRITICISMS OF CULTURAL LITERACY

Before granting that we might use the *Dictionary* in the classroom to make explicit the concept of cultural literacy, there are two major criticisms of Hirsch's list to address: first that it is ethnocentric (white, upper middle class, Western, male, Judeo-Christian), and thus culturebound and elitist; and second, that to promote that list is a form of cultural imperialism, imposing ethnocentric ideas and values on our students. These criticisms lead us to examine how Hirsch compiled his list. He explains that in the process of formulating the list, he and his associates "gave priority to words and phrases found in the front pages and editorial columns of serious newspapers and in the pages of serious books and magazines" (Hirsch 1986, 136). In addition, they selected words and terms which are "*above* the everyday levels of knowledge that everyone possesses and *below* the expert level known only to specialists" (Hirsch 1986, 19). In the *Dictionary* the authors explain the rules they used in selecting entries, citing the criteria just quoted and adding the third rule that "cultural literacy is not knowledge of current events. . . . an item must have lasting significance" (Hirsch et al. 1988, ix). Hirsch calls his list "descriptive" rather than "prescriptive" and says that it presents "the shared cultural schemata that underlie literate communications of the present day" (Hirsch et al. 1988, 135–36). As a result, many of the terms on the list clearly reflect the values and cultural orientation of a specific group of Americans. Assuming that in order to gain power in society one must compete with or join those in power, Hirsch's list directly reflects the values of those in power. The ESL/EFL teacher is left with the problem of how to avoid the cultural imperialism implicit in using such a list.

Hirsch's list has produced at least one reactionary work, Simonson and Walker's *The Graywolf Annual Five: Multi-cultural Literacy* (1988), which supplies about 600 terms as a counterlist to Hirsch's longer compilation. More importantly, however, students need to become aware of a larger need, one which Armstrong has labeled

> "pluralistic literacy"—the ability to deal effectively with cultural differences and to negotiate the competing claims of multiple ways of reading. . . . students must develop the linguistic facility to communicate their beliefs to others whose frameworks are different and to understand views generated by perspectives incommensurable with their own. (Armstrong 1988, 29)

USING HIRSCH'S MATERIAL AS A TEACHING TOOL

The teacher who aims to develop a broader awareness, whether we call it pluralistic literacy or cross-cultural literacy, will find that the limited racial, sexual, political, and cultural perspectives in Hirsch provide excellent fodder for student discussions of cultural literacy in all cultures. Herein lies my first general application of the Hirsch material: to heighten consciousness of the concept of cross-cultural literacy. What list would our students generate for their own cultures? What terms in Thai, Chinese, French, or Serbo-Croatian constitute the knowledge which is "above" the everyday and "below" the specialists' level? What similarity is there between the 2,000 kanji necessary for a Chinese student to read a native language newspaper and Hirsch's list? (Since that list of kanji includes very basic words, there would seem to be only a tenuous connection.) How many terms on their list reflect changes in the knowledge valued by different generations? What terms appear when the older, returning student constructs such a list?

One principle is immediately evident: "the list" in other cultures will not be simply a translation of Hirsch's list. Each list will have its own set of values and assumptions reflected by the terms included there. Each list will reflect what Hirsch calls the "shared cultural schemata that underlie literate communications of the present day" (Hirsch 1986, 135–36) in whatever culture or subculture the students come from. Moreover, how much is the list an instrument to impose one culture's values on all other cultures? And for which subgroup of the culture? A valuable exercise is to scrutinize any list of terms, Hirsch's or those generated by students, applying to each term questions about the culture it represents, the values it carries with it, the generation which uses it, and most important, the world view it represents and the biases it reinforces. Simonson and Walker (1988) point out the *Dictionary*'s male bias in the inclusion of terms such as *penis envy, macho,* and *vasectomy,* but the omission of *mastectomy, gynecology,* or *Georgia O'Keeffe.* Students can easily identify other biases by perusing several of the categories or topics which they flesh out with specific terms. As a final step, they must analyze the biases and world views implicit in the very terms which they have generated. This is not an easy exercise; it is always difficult for us to see our own biases. But as a way to better understand cultural and cross-cultural literacy, it is a powerful tool.

Huenemann (1988) has developed a list of questions about values, cultural maintenance and unity, and challenges to local subcultural unity which provide a thorough checklist for the terms in the *Dictionary*. To use these questions, however, the lists in the *Dictionary* must be broken into smaller sections, divided among members of the class, or rendered more manageable in other ways.

1. How many (which) words are value-laden, value-bearing?
   How many are identity-bearers?
   How many are principle-bearers?

2. Which ones are essential to cultural, social, political, religious, or linguistic unity?
   How does each contribute to unity and identity; counter national fragmentation; or challenge local subcultural unity?

3. What aspect or area of cultural practice does knowledge of each term or element help to maintain or sustain?

4. What cultural configurations are reflected and reinforced by these terms?

5. Which terms or elements have parallels or analogs in other languages? cultures?
   Which ones reflect and carry a unique, specific cultural perspective or world view?
   Which terms/elements in other community languages are unique and specific to that cultural experience and not portrayed by Hirsch's list?

6. Which U.S. subculture does the list represent?

7. What ought to constitute the list for the growing international global workforce? (Huenemann 1988)

By analyzing the nature of any list generated by any culture, students can come to terms with the inherent problems in them. Moreover, such activities will lead to discussions about "dominant" groups trying to impose their cultural values while subgroups may be trying to maintain their values. Obviously, the people in the subgroup are expected to know the terms held important by the group in power; but will the group in power know the terms valued by the subgroup? There is great potential for discussion and new understanding of cross-cultural literacy issues in this application of the Hirsch material. It provides teachers with the satisfaction of taking advantage of an easily available resource, not only without having to buy into the ethnocentric biases of the resource, but with the satisfaction of using the material to broaden (rather than to limit) the students' understanding of cross-cultural literacy.

GOING BEYOND HIRSCH'S MATERIAL

The second general application of Hirsch's material, as a specific tool for building cultural literacy, is also clouded with controversy and debate which create problems for teachers who consider using the *Dictionary*. In *Cultural Literacy* Hirsch argued for his list on the basis of recent English language reading theory research. In one of Hirsch's own studies, an experiment with community college students, students performed poorly when they lacked background information even though "their memory capacities, eye movements, basic vocabularies, and reading strategies—in short, their reading skills—were all up to par" (Hirsch 1986, 47). Since Hirsch's concern is with the American public education system, he does not consult research done in ESL/EFL reading. But similar results have been demonstrated among ESL students (Aron 1986; Carrell 1983; Carrell & Eisterhold, 1983; Connor 1984; Hudson 1982; Johnson 1982; Steffensen and Colker 1982; Steffensen, Joag-Dev, and Anderson 1979). Given that L2 readers have developed good reading skills (memory capacity, eye movement, vocabulary, reading strategy), they may still have trouble reading because of a lack of background knowledge. The terms and definitions which constitute the *Dictionary* are Hirsch's solution to providing background knowledge.

But Hirsch's outrage at the lack of cultural literacy which students display in academic situations needs to be scrutinized in light of the research done by Heath (1983, 1986). Her conclusions from extensive ethnographic study are that people remember and learn that which is relevant to them. The fact that high school students are unable to produce dates and identify names of famous people is more a reflection of the value which students ascribe to such information than an indication of their "ignorance."

Thus, the assumption that learning Hirsch's list of terms will activate schema is one we must question. Many educators saw Hirsch's list as an extended vocabulary list and immediately warned against "teaching the list," that is, focusing on memorization rather than understanding. Indeed, there are vocabulary lists currently available for EFL teachers (Campion and Elley 1971; Francis and Kucera 1979; Ghadessy 1979; Lynn 1973; Nation 1983, 1984; Praninskas 1972; Thorndike and Lorge 1944; West 1953). Admittedly, the list which

Hirsch provides is quite different from those. It does not include just "vocabulary" but places, titles, names, concepts, and other reference to the elements which form the cultural background of a certain segment of American society. But will it transmit that background knowledge to students?

Hirsch admits the danger of too much memorization of the list (Hirsch 1986, 135–36, 142–45); however, he insists that making the list explicit will encourage and energize people. He even makes the rather absurd claim that "only a few hundred pages of information stand between the literate and illiterate" (Hirsch 1986, 143). The kind of literacy which Hirsch is advocating here seems to be simply the recognition of key words (names, concept, works) without an understanding of background. It is, as Grundin argues, "a narrow, test-oriented view that equates literacy with doing well on reading tests" (1988, 1).

Law argues that Hirsch "treats knowledge as discrete, unambiguous pieces of information to be presented for students to absorb" (1988, 33). Cultural background is usually acquired, however, through a complex set of experiences, and sitting down to study a list of 5,000 terms is hardly an exercise which any teacher would assign. Moreover, rote learning of the explanations of names and places listed in the *Dictionary* does not guarantee activation of schema for ESL/EFL or nontraditional students reading English. Background information which leads to activating schema often comes from cultural experience, and reading is only one of many forms of cultural experience. Even though we can acquire some degree of understanding about cultures through reading, Huenemann (1988) points out that there are nonverbal cultural elements and evocative elements which are also important, such as the smell of fresh-baked bread, how far to insert chopsticks when eating, and the taste of pumpkin pie. No dictionary will be able to provide that kind of total information for us.

To investigate our second application, using the Hirsch material as a specific resource and tool in the classroom, let us look first at the section entitled Geographical Designations in the *Dictionary*. The *Dictionary* has reorganized, categorized, and defined the terms that were listed in *Cultural Literacy,* a great improvement over the early list; but even the *Dictionary* functions best as tool rather than as a solution to students' reading problems. Names of towns, cities, rivers, and areas are not important because we need to know their physical locations, but because the students need to know the associations (schema, background knowledge) which each item produces in the minds of native language readers. In the introduction to this section of the *Dictionary*, Kett emphasized that these entries are necessary for "following literate discourse" and "an ability to make the correct associations" about terms (in Hirsch 1988, 375). Many entries are "famous for some distinctive activity that occurs in, on, or near them," while others are "known primarily or exclusively for their associations" (in Hirsch, 1988, 375). In my own informal questioning of people in Colorado and Arizona (I confess they were all TEFL folk) about one American city—Ann Arbor, Michigan—I collected a substantial load of information. People associate

Ann Arbor with the University of Michigan, a pastoral setting, a cold climate, University Microfilms, collegiate sports, a major research facility, and even the beginning of the Peace Corps. The *Dictionary* entry for Ann Arbor, the "window" of information which is between general knowledge (a cold climate) and the details known by specialists (University Microfilms), includes only "City in southern Michigan, near Detroit," and "location of the University of Michigan." (Hirsch 1988, 377) The specific entry from the *Dictionary* is only a starting point for students. A follow up to a list of names of geographical locations would be to interview native speakers about places, as I interviewed EFL teachers, to see what other associations are held by native speakers, and sort through those responses to see which are too specialized and which too general. Students who generate sets of connotations in pairs or small groups will gain relevant and powerful background knowledge, useful schema that will aid their reading on a longer range basis than memorizing a vocabulary list.

The categories in the *Dictionary* have made the list from *Cultural Literacy* considerably easier to deal with in classes:

The Bible
Mythology and Folklore
Proverbs
Idioms
World Literature, Philosophy and Religion
Literature in English
Conventions of Written English
Fine Arts
World History to 1550
World History since 1550
American History to 1865
American History since 1865
World Politics
World Geography
American Geography
Anthropology, Psychology, and Sociology
Business and Economics
Physical Sciences and Mathematics
Earth Sciences
Life Sciences
Medicine and Health
Technology

These twenty-two categories lend themselves to various uses. They provide preview material for any student beginning the study of a new discipline, for instance the EFL student who signs up to take a psychology course at an American university. Another activity using these categories arises from Hirsch's statement that these terms appear in major newspapers and magazines without definition or explanation. One or two paragraphs on medicine or art from *Time* or the local newspaper are manageable texts for students to search, identifying the terms which are listed in those categories of the *Dictionary* and checking the definitions to see if they provide enough background information to understand the paragraph better.

Selecting the *amount* of information which is useful but not burdensome about any one item is another problem which the teacher faces when using the *Dictionary*. How much do students need to know? Our understanding of the complexity of background knowledge and cultural experience warns us that learning a little about a group of American cities will not necessarily activate schema for our students. However, used as a reference rather than as an assignment for memorization, the *Dictionary* provides a beginning, lays the groundwork for students to understand allusions and references that they would not otherwise understand.

A recent study by Wallace and Leki (1988) at the University of Tennessee provides some instructive data on the level of cultural literacy in two sets of college students: one set of native speakers of English and another of foreign students studying at the university. The instrument which was administered checked such items as (1) History: What was the year the Japanese attacked Pearl Harbor? (2) Geographical Locations: In which countries are Seoul, Montreal, Manila? (3) Literature: Who wrote *Hamlet*? and (4) General Knowledge: Who is the current Vice President of the United States? (at the time it was George Bush). On some general knowledge questions, the nonnative students scored higher than the native Americans, but generally, the nonnative students made even more errors than the American students. Cultural literacy was not the strong suit of either group, at least as tested in this sample, and Heath's (1986) evidence that people only remember or learn what they *need* to know certainly applies here. Since the test questions were specifically aimed at identifying cultural literacy in America, the ESL students were being tested in a second language about a second culture. A parallel test of cultural literacy items, administered to American students studying in another country, would provide a reasonable control, as would a test of the nonnative students' cultural literacy about their own cultures, administered in their native languages.

Before we make pronouncements about cultural literacy, either in America or in other countries, we need to engage in some cummunication with each other and with the rest of the world about what information truly is important to all of us. The Hirsch material, if it has done nothing else, has made that discussion vital and necessary. Our classes can benefit from participating in (indeed helping to formulate answers to) that discussion.

Insofar as Hirsch wants to create a "national vocabulary," we must fault him for his argument. As Grundin has so cogently pointed out, "Hirsch confuses cause and effect. Literate people are not literate because they possess certain specific information; they possess the information because they are literate"

(1988, 15). But insofar as Hirsch provides us with research on the items which are currently in popular usage in the serious printed matter in the United States, we should make use of the considerable research which created the list and the dictionary. A study by Aron argues that ESL students who are given reading placement tests may receive scores based on "how closely their background knowledge matches that presupposed by the test rather than based on an assessment of their second language skills" (1986, 140). The two applications of the Hirsch material presented here illustrate that judicious use of the *Dictionary* can help us build the background knowledge that our students need in order to use the reading skills they already have. Even more important, building a clear understanding of cultural knowledge and cross-cultural or global literacy, in part by contrasting it with the limited, test-bound, and ethnocentric version presented by Hirsch, will both beat Hirsch at his own game and serve the wider, more enduring goal of creating and maintaining cross-cultural understanding and communication.

References

ARMSTRONG, P. B. 1988. Pluralistic literacy. *Profession 88.* New York: Modern Language Association.

ARON, H. 1986. The influence of background knowledge on memory for reading passages by native and nonnative readers. *TESOL Quarterly* 20(1): 136–40.

BARNARD, H. 1971. *Advanced English vocabulary list.* Rowley, Mass.: Newbury House.

CAMPION, M.E. and ELLEY, W.B. 1971. An academic vocabulary list. Nzcer: Wellington, N.Z.

CARRELL, P. 1983. Three components of background knowledge. *Language learning* 33(2): 183–209.

_____ . 1984. Schema theory and ESL reading: Classroom implications and applications. *The Modern Language Journal,* 68(4): 332–42.

_____ . 1987. Content and formal schemata in ESL reading. *TESOL Quarterly* 21(3): 461–81.

CARRELL, P. and J. C. EISTERHOLD. 1983. Schema theory and ESL reading pedagogy. *TESOL Quarterly* 17: 553–73.

CONNOR, U. 1984. Recall of text: Differences between first and second language readers. *TESOL Quarterly* 18: 239–56.

FRANCIS, W. N. and H. KUCERA. 1979. *A standard corpus of present day edited American English for use with digital computers.* Providence: Brown University.

GHADESSY, M. 1979. Frequency counts, word lists and materials preparation: A new approach. *English Forum* 17(1): 24–27.

GRUNDIN, H. U. 1988. Cultural list-eracy: What every American does not need. *Reading Today* 5(4): 1, 15.

HEATH, S. B. 1983. *Ways with words: Language, life, and work in communities and classrooms.* Cambridge: Cambridge University Press.

————. 1986. The functions and uses of literacy. In *Literacy, society, and schooling: A reader,* S. DeCASTELL, A. LUKE, and K. EGAN, eds. 15–26. New York: Cambridge University Press.

HIRSCH, E. D., 1986. *Cultural literacy: What every American needs to know.* Boston: Houghton Mifflin.

HIRSCH, E. D., J. F. KETT, and J. TREFIL. 1988. *The dictionary of cultural literacy: What every American needs to know.* Boston: Houghton Mifflin.

HUDSON, THOM. 1982. The effects of induced schemata on the "short circuit" in L2 reading: non-decoding factors in L2 reading performance. *Language learning* 32(1): 1–31.

HUENEMANN, L. 1988, July. *Cultural literacy: A critique and comparison using native American perspectives.* Paper presented at TESOL Summer Meeting, Flagstaff, Arizona.

JOHNSON, P. 1981. Effects on reading comprehension of language complexity and cultural background of a text. *TESOL Quarterly* 15: 169–81.

————. 1982. Effects on reading comprehension of building background knowledge. *TESOL Quarterly* 16: 503–16.

LAW, J. K 1988. Bloom, Hirsch, and Barthes in the classroom: Negotiating cultural literacy. *Freshman English News* 17(1): 33–36.

LYNN, R. W. 1973. Preparing Word Lists: A suggested method. *RELC Journal* 4, 1:25–32.

NATION, I. S. P. 1983. *Teaching and learning vocabulary.* Wellington, N.Z.: English Language Institute.

———— (ed.) 1984. Vocabulary Lists: words, affixes and stems; ELI, Victoria University of Wellington, Wellington, N.A.

PRANINSKAS, J. 1972. *American university word list.* London: Longman.

SIMONSON, R. and S. WALKER, eds. 1988. *The Graywolf annual five: Multi-cultural literacy.* St. Paul, MN: Graywolf Press.

SMITH, J. 1988. Cultural literacy and the academic "left." *Profession 88* 25–28. New York: Modern Language Association.

STEFFENSEN, M. S., and L. COLKER. 1982. *The effect of cultural knowledge on memory and language* (Tech. Rep. No. 248). Urbana, IL: University at Urbana-Champaign, Center for the Study of Reading.

————, C. JOAG-DEV, and R. C. ANDERSON. 1979. A cross-cultural perspective on reading comprehension. *Reading Research Quarterly* 15: 10–29.

SWEARINGEN, C. J. 1988. Bloomsday for literacy: How reactionaries and relativists alike undermine literacy while seeming to promote it. *Freshman English News* 17(1): 2–5.

THORNDIKE, E. L. and I. LORGE. 1944. The teacher's word book of 30,000 words. Teachers College, Columbia University, New York.

WALLACE, R. and I. LEKI. 1988, December. *Defining and teaching cultural awareness through reading: A TESL mission or mission impossible?* Paper presented at Reading, Culture, and Related Issues in Language Teaching, Georgia State University, Atlanta.

WEST, M. 1953. *A general service list of English words.* London: Longman, Green and Co.

XUE, G-Y. and P. NATION. 1984. A university word list. *Language Learning and Communication*, 3(2): 215–19.

Discussion Questions

1. What does the title of this essay mean? Why should we "beat Hirsch with his own game?"

2. Who defines what is "literate" in America? What qualifies those people to make that definition? Who does it in Canada? Or in other countries?

3. Select an article from *The New York Times* or *Atlantic Monthly* and look for terms which do or do not appear in *The Dictionary of Cultural Literacy*. Which terms do you think should be in the *Dictionary* but have been omitted?

4. Construct a list of terms which your parents or friends would need to know in order to be "culturally literate" about your favorite subject (such as rock music, classical music, baseball, dance, rap, etc.).

5. This chapter refers to the concept of "cultural imperialism." What does that mean? What examples of it can you cite? Is it being practiced today? Where?

6. In what ways is *The Dictionary of Cultural Literacy* useful to American college students? To international students studying in America? Could it be used abroad by students who are studying English?

7. Have you ever been made to feel "culturally illiterate" by someone? What did you do in that situation? What would you do now, having read this essay?

8. How "culturally literate" are you about another culture? What responsibility do Americans have to learn about other cultures? What responsibility do international students studying in the U.S. have to be "culturally literate" here?

12

Literacy Practices and Their Effect on Academic Writing: Vietnamese Case Studies

DENISE E. MURRAY and PATRICIA C. NICHOLS

Introduction

Literacy practices differ among cultures. Even more importantly, they differ among individuals within a given culture. Here we introduce eight Vietnamese, each with different experiences in learning to read and write. Some of these experiences have led to success in writing academic English; others have not. These eight different experiences highlight the need to look at individual literacy practices as well as cultural practices. These data show that we can not stereotype cultures; individuals within the same culture experience literacy in differing ways.

BACKGROUND

At our campus in northern California, the Vietnamese student population is one of the fastest growing (currently 1,200 students). Many of these bilingual

Vietnamese students are not successful with college level writing, failing to pass the university-wide sophomore level writing skills test (WST) at far higher rates than other groups (50 percent failure rate for Vietnamese compared with 5.7 percent for native English speakers). Previous research has identified age as a primary factor in success with academic English (see Collier 1989 for an overview of such studies). But we were interested in identifying other factors that might contribute to academic literacy, since our Vietnamese students began acquiring English at different ages and in different contexts. We hoped to uncover practices that could inform teaching and learning, ones that instructional programs and individuals might use.

Literacy Community

Our study found that successful students used a range of practices, all entailing active and enthusiastic participation in literacy communities: some were avid readers (of novels, environmental books or books about geniuses) when young, some write letters now, some read and write extensively in their part-time jobs, one is a poet, and several spent as long as a year observing language used in context before becoming active participants themselves. Unsuccessful students, on the other hand, did not become active members of literacy communities. Nor did they develop a love of reading and writing.

Our notion of literacy community mentioned in the last paragraph combines and builds on both Heath's construct of literacy event and Cummins' construct of cognitive academic language proficiency (CALP). In *Ways with Words,* Heath points out that many of the texts read and written in certain communities are part of a literacy event—those events that "have social interactional rules which régulate the type and amount of talk about what is written, and define ways in which oral language reinforces, denies, extends, or sets aside the written material (Heath 1983, 386)." Literacy practices, then, are socially constructed and culturally embedded, a pattern which Street (1984) characterizes as an "ideological" model of literacy. Since literacy is culturally embedded, different communities practice different literacies (see Heath 1983, Scribner and Cole 1981; Street 1984; and chapters in this book for detailed examples of literacy practices in different settings). However, not all literacy practices foster academic school literacy. Scribner and Cole (1981), for example, show that the Vai people (Liberia) who were literate in Vai were not able to engage in some of the schooled tasks they assigned them and thus could not display literacy skills on these tasks. Such tasks were not part of their literacy repertoire.

To apply the notion of literacy events to the use of language required for academic settings, we can look to Cummins' notion of CALP (e.g., 1982): that use of language which is cognitively demanding and makes use of decontextualized information. According to Cummins, such uses of language can be oral or written, although they more often occur in written genres. Thus, when students are in an academic setting like the university, participation in a literacy community requires interaction around written texts. Literacy, then, entails *both* cognitive and linguistic activities *and* social and cultural activities (see Johnson and Roen 1989 for a collection of articles dealing with both sociocultural and cognitive aspects of writing). Students must actively participate with others in the academic community in the *use* of academic language if they are to be accomplished members of such a literacy community.

EIGHT ENCOUNTERS WITH LITERACY

We decided to focus on Vietnamese literacy practices because Vietnamese students were failing the WST at such high rates. We chose eight Vietnamese students who were willing to participate in this study: three successful males, two successful females, two unsuccessful males, and one unsuccessful female. Successful students were those who had passed the WST, which consists of an objective section (Educational Testing Service's Pre-professional Skills Test) and a direct writing sample, rated holistically on a six-point scale and read by two readers. A passing score on the WST requires either a score of seven on the essay *or* a score of twenty-two on the objective section. To ensure that we did capture clear failures and clear passes, failures had to receive a score of five or less for the essay and passing students had to receive a score of eight or more. To ensure that participants planned to stay in the U.S., where written English would be essential to a successful career, we chose only permanent U.S. residents.

The eight students were asked to keep a journal of language use over two days—one weekday and one weekend day. We chose two different days to capture these students' language use in both the school and the community setting. Trained linguistics students interviewed the participants, with whom they were matched for age and gender. These one-hour interviews were audiotaped and later transcribed. In addition, the students' WST essays were analyzed for organization, grammar, and vocabulary (the major criteria used to evaluate these essays).

Since all eight students have a unique story to tell, we will first provide narratives, based on the journal and interview data. (Names have been changed to protect students' privacy.) Most of the data we have selected demonstrate the students' literacy practices and attitudes. However, we have also included some uses of oral language (e.g., code switching) to give a more complete picture of these individuals' language use. We hope that reading about their language experiences will help readers get to know these students intimately as we have gotten to know them.

The Successful Academic Writers

All five successful writers demonstrate their facility with written English in their essays. Although they often show awkward uses of late-acquired forms, they all demonstrate their understanding of the conventions of written English: their essays are well organized, use complex structure and sophisticated vocabulary.

Thu-Hồng, a twenty-two-year-old Vietnamese arrived in the U.S. at age eight knowing no English. When she arrived, although of age to enter third grade, she was placed in second grade to be closer to her sister who was in first grade. Because of her success in acquiring English, she skipped third grade and so began fourth grade with her age cohorts. Thu-Hồng says she and her siblings learned English largely by watching TV. Her mother, who had worked for an American company in Vietnam and her father, who held a government position in the U.S., also could read and write English. So, at home the family code-switches between English and Vietnamese. Thu-Hồng also learned French in elementary school in Vietnam and took it up again in high school in the U.S. She recalls learning to read in Vietnamese by sitting on her father's lap while he was reading the newspaper aloud "and all of a sudden one day I remember I was following along. I just picked it up."

Thu-Hồng always loved reading and going to the public library in Vietnam. "Every weekend I would get a new book." She is still an avid reader—now in both Vietnamese and English. When she first arrived here " . . . there were no Vietnamese books . . . so in order for me to read, I have to learn English and I think that was what I wanted to do, was to read, see, cause I always loved to read and that's why I picked it up." She read C. S. Lewis, Nancy Drew, Beverly Cleary, Judy Blume, and all the Agatha Christie books.

During her first year in elementary school in the U.S. she " . . . never opened her mouth. . . . I was so busy trying to listen all the time, that's all I did was just listen and try to remember." Thu-Hồng writes many letters in English to friends, one of whom she's been writing to for six years. She did a lot of writing in English in high school, more than she does in college where she is a business major. As well as required writing for her classes, Thu-Hồng also contributed to the semiannual publication of her high school's Vietnamese club. Her friends are primarily Vietnamese and they code-switch. Her parents, because of their work experiences in Vietnam, are "pretty liberal . . . never that old-fashioned," allowing the children to use English in the home. Now the children are older, however, they want them to use more Vietnamese because "they're afraid their grandchildren aren't going to speak any Vietnamese."

Lan, a twenty-three-year-old Vietnamese, arrived in the U.S. at age nine knowing how to read in Vietnamese but knowing no English. She repeated the third grade in a private school in "northern Dakota," where "basically the first year I was there I didn't do any work at all. . . . All I did, I sat there, listening." She attended a special ESL class, where they matched pictures to words, but in the regular classroom she understood only math and music. She learned English so quickly, however, that she was soon helping her parents' teacher at the night class they attended. After two years, the family moved to California, where she entered the sixth grade. By this time Lan was fluent in English. She memorized the words to popular songs she heard on the radio and read books, newspapers, and teen magazines—some in Vietnamese, but most in English. She remembers fondly the books of Beverly Cleary, especially *Ramona the Pest.* Her parents subscribed to Vietnamese newspapers.

In college she has time for only the front page of the newspaper, largely because of her two part-time jobs, one of which entails extensive reading and writing. Beginning as a secretary with a law firm, she has been promoted to the position of paralegal. She writes summaries of cases and uses a medical dictionary extensively, as well as talks with clients, insurance adjustors, and lawyers, all in English. Occasionally she is asked to translate for Vietnamese clients, but never writes Vietnamese for them. "The only time I write Vietnamese is to leave notes to my parents on the refrigerator!" Although her major in college is business, she is "really interested in the law firm job. It's really interesting, and I'm learning a lot." Her other part-time job is with a Vietnamese travel agency, where she speaks to customers in Vietnamese but writes their itineraries in English. At home she speaks Vietnamese with her parents, but code-switches with her brothers. At school she uses mostly English, even with her Vietnamese friends. In addition to her business classes in her major, she studies French and Mandarin at the university.

Hùng, a twenty-three-year-old Vietnamese, arrived in the U.S. at age ten knowing a few words and phrases in English. In Vietnam he attended a private school, where he thinks he may have been read to in kindergarten. Although he does not think he was read to at home, he remembers that there was always something to read around his house, especially magazines. He did a lot of reading when he was younger, but believes he now does not read in Vietnamese as well as he did then.

When he entered fifth grade in California, he was with many Asian children attending a special ESL program where " . . . you sit in a class, and then a certain time of day you leave that class to go to this other class, you know, to learn English . . . I learned a lot from that program."

He now lives at home with his parents, speaking both English and Vietnamese to them. His mother was born in China and speaks Chinese as well as Vietnamese; she understands English but does not speak it well. His father, an interpreter in Vietnam, speaks English well. With his four older brothers, Hùng code-switches between English and Vietnamese; with his three younger sisters he uses more English. Hùng has a Filipina girlfriend who speaks very little Tagalog, and they use English with each other and with her family. He uses only English at work and with his friends, who are all non-Vietnamese. At school he has been working on a senior project with other students in Electrical Engineering, his major, and with them he uses English. His television watching is all in English, although his mother watches the news in Vietnamese and rents movies in Chinese, which he does not understand at all. He writes letters to his friends in English but does not write to his Vietnamese relatives at all.

Steven, a twenty-two-year-old Vietnamese, arrived in the U.S. at age six knowing only Vietnamese. The family hired an aunt who was an interpreter to tutor him when he began school in Florida. After a year in school and a summer vacation during which he played with children in his neighborhood, he "pretty much knew what was going on." By the second year in school he knew what the teacher was saying, knew what to write and what certain words meant. By the sixth grade he was "pretty well off," using the encyclopedia, dictionary, and other source books and writing essays and short stories. He read extensively for pleasure: "environmental stuff"; books on pets such as birds, dogs, and cats; books on hobbies like airplanes. He became interested in tidepools and the ocean. However, "the time I was in high school I was so overwhelmed with all the stuff I had to do, homework and stuff like that I didn't really have time for outside reading, so . . . just concentrated on school material." He was placed in honors English classes, where he had the same teacher for four years. She and his classmates critiqued his writing and encouraged him to write more of what he felt. He remembers her telling him, "You're writing to impress somebody, there's no reason why you should do this, just write what you feel."

In college he kept a journal, hated doing it, but could see that his writing improved because of it. He did little writing outside of school until he took a job with one of the major airlines. There he wrote daily reports as part of his job. He wrote his report last so that he could use those written by his co-workers as a guide, making sure that he did not make the kind of grammatical errors that they did. He thinks that the peer reviews in high school helped his writing; he learned that a writer must think of the reader, "[you] gotta tell the reader, take him by the hand."

His reading now consists of *Aviation Week,* the premier journal in the aviation world, as well as safety reports and manuals on systems for new airplanes. He cannot read or write in Vietnamese, although he remembers that both his mother and his grandmother read to him in Vietnamese. He judges his Spanish to be better than his Vietnamese in all categories except listening. His parents use Vietnamese with each other but both English and Vietnamese with their children. He is majoring in aviation, having made the choice between that and marine biology on entering college. His goal is to become a pilot, manager, air traffic controller—almost anything connected with aviation except flight attendant.

Trung is a twenty-year-old Vietnamese with three grandparents who were born in China. He entered the U.S. at fourteen, having studied English for two years in Vietnam in private classes. His father was imprisoned for three years but escaped and did the paperwork necessary for Trung to be flown to the U.S., where he went to high school and then a community college before entering the university. In high school he made Vietnamese friends and did not speak much English. He keeps in touch with his high school friends and continues to speak Vietnamese with them, although he uses English for school work and for expressing intimate feelings not usually articulated in Vietnamese. He uses English because "[it] is very easy to express feelings, you know, when I get mad with my mom, when I want to say intimate things, I tend, I tend to speak English more than Vietnamese, it's quite easy, you know . . . I can't, I can't tell my mom 'I love you' in Vietnamese, you know, I can tell her in English easily. . . . Because, you know, Vietnamese people tend to not to express their feelings, you know." He resists his girlfriend's pressure to tell her that he loves her in Vietnamese "because it's so damn hard, you know, you can see that it's more committed."

A business major, Trung also sees himself as " . . . a poet and a writer." He began writing as a child in Vietnam and was much praised for his work. Both parents were teachers and would not allow him to watch television because of the war news, so he read a lot. His favorite books were about "geniuses," who in Vietnamese culture all know a lot of poetry. He feels that his writing in Vietnamese "really got good recently." He belonged to a Vietnamese club at a community college, which exchanged its club newspaper with other clubs; through these exchanges his writing has gotten wide circulation—"girls love them, they fall over me for that." Once he went to a Vietnamese bakery which had a "really stinky poem" on the wall, so he made a good poem to give to the owner; the owner displayed his poem and now he gets "like 50 percent discount."

He remembers reading the newspaper when he was three years old, and later lots of books. No one read to him as a child because he could read himself. He studied French for six years but has forgotten it because he "never liked French." After the tenth grade he went without schooling for two years before he arrived in the U.S. His reading now consists of English and Vietnamese newspapers, but his writing is extensive: poems, short stories, political essays, and correspondence with his many readers. He writes in English for school work, but in Vietnamese for his published work and correspondence. He keeps a journal in his university writing class, but hates it. He made A's in his two English composition classes at the community college, and says that his teacher frequently read his work to the class. He used writing to express himself in that context more than speaking, observing "I was shy in that class, you know, cause I'm the only Vietnamese, most Vietnamese dare not to take it." A stand-up comedian in his native language, he chooses humor as a vehicle for reaching his American readers, telling his interviewer "I joke at everything. I write as probably the teacher love, like humor."

This humor is reflected in his test essay, which is well organized but reflects surface-level errors of word choice and grammar. His perception is that he did well on the writing test "because I'm a writer and poet, and because I'm solid in grammar—I took it in Vietnam and I know that vocabulary simply is not enough, one *must* know the grammar of the language if he is to do well." In fact, his vocabulary and command of idiom is stronger than his grammar in this essay.

The Unsuccessful Academic Writers

The experiences with reading and writing are markedly different for the three unsuccessful writers. They did not become part of a literacy community; nor did they develop a love of literacy. These three writers also have not acquired the conventions of written English. However, their problems differ. Both Kevin and Diane's essays are disorganized, with weak sentence grammar and only basic vocabulary. Danh, however, shows a sophisticated understanding of the rhetorical conventions of written English and an extensive vocabulary; his sentence-level structure is inadequate for the task.

Kevin, a twenty-three-year-old Chinese-Vietnamese, arrived in the United States at age fourteen and entered a California high school as a freshman. His previous schooling had ended after two months of fifth grade, primarily because his family needed help running their coffee store. He first went to a private Chinese school where he received only two hours of instruction in Vietnamese a week. After four years in Chinese school, he transferred to a Vietnamese school, which he left after two months. Because of this interruption to his schooling in Vietnam, his reading and writing experiences in both Chinese and Vietnamese have been minimal.

Because he has associated more with Vietnamese than Chinese, he has used primarily Vietnamese for spoken communication. Even with his parents he uses Vietnamese more than Chinese. Now that the family is in the U.S., the children use English extensively in the home. Kevin's parents did not really care about preserving their culture—either Chinese culture in Vietnam or Chinese and Vietnamese culture in the U.S. For them now, "the most important thing is English."

Kevin first began acquiring English when he entered high school in the U.S. But even at school his experiences with writing English were limited. "I have only written about four reports, papers in the whole four year of high school." And, of these, two were not formal papers—one was for math and the other was a personal account. Even so, Kevin says his strongest written language is English. But he does not have sufficient facility with written English to pass the test.

Kevin himself recognizes his problems when writing English. "[I]t's really tough for me at first to try to put my ideas down on paper . . . and even I do have I have a lot of ideas . . . and after I put it down I keep reading it back, and it, the process take me a lot longer . . . I don't feel good about whenever I try to write something." He does find the technical writing required at work is less problematic. He works for a computer company (he is a computer engineering major) and has to report problems with the program for which he is responsible. The problem is there and so he "just put[s] it down." With his job and college studies, Kevin has no time to read for pleasure. Kevin shows great insight into the causes of his current dilemma when he says "I notice my problem was that I didn't do a lot of writing when I was young." Even now, he says he has "let English skip by," by focussing on his technical classes to the exclusion of English classes.

Diane, a twenty-four-year-old Vietnamese, arrived in the United States when she was eighteen. She had had extensive English instruction in Vietnam, attending a school where English was taught five hours a week from grade six. The focus of instruction, however, was on grammar-translation, with no use of oral English. Diane cannot remember her parents or older sisters reading to her as a child. "They [Americans] read when you go to bed, when little, but not in Vietnam we don't." However, she does recall reading stories, picture books, and some newspapers in Vietnamese. Diane read newspapers aloud. " . . . Parents and grandparents would love for us to read newspapers for them. They love seeing you reading." She can't remember whether she understood what she read, but she was proud to "read aloud." As she grew older, her newspaper reading became less and she read stories, books, and textbooks. She wrote in Vitenamese, primarily writing required for school. However, she did write letters to friends and still does.

Her English acquisition continued during her two years in a refugee camp, where classes were conducted by Vietnamese. Her arrival in the U.S. was difficult because the English instruction in both the refugee camp and the high school in Vietnam focused on reading, writing, and translation, with no speaking. Because she had graduated from a Vietnamese high school, as soon as she arrived in the U.S. she was able to enter a community college, where she took ESL freshman composition classes. She worked part time in a campus office, helping both Vietnamese and American students. The files she kept on students were all in English. She then transferred to the University of California, Berkeley, where she lived in a dorm with an American roommate.

She feels her English has deteriorated since she transferred to San José State University and began living at home again. Diane, now a full-time student in industrial and systems engineering, mixes with both Vietnamese and American students. With her Vietnamese friends and her parents she uses Vietnamese. With her younger brothers, nieces, and nephews, she code-switches. In addition to the writing required of her at school, she sometimes writes " . . . something, just anything in English . . . just for fun."

Danh is a thirty-four-year-old Vietnamese, studying for a degree in environmental studies. He used English extensively in Vietnam, in high school, with the American-Vietnamese Association, and then in medical school. In medical school, most professors were American and the textbooks were in English. However, after graduating, he did not use English for the three years he practiced medicine before escaping from Vietnam. After escaping, he spent three years between refugee camps in Indonesia and Thailand, where his eldest daughter was born. Because of his knowledge of English, he taught English to younger people in the refugee camps, but received no further instruction himself.

Danh was twenty-six when he arrived in the U.S. He took the medical board test and passed, hoping to practice medicine in the U.S. However, he has been unable to get an internship "because of language barrier and second because the competition is very high here." So, he has switched to environmental studies, intending to become a health inspector. As well as studying, he currently has a full-time job in a nonprofit organization for the mentally ill. Most of his clients are Vietnamese, as is one of his co-workers. Thus, he is able to use Vietnamese on the job. All reports on his clients are written in English, however. He uses Vietnamese with his wife, parents, and in-laws, but code-switches with his two young daughters. Just as he was read to by his parents in Vietnamese, he reads to his daughters in English. He also reads an English newspaper daily and sometimes a Vietnamese newspaper. Danh has mainly Vietnamese friends.

Danh is clearly frustrated that he is unable to practice his original profession, and now that he has switched professions, his graduation is being held up because he cannot pass the test to take the required upper division writing class in technical writing. "I can find a job in the working place, but all it is, I can't pass the one course." He in fact took the class before the entrance test was a requirement, but failed the course. He complains that his teacher's advice was to use English at home, but "I cannot speak English with my older generation, you know." He is very aware of the age difference between him and other students and that his daughters are so successful learning English that they even correct his pronunciation. "You have to think about the English. . . . But you know, for the older generation, we used to thinking in Vietnamese, thinking, and then you translate into English. That's not correct."

DISCUSSION

The Successful Academic Writers

Because most academics read alone and silently, we forget that the acts of reading and writing are actually exchanges between partners, that is, they are activities of a literacy *community* (Heath 1983). Although the partners may be, and often are, unknown to each other, they nevertheless engage in a joint activity over time and space. All of the proficient university-level writers in our study became members of literacy communities as children and actively maintain memberships in them as adults.

Thu-Hồng, Lan, Hùng, and Trung developed literacy in Vietnamese before arriving in the U.S.—Thu-Hồng learned to read in Vietnamese while sitting on her father's lap as he read the paper aloud; as a child, Trung read books about famous Vietnamese and began writing poetry at an early age. After arriving in the U.S., Thu-Hồng, Lan, and Hùng became active members of English literacy communities: Thu-Hồng is an active writer in English, currently having one letter-writing partner of six years' standing; Lan read avidly in English as a teenager, remembering *Ramona the Pest* as one of her favorite books and now she reads and writes extensively in English for her job in the law firm; Hùng now reads newspapers, magazines, and sometimes science fiction novels in English, and he writes letters to friends in English. Trung's experience with English literacy is different. Although he wrote in community college, he is not as active a participant in English literacy communities as the other three successful students; however, he continues to write and publish Vietnamese poetry and correspond with his fans. Steven, who left Vietnam at age six, has also had different experiences: he can neither read nor write in his native language, although he remembers having been read to as a child by both his mother and grandmother in Vietnamese. However, he reads English voraciously as a child, choosing books on the environment and airplanes. In high school he wrote frequently and discussed his and his classmates' writing. As a college student, he has written daily reports as part of his job, and he currently reads journals, safety reports, and operating manuals related to aviation. Thus, he is and has been an active participant in a number of English literacy communities. In each of these cases, then, the successful writers actively interacted both with print and with other individuals in literacy communities.

Also, several of the students who are proficient in academic English exhibit in their behavior or comments some very positive attitudes (Edwards 1982) about their participation in literacy communities: Thu-Hồng's joy in reading in Vietnamese and her learning to read in English in order to continue her positive experience with books; Lan's remembered pleasure in reading the books by Beverly Cleary and her present enjoyment of her work in a legal office; Steven's childhood pleasure in reading about tidepools and "environmental stuff"; and Trung's delight in his successes as a writer in both Vietnamese and English. This joy of literacy clearly motivates their participation in literacy communities.

The Unsuccessful Academic Writers

Unlike their more proficient peers, Diane, Danh, and Kevin have not developed the love of literacy that compels people to become active members of literacy communities as children or as adults. Both Diane and Danh arrived in the U.S.

later in life (at eighteen and twenty-six, respectively), after having developed literacy in Vietnamese. While late age of arrival can be identified as one factor in Diane and Danh's failure to develop literacy skills in English, other factors are equally important.

Diane does not seem to have the love of reading and writing that would encourage her to read and write English outside her school assignments. She says she was not read to as a child and notes that this is an American custom, not a Vietnamese one; yet she relates that she read newspapers to her parents and grandparents, but cannot recall whether she actually understood what she read. Also, the evidence from other students shows that some Vietnamese families do read to their children. This ambivalence towards written language indicates that Diane enjoyed the display of literacy rather than the interaction with text. Unlike three of the successful writers, Diane did not have a time of extended listening to English in context, a practice that enhances second language acquisition (see, for example, Krashen and Terrell 1983). Although she learned English in Vietnam, it was not used for communicative purposes. Diane first learned English through grammar-translation and transferred immediately from a Vietnamese high school to a U.S. college, where she has chosen a major requiring little proficiency in English.

Although Danh was highly literate in Vietnamese and could read medical texts in English, his experiences with English in Vietnam were only with medical English in an academic setting. Danh writes reports in English for his job, but feels inadequate compared with the younger generation. For Danh, now an older person worthy of respect and with a highly valued occupation in Vietnam, his experiences since fleeing Vietnam have all contributed to lower his self-esteem: his inability to get an internship; his inability to finish school and graduate; and his daughters' fast progress in English (see Freeman 1989 for discussion of status and age as factors in cultural adjustment of Vietnamese in the U.S.). Danh feels he is too old to be making the struggle required to master the variety of English needed just to pass one course. Yet he understands the need for literacy in English, reading American bedtime stories to his daughters every night. His test essay reflects the poignant struggle of a man with complex ideas but language that does not allow those complex ideas to be readily conveyed to others. A close reading of his essay shows a mature response to the topic; but reading the essay is like pushing through tangled undergrowth.

Unlike Diane and Danh, Kevin developed only limited literacy skills in both Chinese and Vietnamese while in Vietnam, largely because his education was interrupted in the fifth grade. In four years at an American high school he wrote only four papers, and he has chosen a major in college requiring little proficiency in written English. Thus, Kevin fits one of the profiles for probable poor academic achievement, as described in previous research: an adolescent arrival with no L2 exposure and who does not continue academic work in L1, does not have the time in high school (without special assistance) to make up lost years of academic instruction (Collier 1989).

Conclusion

Participation in a literacy community is not automatic. Participants must have both opportunity and perceived need to belong. Using the case study approach, we have been able to see the individual differences in opportunity and attitude that result in membership in a literacy community and thus affect success in academic writing. We have been able to uncover the more complex interrelationships between social and attitudinal factors associated with cognitive academic language proficiency for specific individuals. Clearly, paths of acquisition vary; they are not entirely predetermined by age or cultural practices. Well-planned academic programs can create literacy communities that provide students with both opportunity and a need to belong (as Steven's high school English classes clearly did), and individuals can create for themselves such communities outside the academic setting (as Trung has done with his poetry). The practices of the five successful students provide invaluable guidelines for programs and individuals alike.

ACKNOWLEDGEMENTS

This research was funded by a California State University faculty research grant in 1988-1989. We gratefully acknowledge this institutional support of research for improvement of teaching and learning. We also acknowledge the invaluable assistance of San José State University Linguistics students in this project: Connie Rao, who served as Chief Research Assistant; Rod Cardoza, Susan Crandall, and Bruce Hull, who interviewed the Vietnamese students; and Susan Crandall, who transcribed the tape recordings of these interviews. The Vietnamese students who contributed their time and thoughtful reflections on their own language experiences did so with the expressed hope that other students will benefit from our collective study. It has been our privilege to be part of this community of researchers.

References

COLLIER, V. 1989. Academic achievement in a second language. *TESOL Quarterly* 23(3): 509-31.

CUMMINS, J. 1982. Tests, achievement and bilingual students. *FOCUS*: 9. National Clearinghouse for Bilingual Education.

EDWARDS, J. R. 1982. Language attitudes and their implications among English speakers. In *Attitudes towards language variation: Social and applied contexts,* E. B. RYAN and H. GILES, eds. 20-33. London: Edward Arnold.

FREEMAN, J. M. 1989. *Hearts of sorrow: Vietnamese-American lives.* Stanford, Calif.: Stanford Univesity Press.

HEATH, S. B. 1983. *Ways with words: Language, life and work in communities and clasrooms.* Cambridge: Cambridge University Press.

JOHNSON, DONNA M. and DUANE H. ROEN, eds. 1989. *Richness in writing: Empowering ESL students.* New York: Longman.

KRASHEN, S. D. and T. D. TERRELL. 1983. *The Natural approach.* London: Pergamon.

SCRIBNER, S., and M. COLE. 1981. *The Psychology of literacy.* Cambridge, Mass.: Harvard University Press.

STREET, B. V. 1984. *Literacy in theory and practice.* Cambridge: Cambridge University Press.

Discussion questions

1. Reflect on your own experiences with literacy. Have you been (or are you still) a member of a literacy community? How did you become such a member, for example, did your family or a teacher encourage you to read and write?

2. We have claimed (with others) that literacy is a social construct and that there are many literacies. Reflect on your own uses of literacy. Explain how your uses are socially constructed. Are all your literacy uses the same? If not, how do they differ?

3. If you were teaching a student such as Danh, how would you build his self-esteem and also help develop his literacy in English?

4. Given the types of experiences the successful Vietnamese students had with reading in their families as children, how might educators build on these cultural experiences (for example, reading the newspaper aloud)?

5. We have introduced the notion of literacy community to explain the ways students developed literacy and cognitive uses of language. How might this concept be expanded to cover all group uses of literacy events? How then could the type of literacy required for academic success be distinguished from this more general notion?

13

Perceptions of Reading Among English- and Spanish-Speaking Adult Basic Literacy Students

MARGARET LEWIS

Adult learners come to literacy programs from a variety of backgrounds. If program designers, administrators, tutors, and policy makers were more familiar with adult literacy students' expectations for their classes, their prior experiences with school, and their beliefs about reading, instructional practices could be adjusted to make the learners more comfortable and the sessions more productive. This, in turn, would result in greater learning and retention of students. Input gained directly from the adult learners can provide valuable information relevant to improved programs and instruction. This paper presents the findings of a study in which two groups of first-language (English and Spanish) literacy students were interviewed about their family literacy and schooling backgrounds, expectations for literacy classes, and beliefs about the reading process.

In the United States, most native English speakers have had some prior experience with reading instruction; for many, these experiences have been negative. In contrast, many adult immigrant literacy students have very little or no prior school experience. Having failed to read in childhood, whatever their prior school experience might have been, adult learners often feel that they are unable to learn to read. These prior experiences (or lack thereof) contribute to the adult learners' expectations about how the reading class will be conducted. Since most adult literacy students attend classes of their own volition and since adult lives are full of obligations (work, home, family, etc.), literacy students are likely not to continue their classes if their expectations are not met. Heathington, Boser, and Salter (1984) report that 100 hours of literacy instruction are needed to increase an adult's reading level by one grade level. However, many adults drop out before completing 100 hours of instruction and, thus, meet neither their own nor the program's expectations for improvement in reading and writing abilities.

In addition to the expectations about teaching and learning that the adult brings to the class, s/he also carries an idea of what reading is, that is, of how people read. According to Canney and Winograd (1979) many less able readers may not realize that reading must include getting meaning from print.

Schema theory provides a framework for understanding reading as a meaning-making activity. A schema incorporates interrelated components of a larger idea into a cognitive structure. The pieces of that larger idea are placed into slots; as the slots are filled and their interrelations are formed or confirmed, comprehension takes place. Thus, prior knowledge forms a frame into which facts, impressions, and attitudes combine with new knowledge from the text to complete the larger idea. Sub-schemata may exist within the larger framework as well. A schema for reading, for example, would include slots and sub-schemata for sound/symbol correspondence, for knowledge of grammar, for predicting events in the text, for making inferences about the author's intent, etc. Perhaps because of initial reading instruction which focused too heavily on subskills of reading or phonics, or perhaps because of a lack of being involved with reading for meaning either at home or at school, poor readers may never have incorporated slots for comprehension into their reading schema; they may believe that reading is nothing more than recognizing or sounding out words, and not be aware that reading includes understanding a message, not just pronouncing the words correctly.

Several studies have been done with children, asking them what they think reading is. Canney and Winograd (1979) asked good and poor readers in elementary school about their perceptions of reading. The good readers were much more aware of the meaning-getting or top-down nature of reading, while the poor readers referred more often to surface level or bottom-up facets of reading.

Guzzetti (1987) asked 161 high school students who were either in senior advanced placement (AP) English classes or in auto mechanics classes what they thought reading is. Over half (36 of 64) of the AP English students gave responses which mentioned meaning or comprehension, while only 3 of the 97 auto mechanics students did so. Her results support Canney and Winograd's hypothesis that poor readers do not include comprehension in their schema for reading. To date, few or no studies have looked at reading schemata of adult non- or low-readers.

For the purposes of this paper, an adult is any person over the age of eighteen. Immigrant refers to any person who has come to the United States planning to reside and work for an extended period of time, regardless of their legal status with the Immigration and Naturalization Service. Literacy is the ability to read and write at a level considered necessary by an individual for successful functioning in daily life. An illiterate is a person who lacks that ability. Tutor refers to the provider of literacy instruction. Tutor is used rather than teacher because most initial literacy instruction for adults is provided by literacy volunteer tutors. In the Adult Basic Education (ABE) reading lab interviews, tutor was replaced by teacher to make the questionnaire more appropriate for that class.

This paper reports the results of interviews with adults who had recently begun attending literacy classes. They were asked about their family literacy backgrounds, their perceptions of reading, and their expectations for the literacy instruction they were starting. Their responses were sought in order to provide information on the following questions:

1. Do most illiterate adults have a family history of illiteracy?

2. Why did they not learn how to read when they were children?

3. What motivates illiterate adults to seek literacy instruction?

4. What kinds of materials do adult literacy students want to be able to read?

5. Do they want to learn to write at the same time?

6. What do illiterate adults think reading is?

7. What do the illiterate adults expect will happen in their literacy classes?

8. How do the students think they can help themselves learn to read better?

LIMITATIONS

The number of students interviewed is smaller than I had intended. Gaining access to Spanish-speaking literacy students was relatively uncomplicated, facilitated by my work in Los Angeles with BASE (Basic Adult Spanish Education). [BASE is an adult literacy program which teaches basic reading, writing, and arithmetic in Spanish. English instruction is included in some centers but is a minor focus of the program.] Locating English-speaking literacy students who fit the parameters of the population described in the design of this project was difficult. First, a limited number of centers provide very basic literacy instruction. Seven adult schools were contacted and asked about their beginning literacy instruction for adults. All seven require at least a third-grade reading level for entry into their programs. Second, many directors of library-based and of small community-based programs (YMCAs and churches) have a strong inclination toward protecting the privacy of their students. Several directors mentioned the great shame their students feel about being illiterate. The most recent entrants are the students that directors feel most protective towards. During the actual interviews, however, the students seemed pleased that someone would take an interest in their histories and thoughts. What I expected to be ten-minute interviews often lasted half an hour or more.

Another possible limitation is the reliance on self-report for discussion of reading ability. The only measurement of the participants' reading ability was their response to the question, "Can you read in that language?" Literacy instructors had been asked to indicate people who were "very beginning readers." Some of the participants said they could read a little, but there was no measurement of what that "little" reading ability was. Garcia et al. (1988), in their study of two Spanish-speaking communities in New York described one possible drawback to self-report. "Undereducated speakers may frequently overestimate their literacy ability, and educated speakers may frequently underestimate it" (Garcia et al. 1988). These discrepancies between real ability and reported ability are based on different underlying perceptions of standards for literacy.

METHODOLOGY

Interviews were carried out with thirteen adult students who have been attending literacy classes for less than two months. The interviews were done in a variety of literacy classes: an ABE (Adult Basic Education) reading lab, three Laubach tutoring sessions, and two BASE (Basic Adult Spanish Education) centers. The thirteen participants were adults learning to read in their first language—eight were Spanish speakers and five were English speakers. All eight of the Spanish speakers are immigrants: Five were from Mexico, the other three were from El Salvador. Four were women and four were men. All of the English speakers were born in the United States. Two were women and three were men. The ages of the thirteen participants range from nineteen to sixty-three.

All participants reported low SES (Socio-economic Sector) jobs for themselves, their spouses, and their parents. The jobs included such positions as cook's helper, housekeeper, baby sitter, painter, construction worker, and field hand. Many of the mothers of the students had not worked outside the home (100 percent Spanish; 40 percent English.) The incidence of unemployment reported by the interviewees was lower than might have been expected (two out of thirteen), given the high incidence of illiteracy often reported among the unemployed.

Since the focus of the study is on first language literacy students, no ESL literacy students were included, though some of the Spanish-speaking students were also learning English. All interviews were conducted in the adult learner's first language by a bilingual interviewer. A set interview schedule of open-ended questions was used to initiate discussion about each of the research questions. Thereafter, probing questions and natural responses to the content of the responses were used in order to clarify and elicit further information, and in order to allow a deeper understanding of the respondent's ideas and life story. Subsequently, all Spanish responses were translated into English by the interviewer.

RESULTS

First the backgrounds of the adult learners are compared. Then information about their perceptions about reading is presented. Finally student expectations about what will happen in the classes, about how long becoming literate will take, and about homework and independent study are reported.

Family Background

The two groups differed markedly in their family literacy histories. Three-fourths of the Spanish speakers' parents were reported as being illiterate while only three out of the ten (30 percent) parents of the English speakers were reported as being illiterate. Of the Spanish speakers, 75 percent are married, while only 40 percent of the English speakers have spouses. Of these, four of the six Spanish spouses and one of the two English spouses can read, though most responses included the qualifier "can read a little." The interview did not include questions about their children's literacy.

School History

The two groups showed a substantial difference in their average years of schooling. The Spanish speakers' years of schooling ranged from none to three. The Spanish speakers reported not having had access to schools as children. Living on a remote ranch, being female, and having to go to work at a young age were the reasons given. Most of the Spanish speakers expressed having had a desire to study as a child, although one man said that he had had the chance to go to school, but had preferred to work in the fields with his father. Three of the four women said that their brothers were allowed to study, but their fathers believed it unnecessary for women to be educated. "Schools just fill girls with bad ideas about liberty. Then no one wants to marry them!'' one woman quoted her father as saying.

The English speakers had all reached at least the seventh grade, with one having graduated from high school. Two had dropped out in eighth grade, and one in the tenth. Those who dropped out without completing junior high school (less than ninth grade) had all repeated at least one year of school. These learners reported having had poor attendance because of family instability, illness, and lack of interest in school. Family instability included moving often or being shifted frequently from one relative to another. One man reported having attended seven schools in different states before third grade. One woman became pregnant in ninth grade, dropped out, and "never needed to read much."

All of the English-speaking illiterate adults stated or implied that they had not liked school—not a surprising admission since they were not functioning successfully there. Poor attendance, reported as the major reason for their nonliteracy, may have been a factor. Possibly the students did not attend school regularly because they were not successful in the classroom, and, due to absence, fell even further behind. Or, perhaps these students had always disliked school or found the classroom activities irrelevant, had not attended regularly, and this lack of attendance prevented them from learning to read well.

Reasons for Studying Now

For the BASE students, reasons for learning to read and write now included finally having an opportunity to study (four of eight); the necessity of studying to qualify for legal residence under the amnesty law (the IRCA act of 1986) (two); and the greater need for literacy in the U.S. than in their home countries (two). [This study was done just as the new IRCA regulations were being established; more students than this data would indicate are currently enrolled in BASE classes in order to satisfy the legalization requirement of forty hours of instruction.]

Several of the BASE students stated that they had tried to attend ESL classes at an adult school, but those classes assumed that the students could read, so the nonreaders could not keep up with the class and dropped out after a few weeks. As one man explained, "The very first day they gave us a book and wanted everybody to read. It made me feel stupid, so I never went back. But, I kept the book. I wanted to read it so much. Now I think that after I learn to read Spanish and to speak English, I will go back and try again."

The five English-speaking students had different reasons for enrolling in literacy classes now. Three were job-related. One woman worked in a factory that was eliminating many jobs because of automation, but which wanted to save a few valued employees to run the computers. The new position will not require a high level of literacy, but some reading will be necessary. When offered one of the computer jobs, she confessed her illiteracy. Her supervisor agreed to hold one of the positions open for her until the changeover was complete, if she would try to learn enough reading to run the machines. She was determined to accomplish her goal of finishing the third Laubach skill book by then. "I been working there for 17 years. I'm too old to get a new job. I thought I was dumb, but I'm smart enough to see I need to learn to read. It's my future."

The other two said that they do not want their children to be illiterate when they grow up. These two expect to be able to read with their children and to help them with their schoolwork. One man said,

> I looked at my little boy and saw that he was starting to be just like I was in school—goofing off and being a smart-ass to the teacher because he didn't know how to do things. I just couldn't stand it. I want him to be better than me. But I can't tell him. No one could tell me. My old lady tried. I have to show him. I have to learn to read.

Several respondents gave more than one answer when asked why they want to become literate now. Enhanced self-esteem is a motivating force mentioned by a majority of each group (five Spanish and two English). One man said,

> "When your friends find out you can't read, they start treating you different, even if you've known each other for 10 years. I don't want to be hiding any more. I want to feel like normal people who can go anywhere without worrying if their girlfriend's going to pass them a little note or something and then they'll feel dumb. I'm not dumb, but they sure can make me feel like I am."

Most participants (ten out of thirteen) want to be able to read all types of printed material. Of those who expressed an interest in a particular type of reading matter, two want to read job-related or "useful" materials and one is particularly interested in reading the Bible.

A subsequent study (Lewis and Madrigal 1988) was done in which twenty-eight BASE students were shown a variety of functional and recreational reading materials: newspaper, cookbook, TV program schedule, comic-book-format biography of Pedro Infante, second-grade reader, women's fashion magazines, sports magazie, do it-yourself home electrical projects, *fotonovela*. The students were asked to indicate which materials they most would like to be able to read. Overwhelmingly, the chosen materials featured big print and colored pictures. The subject matter influenced the students' choices less than the appearance of the materials. The materials need to "look easy."

After discussing what they want to be able to read, the participants were asked how long they think they will need to study before being able to read the materials they want to read. Three replied they do not know, four said less than a year, two said between one and two years, and four said more than two years.

Reading and Writing

Nine of the participants want to learn to write as well as to read. Two were unsure, and two stated a preference for learning to read before tackling writing. The majority of each group reported that writing is linked to reading. The close relation of the two seemed so obvious that the question seemed silly to some of the learners. "They're two sides of the same coin," said one woman when asked why she thought it was best to learn the two skills together.

Perceptions of the Reading Process

On the question of what it is that people do when they read, the Spanish-speaking group was more aware of the meaning-making nature of reading. More than half included some reference to understanding what the author is trying to say or comprehending the message in their description of what reading is. Only one of the English speakers did so. Following Canney and Winograd (1979), the responses (shown in Table 1) are separated into four categories: *meaningless, bottom-up, to-down,* and *both. Meaningless* includes responses such as "I don't know" or "They just read." *Bottom-up* includes all responses which emphasized knowing sounds, knowing all the words, or pronouncing everything correctly. *Top-down* includes all responses in which the description of the reading process included reading for meaning, understanding, or trying to get what the writer meant when s/he was writing. *Both* is a category added to the original three categories to include the responses which indicated that both types of strategies (bottom-up and top-down) are used when a person reads.

TABLE 1
Student Perceptions of the Reading Process

Responses	Meaningless	Bottom-Up	Top-Down	Both	Number
Spanish Speakers	1	2	3	2	8
English Speakers	2	2	0	1	5
Total	3	4	3	3	13

Expectations for the class

The majority said they expected the tutor to help them read. When asked how the tutor would help them, most (eight) gave answers which reflected expectations for bottom-up teaching and learning activities: "Explain the letters and their sounds," or "Help us pronounce the words." Three people said the teacher would show them how to understand what the text said. Two people said they did not know.

All students expected the literacy classes to be different from school, even those students who had never attended school. Most mentioned that there was much more individual attention, and that the classes were small. One student said, "I'm the one who sets the pace. If I don't get it, we don't go on." Another said, "It has to be different. I'm not a kid." (Because the control for length of time in the program had to be abandoned, most of the students had been in their class for over a month. Thus, this question was answered less on the basis of expectations and more on the basis of their knowledge of how the classes are operated.)

All students expected to have homework, although three said that they hoped there would not be very much because they did not have time to study. Memorizing words and letters was mentioned six times and practicing reading and writing was mentioned five times in response to "What kind of homework do you think you'll have?"

Helping Themselves Learn

When asked how they might help themselves learn to read better, few students had specific answers. Most responded that they should do what the tutor tells them to do. The woman whose job depends on her learning to read said that she is trying to read everything she can, looking for words she knows, and trying to guess the rest. Her tutor had suggested the strategy, and she was discovering that she could understand much more than she had expected. Two men said that they try to read the sports section of the newspaper. When they cannot understand something, they ask somebody to help them. They believed that the sports section is the easiest to read because often they have seen the sports event on television and already know what happened.

The two groups (English speakers and Spanish speakers) showed different patterns for their family literacy histories. Also, there were wide differences between the schooling backgrounds of the Spanish and English groups. The two groups differed in the reasons for attending classes now. The types of materials they wanted to be able to read were similar. As for the expectations about what the tutor would do in the class, both groups responded in a manner that indicated that they expected to be helped in reading and understanding materials as well as instructed in basic skills: sound and symbol correspondence, pronouncing the words.

DISCUSSION

There are significant differences between the backgrounds of the Spanish-speaking and the English-speaking illiterate adults who were interviewed in this study. For a variety of reasons, fewer children attend elementary schools in Mexico and Central America than in the U.S. This is also the case in much of Asia and Africa. Therefore, it is possible that many immigrants have not attended school and are illiterate in their first language. While they are free of the negative conditioning that long years of failure to learn can cause, neither do they have "school culture." Although no ESL literacy students were interviewed in this study, recommendations for beginning ESL classes can be made based on the results reported here. ESL students who are illiterate in their language should have separate classes from those who are able to read in some language other than English. Many students in Spanish literacy classes report having dropped out of ESL classes because they could not keep up with their literate classmates. Illiterate ESL students need to be taught with special techniques which literacy tutors can learn.

Since the majority of both groups reported wanting to be able to read anything they find interesting or useful, literacy classes should provide a wide variety of reading material. Students might be encouraged to bring what they want to read to class, where the tutor can assist them in reading that material. Rigg and Kazemek (1984) have shown that student interest is more significant than level of difficulty in reading instruction.

All of the learners interviewed in this study want to learn to write as well as to read. Most believe that it is best to learn the two simultaneously. Some literacy programs postpone writing until some degree of proficiency in reading has been attained. Both the findings of researchers (Jensen 1984) and the beliefs of the students suggest that simultaneous instruction is preferable to sequential instruction. Reading and writing are seen as inseparable by most students.

The results of this study support the hypothesis of Canney and Winograd (1979) that poor readers may not have a schema for reading which includes comprehension. Fewer than half of the participants (six out of thirteen) mentioned comprehension or understanding as part of what people do when they read. Only one of the English speakers did so. The finding that the English speakers, the group with the highest average years of schooling where they presumably received instruction in reading, appear so much less aware of the meaning-making nature of reading is most intriguing.

Many remedial reading classes concentrate the efforts of the poor readers on phonics and skills practice while the good readers are allowed to go to the library and choose their own books. Such practices may be based on the mistaken belief that good reading consists primarily of rapid, accurate translation of sound into meaning via mental pronunciation of each word. However, Goodman (1967), Smith (1982), and many other leading reading theorists have pointed out the physiopsychological reasons why this view of reading is untenable.

Research is needed into the relative merits of phonics and workbooks compared with real reading of student-chosen materials with a concentration on interest and comprehension to determine the best way to help those students who are not reading at a satisfactory level.

It would appear that specific instruction in getting meaning from print is needed. Literacy tutors should be trained in methods which allow them to demonstrate the meaning-getting strategies that they themselves use. Meyer, Keefe, and Bauer (1986) suggest methods for making literacy tutors aware of their own use of prediction and context as meaning-getting strategies in reading. Instruction in these and other similar strategies, as well as consistent emphasis on the meaningful aspects of reading, should be an essential component of all literacy classes.

The students expect their literacy classes to be different from their school experience. They expect small classes with individual attention. They expect to be treated as adults. Implications of these expectations for instruction are obvious. The classes must be student-centered, conducted at a pace attuned to the ease or difficulty with which the student is progressing, and focused on topics and materials that are of use to the student. Eberle and Robinson (1980) used quotes from illiterate and formerly illiterate adults to support their account of and recommendations for student-centered, nontraditional tutoring using a variety of materials. Moriarty and Wallerstein (1979) describe ways in which community issues can be used to generate reading, writing, and critical thinking.

Almost all of the students had quite limited repertoires of strategies to use to help themselves improve their reading. Two had discovered a strategy that incorporates background knowledge (they have already seen the sports events on TV), practicing the reading skills they already have, and asking for help if they need it. All of the learners interviewed are fairly recent entrants into literacy classes. The tutors need to help their students develop self-help strategies and encourage their use. One tutor had shown such a technique to her student. The woman was using it, was looking for words she did know, and had felt encouraged that she was able to read so much. Asking for help with a tough selection, expecting to find readable words, attempting to read material dealing with familiar topics—these are strategies which poor readers can be taught to use to strengthen their skills. People who are learning to read need to have meaning-getting strategies taught to them and demonstrated for them. Literacy instructors have an obligation to emphasize these strategies in their classes so that students have a complete schema for what reading is.

Conclusion

This study has attempted to investigate the perceptions of reading and the expectations for literacy classes of adult learners who are new participants in literacy instruction. In the process of this investigation, the English- and Spanish-speaking groups were found to differ in family and school backgrounds, in their motivation for studying, and in their perceptions of the reading process. In this study, only students in first-language literacy programs were interviewed. Further investigations into the perceptions and expectations of illiterate students in ESL programs are needed. What are the differences between those who enter ESL literacy programs and those who are first-language literacy students? What role does oral proficiency in English play in deciding what kind of program to enroll in? Do the differences found between the two language groups in this study hold for other immigrant groups?

There is much to be learned about the nonliterate population of the United States. This study has revealed some significant differences among two of the many diverse groups who are not literate. Their different views of what reading is may be related to their different schooling backgrounds. That the educational attainment of the immigrant group tends to be low is not surprising to many ESL classroom teachers who have worked with beginning ESL classes. The implications of that lack of school experience, however, seem to have received little attention. Recommendations based on these findings include the following:

1. Placement into ESL classes should not be based solely on oral proficiency. Some assessment of the first-language literacy of the student should be made. College graduates and unschooled farmers are placed in classes together on the basis of their oral proficiency. However, due to their vastly different school experiences and literacy abilities, the class soon abandons one or bores the other.

2. Teachers of ESL classes, especially the lower levels, need to be careful not to assume that all their students can read and write in some language. Simple techniques such as not mixing cursive and print forms, pointing out distinctive features of letters in words being used, and remembering to erase the board frequently can assist the nonreaders.

3. Teachers of all types of literacy classes—first language and ESL—need to focus on reading as a meaning-making activity. Reading aloud to your students or using paired reading techniques followed by discussion is one way of emphasizing that reading means getting a message, even with the very beginning reader. Using reading material to gain information which can be applied to daily life situations (for example, the Yellow Pages, mail order catalogues, want ads) is another.

4. Adult education administrators and policy makers should be made aware of the differences in schooling background and literacy of many of the ESL and immigrant students. Programs should be organized in ways that allow for consideration of the needs of such students. For example, unschooled adult students often require more time to achieve program goals, due to their unfamiliarity with the process of schooling. Such students also benefit greatly

from individual attention when beginning to read and write. While classes with fifty or sixty students do not establish a supportive learning atmosphere for any students, such large classes are especially difficult for nonliterate students. Funding for programs with substantial percentages of nonliterate students should provide for classes of no more than twenty-five students.

5. First-language literacy classes should be considered for unschooled adults who are speakers of languages which have a written tradition and are used widely in California. Becoming literate in a language you speak is much faster than becoming literate in one you do not speak. Spanish, for example, has a long written history, is a language in which printed materials are readily available in California, and is the language of large numbers of nonliterate adults. Offering basic literacy and numeracy instruction in Spanish will both increase immediate participation in the literate lifestyle and facilitate eventual acquisition of literacy and basic education in English.

6. Nonliterate and formerly nonliterate adults should be asked to provide input into programs, materials, recruitment efforts, and evaluation of both individual progress and program effectiveness. Much of the funding designated for literacy has been spent inappropriately because of a lack of experience on the part of planners, funders, and administrators with not being able to read and write. The experts on nonliteracy include the people who are living the nonliterate reality as well as the literacy teachers and researchers.

There is no "typical" nonliterate. All of us who work with literacy issues, whether as teachers and tutors, administrators, policy shapers, or researchers, need to keep this in mind. We need to learn from the adult nonreaders in order to develop programs, materials, and attitudes based on the realities of nonliteracy rather than on our suppositions of how we would be likely to experience nonliteracy. The adult nonliterates have much to teach us about their worlds, and about the role of literacy in those worlds.

References

CANNEY, G., and P. WINOGRAD. 1979. Schemata for reading and reading performance comprehension. (Tech Rep. No 120). Champaign: University of Illinois, Center for the Study of Reading.

EBERLE, A. and S. ROBINSON. 1980. The adult illiterate speaks out: Personal perspectives on learning to read and write. NIE, Washington, D.C. ERIC ED 197771.

GARCIA, O., I. EVANGELISTA, M. MARTINEZ, C. DISLA, and B. PAULINO. 1988. Spanish language use and attidues: A study of two New York City communities. *Language in Society* 17:475–511.

GOODMAN, K. S. 1967. Reading: A Psycholinguistic guessing game. *Journal of the Reading Specialist:* 126–35.

GUZZETTI, B. 1987, October. Reading as a process. Workshop at the Literacy Outreach Conference by the Teacher Preparation Center at California State Polytechnic University, Pomona.

HEATHINGTON, B. S., J. A. BOSER, and T. SALTER. 1984. Characteristics of adult beginning readers who persisted in a volunteer tutoring program. *Lifelong Learning* 7(5):20–22.

JENSEN, J. M., ed. 1984. Composing and comprehending. Urbana, IL: ERIC Clearing House in Reading and Communication Skills.

KEEFE, D., and V. MEYER. 1980. Adult disabled readers: Their perceived models of the reading process. *Adult Literacy and Basic Education* 4:120–24.

LEWIS, M. and L. MADRIGAL. 1988. Reading materials preferences of adult literacy students. Unpublished manuscript. University of Southern California.

MEYER, V., D. KEEFE, and C. BAUER. 1986. Some basic principles of the reading process required of literacy volunteers. *Journal of Reading* 29:544–48.

MORIARTY, P. and N. WALLERSTEIN. 1979. Student/teacher/learner: A Freirean approach to ABE/ESL. *Adult Literacy and Basic Education* 3:193–200.

RIGG, P., and F. KAZEMEK. 1984. A last chance at literacy: Real world reading comes to a a Job Corps camp. *Journal of Reading* 29:328–36.

SMITH, F. 1982. Understanding reading. 3rd ed. New York: Holt, Rinehart, & Winston.

Discussion Questions

1. What are some of the characteristics of adult basic literacy students? How do their expectations about reading affect their participation in adult literacy learning, either as tutorees or as students in literacy classes?

2. In what ways is the attitude of shame connected with adult nonliterates? Did Lewis consistently find this attitude manifested by the people she interviewed?

3. Why does the author emphasize the importance of ''meaning-making'' in reading? Do you know of adult literacy programs which either minimize or maximize meaningful reading? What are classroom learning-to-read activities which characterize these opposite approaches?

ABOUT THE AUTHORS

Fraida Dubin, Associate Professor of Education at the University of Southern California, received her Ph.D. in sociolinguistics at UCLA. As a language and education specialist, she has published textbooks for English language learners, as well as reference books for teachers. She has taught and lectured widely in the United States and in countries where English is taught as a language for wider communication. Her research interests are in the sociolinguistic aspects of reading and writing.

William Eggington is an assistant professor in the English department at Brigham Young University, Provo, Utah. His research interests include literacy among oral cultures, contrastive rhetoric, language policy and planning, and sociolinguistics. He has published nationally and internationally in these areas. He has also lectured at the Northern Territory University, Darwin, Australia, where his research interests focused on aboriginal educational linguistics. He has taught ESL at the university and adult basic education levels in Austrailia, Hawaii, California, and South Korea.

Mary Lee Field is an associate professor at Wayne State University, Detroit, Michigan, in the Interdisciplinary Studies Program, a re-entry program for working adults. She teaches writing, cross-cultural communication, and introduction to language. She has also taught EFL in Greece, Japan, China, and Yugoslavia. Her research centers on culturally shaped beliefs about reading, a topic on which she has published in *ON TESOL '84* and in the *Journal of Reading*. The most recent phase of this work includes data collected from teachers and students in Yugoslavia, Hungary, Turkey, and Egypt.

Rosemary C. Henze is an educational ethnographer whose research and teaching focus on learners acquiring language and literacy skills in cross-cultural settings. She has taught ESL and composition to university students from many backgrounds and has conducted research in settings which include an Arabic language classroom, a Lao community in San Francisco, a village in central Greece, secondary schools in California and Arizona, and a bilingual education program in southwestern Alaska. In her current position at ARC Associates, Oakland, CA, she provides training for teachers on intercultural communication, language development, and effective schooling for language minority students. Her doctorate in Education is from Stanford University, Stanford, CA.

Nobuyuki Hino is Assistant Professor, Faculty of Language and Culture, Osaka University, Japan. He has published extensively, including articles in *World Englishes* and *Georgetown University Round Table on Languages and Linguistics*. He received his graduate degree in TESL at the University of Hawaii, Manoa, and has presented at TESOL and JALT conferences.

James Kohn has been training EFL/ESL teachers at San Francisco State University since 1975, focusing on the relevance of sociolinguistic issues to the teaching of English. he has given several presentations at TESOL on issues in sociolinguistics, reading, and composition for ESOL teachers. He also has taught courses in ESL reading and composition since 1967. With his wife, Elaine Fischer-Kohn, he spent the academic year 1984 to 1985 training teachers in Shandong, China. His latest interest is in the literature of EFL students—writing in English from postcolonial countries.

Natalie A. Kuhlman is an associate professor in the Policy Studies in Language and Cross-Cultural Education Department in the College of Education, San Diego State University. With Fraida Dubin, she has co-chaired the Cross-Cultural Literacy Colloquium at TESOL conventions since 1984. Her research interests include interactive journal writing of first-grade Spanish-English bilingual children, acquisition of writing skills by adults learning English as a second language, language assessment, and language policy. She spent the 1986 to 1987 academic year as a Senior Fulbright Lecturer in Krakow, Poland.

Chunok Lee is a graduate student in applied linguistics at the Monterey Institute of International Studies, Monterey, CA. She received B.A. degrees from Yonsei University in Seoul, Korea and from the University of California, Irvine. Her publications include "Different Paths to Writing Proficiency in a Second Language," 1989 (with R. Scarcella), in M. Eisenstein ed., *The Dynamic Interlanguage: Empirical Studies in Second Language Variation,* 137–53. New York: Plenum Press.

Margaret Lewis has taught adult literacy classes in both English and Spanish for native speakers and has worked with adult ESL students at all levels. A doctoral candidate specializing in Adult Literacy at the University of Southern California, she founded the Adult Literacy Colloquium held annually at USC and is active in literacy efforts in Los Angeles and Sacramento, CA, her current work place and residence.

Lynellen D. Long is working for the Office of Technology Assessment, U.S. Congress, on a national study of literacy and technology. She is also conducting research on refugees as a postdoctoral fellow in anthropology at Johns Hopkins School of Public Health and teaches Comparative and International Education in the graduate program at American University, Washington, D.C. Her research and publications have focused on refugees, literacy, and gender issues. After completing her fieldwork in the Thai camps, she did studies on refugees and displaced persons in Sudan, Kenya, Malawi, and Guinea for the Agency for International Development and the United Nations High Commissioner for refugees.

Susan Meisenhelder is Professor of English at California State University, San Bernardino. In 1986 to 1987 she taught at the University of Botswana as a Fulbright Professor. In addition to her work on literacy programs in Botswana, she has written on literacy in Nicaragua and the USSR. She has also authored a book on William Wordsworth's poetry, *Wordsworth's Informed Reader: Structures of Experience in His Poetry,* and is currently working a book about Zora Neale Hurston.

Denise E. Murray is Associate Professor and Chair of the Department of Linguistics and Language Development at San Jose State University and coordinator of the university-wide sophomore-level writing test. She teaches courses in sociolinguistics, literacy, and TESOL methods and testing. Her research interests include language, literacy, and culture and their interaction with technology. Her publications include *Conversation for Action: The Computer Terminal as Medium of Communication* and numerous articles on literacy, ESL, and computer-mediated communication. She is coeditor of *The CATESOL Journal* and cochair of the statewide Bilingual Advisory Panel to the California Commission on Teacher Credentialing.

Patricia C. Nichols is Professor of English at San Jose State University where she has served as associate director of the Writing Center, coordinator of teacher education in English, and director of a summer program for ESL teachers. Her research interests have focused on language contact in colonial South Carolina between Europeans, Africans, and Native Americans. She has published articles on Gullah, a creole spoken in South Carolina and Georgia; on dialects of the American South; on gender and language; and on teaching in multicultural settings. She has been active in the organization of ESL professionals within the nineteen-campus California State University system.

Ted Plaister was a University of Hawaii faculty member for twenty-four years where he was the founding chair of the Department of ESL. For many years he was the director of its English Language Institute. He has done ESL teaching and teacher training in Thailand, American Samoa, Japan, and micronesia, and has conducted numerous workshops on language teaching for Hawaii's Department of Education. Professor Plaister received his B.S. from the University of California, Davis, his M.A. from the University of Michigan, and his doctorate from Sussex College of Technology, England. He is retired and resides in Aptos, California.

Robin Scarcella is Associate Professor of Teacher Education and director of the ESL program at the University of California, Irvine. Her publications include *Teaching Language Minority Students in the Multicultural Classroom* (Prentice Hall, 1990). Her ongoing investigation of the home literacy practices of Korean-American children (with Sung-Chul Lee) is funded through the University of California's Center of Cultural Diversity and Second Language Learning.

The late **John Mark Summers** completed his undergraduate work at Indiana University, an M.A. in ESL at the University of Hawaii, an M.Ed. at Columbia University and his Ed.D. at the same university. For over twenty years he was an instructor at Kauai Community College teaching ESL, English, and cross-cultural studies. Summers had extensive overseas experience in the Peace Corps (Philippines), Micronesia (contract teacher on Truk), and as a Fulbright fellow in Indonesia in 1975 to 1976 and more recently in West Africa in 1986. In 1987 to 1988 he was on the faculty of Kansai University, Osaka, Japan.

Donald M. Topping is Director of the Social Science Research Institute, University of Hawaii, Manoa. As a linguist, he has published widely on the languages of the South Pacific area and has been a friend of the Cross-Cultural Literacy Colloquium since its inception.

INDEX